FIRST FAMILIES

OF

BLEDSOE COUNTY TENNESSEE

Elizabeth Parham Robnett

Heritage Books
2024

HERITAGE BOOKS
AN IMPRINT OF HERITAGE BOOKS, INC.

Books, CDs, and more—Worldwide

For our listing of thousands of titles see our website
at
www.HeritageBooks.com

A Facsimile Reprint
Published 2024 by
HERITAGE BOOKS, INC.
Publishing Division
5810 Ruatan Street
Berwyn Heights, MD 20740

International Standard Book Number
Paperbound: 978-0-7884-8799-6

TABLE OF CONTENTS:

FOREWARD

Bledsoe's First Families include several, but not all, the pioneer families that settled in the Valley or on the Cumberland Plateau in the early 1800s.

Several families were in the frontier county a short time before moving to new states or counties. Several, thirty or more veterans of the American Revolution, found Bledsoe County their last home.

The families included in this book are some of those who remained in the county and their descendants who contributed to the development of the area.

The family information in this book is not to be taken as a "Family Tree".

This book was written in 2007 on the 200th anniversary of the date of the passage of the act to establish Bledsoe County.

This book is to be published in 2008 on the 200th anniversary of the official beginning of Bledsoe County.

Every effort has been made to avoid any mistakes, the spelling is used as it was at the time it was written. This may or may not differ from the present spelling of names and/or locations.

ii

ACKNOWLEDGMENT

The writer wishes to express sincere appreciation to all that have contributed their families' histories in any small way.

As County Historian and history teacher, I had in my library much information that I have collected over the years. To all others that have helped in any way, we thank you. Hoping this information may be a help to the future generations who may be searching for an early ancestor in Bledsoe County.

My appreciation, especially to Santos (Rodriguez) Mercer who did the word processing and the final compilation of the manuscript.

To Mr. James L. Douthat for his kind words, patience, encouragement, helpful suggestions and understanding.

To Vickie S. Kelly for the cemetery photographs.

To Sue Robnett, Alfred Terry, Frank Boring and Mr. And Mrs. Steve Thurman.

iv

DEDICATION

This book, "Bledsoe's First Families" is dedicated to the first families, men, women and children found their way into a wilderness, uncultivated and uninhabited land.

They left a more settled and civilized area to withstand danger and hardship. They were "hungry for land and opportunity."

Who were the first families? Old American, these first families' ancestors had been in the American colonies for a hundred years, before crossing over the mountains. Several were veterans of the War for Independence. "Let's thank those who came before us!"

IN THE BEGINNING...

In the beginning God created the heaven and the earth
And the earth was without form and void; and
darkness was upon the face of the deep,
and the spirit of God moved upon the face of the waters.
Genesis 1:1-2

In the beginning, John McClellen and Charles McClung explored the Sequatchie Valley - 1795.

The State of North Carolina granted 80,000 acres of land, "Eastern District to Stockly Donelson, North side of Tennessee River - other side - Cumberland Plateau - crossing Crow Creek. [Sequatchie River]"

The land was divided into 16 lots of 5000 acres each and sold to Charles Love of Virginia for $50,000.

By the time of the American Revolution 1776-1781, the population of the British Colonies had reached the Appalachian mountains.

After the peace treaty was signed with Great Britain in 1783, the American settlers began to move over the mountains from the eastern seaboard states. Tennessee was in the path of the great "Western Movement." In this southwest path or route was Sequatchie Valley and Bledsoe County.

Just as Tennessee became a "gateway" to the west by the Cumberland Gap, Bledsoe County became a "gateway" to the southwest by way of Sequatchie Valley.

viii

SEQUATCHIE VALLEY

Sequatchie Valley is located in the southeastern part of Tennessee in the Cumberland Plateau. Walden Ridge separated the East Tennessee Valley from the Sequatchie Valley. This valley is about seventy miles long and an average of from three to five miles wide. It is said that the "Cumberland Plateau and the magnificent Sequatchie Valley encompasses one of the world's most unique geological formations."

Another description of this famous valley, Sequachee [old spelling], "it is in the western part of East Tennessee and one of the prettiest valleys and best farming region in the United States."

The valley is hemmed in on both sides and one end by cliffs approximately one thousand feet high. The valley floor, a gently rolling plain, is interrupted throughout by a chain of low rounded hills averaging about three hundred feet in height. Sequatchie Valley has been compared to the well-known Shenandoah Valley of Virginia.

The word, Sequachee/Sequatchie, is of Cherokee origin. The first mention of the word is made in the famous Spanish explorer, DeSoto's account of his journey through what is now the southern states, in the sixteenth century. Some historians say the word in Cherokee language meant "hog trough" and others say the word means "opossum".

The valley is drained by the Sequatchie River and its tributaries. The river, after entering the valley from Grassy Cove, follows a meandering course down the middle of the valley until it flows into the Tennessee River not far from the Alabama state line. Since the river flows nearer the east side of the valley, most of the larger tributaries come from the west side. This is also true about the springs. The strongest springs are located on the west side. The valley runs from the north-east direction opening up into north Alabama.

The Sequatchie River, a north branch of the Tennessee River, has its source at the head of the Sequatchie Valley. A small stream, Mill Creek, which drains Grassy Cove enters a large cave and is lost for eight or ten miles under the mountain. At the head of the valley the stream breaks out in a clear spring which is called the "head of the Creek."

John McClellan and Charles McClung explore the northern part of Sequatchie Valley in 1795. After returning to Knoxville, the territorial capital of Tennessee, they wrote an account describing the area which was signed by William Blount, governor of the Territory South of the River Ohio. The description in part is, "...the land on Crow or Sequatchie Creek is excellent quality, the valley from one to three miles wide, covered with lyn, buckeye, walnut, and almost all other kind of timber natural to a rich soil, a large portion of it I conceived to be equal to any land in the world."

John Sevier, first governor of Tennessee, once owned land in Sequatchie Valley. In 1795 the state of North Carolina granted John Sevier 10,500 acres of land described as "...lying in the Eastern District on Crow Creek called by some Sequache adjacent to Stockly Donelson's 5,000 A."

In 1805 by the Treaty of Tellico, the Cherokee Indians ceded the upper part of Sequatchie Valley and a large area of the upper Cumberland Plateau to the United States government. Chief Sequatchu whose home was in the Sequatchie Valley, signed the Dearborn Treaty in 1806. In the Jackson and McMinn Treaty of 1817, the Cherokee Indians gave part of the southern area of the valley up to the white settlers. By the Calhoun Treaty of 1819 the remainder of the land in Sequatchie Valley was ceded to the Government.

Bledsoe was the first county to be formed in Sequatchie Valley, this being in November 1807. Marion County was created in 1819 and Sequatchie County in 1857. Therefore, Bledsoe County is the oldest political division of the Valley. Pikeville, the county seat of Bledsoe, is the oldest town. Other towns are Dunlap, county seat of Sequatchie County and Jasper, county seat of Marion County. Whitwell and South Pittsburg are also in Marion County. All five incorporated small towns are located on the west side of the river. The railroad built in the late 19th century also was constructed on the west side of the Sequatchie River.

Isaac Stephens probably was the first to make Sequatchie Valley known outside of the valley. He was elected to the Tennessee House of Representatives in 1813, while living in Bledsoe County.

James Standefer was probably the first to make it known outside the state. He was elected to the U.S. Congress in the late 1820s while living in the frontier - isolated county of Bledsoe in northern Sequatchie Valley. He was elected to serve six terms. He served with many famous Tennesseans and was congressman when Andrew Jackson was elected president twice.

Gerard Troost was the first to make known the mineral wealth of Sequatchie Valley. In the spring of 1834, European born and educated, set out on a trip to East Tennessee. Mr. Troost had recently been appointed Tennessee's first official state geologist. He explored the valley from Jasper to points north of Pikeville. He collected samples of coal, limestone and fossils. Before returning to Nashville, he also took note of life in the valley. He was met and accompanied on some of his side trips by some of the prominent citizens of the valley.

Mr. W. M. Browne, a British explorer, said in 1888 that he found Sequatchie Valley and before this no one outside the area knew where the valley was and a few knew then. He traveled by railroad to Dunlap, at that time was the terminus; by horse and buggy and in the saddle and on foot to the head of the valley. He wrote of the scenery, "I have stood on vantage points in different parts of the world, many of them renowned in song and story, and have found scenery in Sequatchie Valley and it surroundings by no means inferior to much of the world prizes."

What drew the pioneer families to the frontier land in

Sequatchie Valley? The "hunger for land and opportunity". However, "they were not deterred by the danger of the frontier or by the presence of Indians", who held the land until the Indian Treaty of 1805. This Tellico Treaty, the Cherokee Indians ceded the upper part of Sequatchie Valley and a large area of the Cumberland Plateau to the United States.

Let's thank those who came before us.

Bledsoe County, in Sequatchie Valley was settled by "old American families". The majority of the families' ancestors had been living in America for a hundred years before migrating to the valley and the Cumberland Plateau.

THE CREATION OF BLEDSOE COUNTY, TENNESSEE

Bledsoe was created in the First Session of the Seventh General Assembly of Tennessee 1807. Knoxville was the capital of the state at that time. However, during this session the capital was moved to Kingston for one day and back to Knoxville. This no doubt caused confusion. John Sevier was governor.

Roane County was created in 1801 from part of Knox County. The size of Roane embraced "all land south and west of the southern line of Anderson County between the Tennessee River and the Cumberland Plateau to the Alabama and Georgia state lines." However, a considerable portion of Roane County at this time was still embraced in the holdings of the Cherokee Indians.

October 29, 1807 - Senator George Preston introduced a bill in the state legislature to "...reduce the territory of Roane County to its constitutional limits and create two new counties of the area detached."

This, the Preston Bill, suggested Bledsoe and Cumberland for the names of the two new counties, Bledsoe on the west and Cumberland on the east.

November 4, 1807 - Wednesday, four days later, Preston's Bill was discussed briefly in the senate; laid on the table.

November 5, 1807 - Thursday, Preston's Bill not called up, no explanation given.

November 6, 1807 - Friday, Senator Preston was granted leave of absence for a few days.

November 11, 1807 - Wednesday, Preston's Bill taken up, explained, passed and sent to the House of Representatives.

November 12, 1807 - Preston's Bill was withdrawn by Mr. Kirby who was a Representative from Roane County for an amendment. Here in the House, the bill aroused considerable interest.

November 17, 1807 - Four days later Preston's Bill returned to the House and was taken up for discussion. Representative John Cocke moved to strike out the word <u>Bledsoe</u> and insert the word <u>Rhea</u> in Senator Preston's Bill.

John Cocke lived in Grainger County in the district represented by Congressman John Rhea. He wanted to honor his congressman by naming a county after him. The motion was voted down.

Willie Blount (Governor elect), moved to strike out the word Cumberland and insert the word Rhea. This was satisfactory to the Bledsoe contingent. Mr. Blount lived in Montgomery County, which was next to Robertson and Sumner counties where the large well-known Bledsoe families lived. Mr. Blount did not want to leave his neighbors out.

The Preston Bill was agreed on by the House and sent back to the senate.

November 21, 1807 - The Preston Bill again was considered in the senate. The House amendment was accepted. This suited Mr. Blount to honor both the Bledsoe family and Congressman Rhea. The bill was again sent back to the House and the same day engrossed (prepared for final text, an official document).

The act was passed and was signed by the Speaker of the Senate, Joseph McMinn and John Tipton, Speaker of the House. The bill was sent to the governor, John Sevier and signed November 30, 1807.

However, Sequatchie Valley, Bledsoe County was under the jurisdiction of Roane County until January 1808.

In the year 1807, the 7th General Assembly (The Tennessee State Legislature), was meeting in Knoxville, created seven new counties, Rhea, Bledsoe, Bedford, Hickman, Franklin, Warren and Maury.

The boundary for Bledsoe County was set out by the 7th

General Assembly Acts - Chapter IX Sec. 3 - "Beginning on the northeast end of corner of Rhea County where it strikes the road leading to West Tennessee; thence north forty-five west to Overton County line; thence southwardly with said line to White County line, and with that line to the southern boundary of the state; Thence eastwardly with said line to corner of Rhea County line; thence with said line to the beginning."

Sec. 8 - "John Tollett, Joseph Hoge and James Standefer were appointed commissioners to fix on most suitable place for holding court, until otherwise provided by law."

****

PIKEVILLE AND MADISON
IN BLEDSOE COUNTY
SHOWN ON THE 1821 MAP OF EAST TENNESSEE

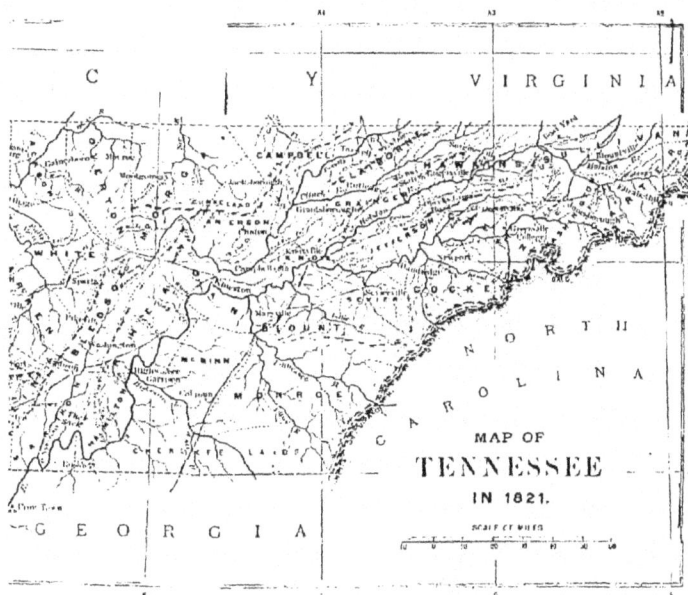

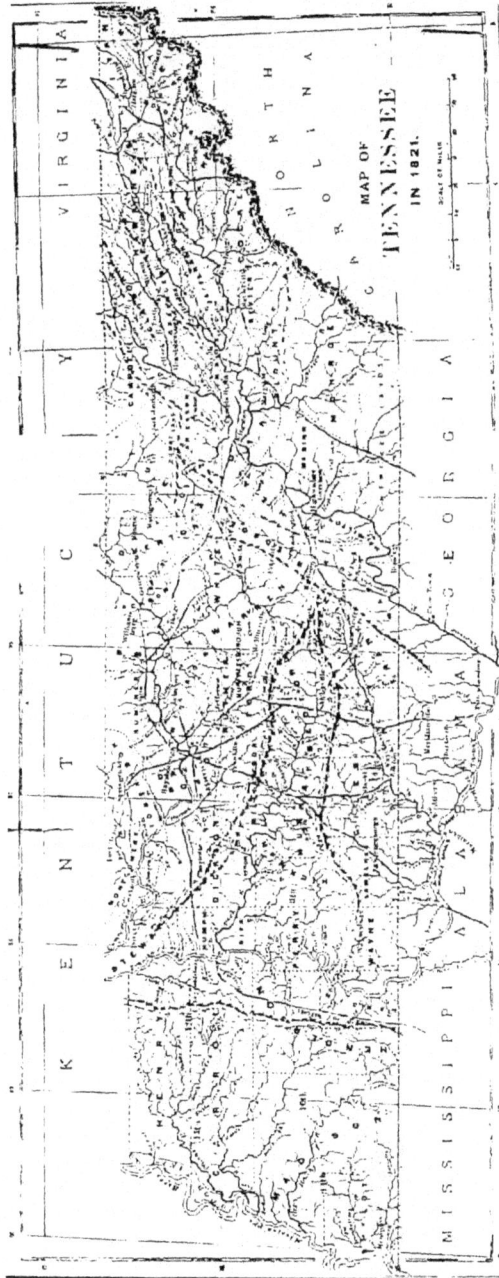

MAP OF
TENNESSEE
IN 1821.

BLEDSOE COUNTY SETTLED

Bledsoe County was settled during one of the most interesting periods in American History. The period between the American Revolution and The War Between the States.

After the American Revolution (1775-1781) the western movement began. The population of the seaboard states began to move west and south over the Appalachian Mountains. During this period important events took place. The Louisiana Purchase, the Lewis and Clark Expedition, The War of 1812, the Texas Revolution, The Mexican War, Tennesseans in the White House and Congress, the extension of the nation to the Pacific, manifest destiny had been achieved.

Just as Lewis and Clark were making their historic journey over the Rocky Mountains 1803-1806, Bledsoe's first families were making their journey over the Appalachian and Cumberland Mountains into Sequatchie Valley. The first settlers that came into Bledsoe County were brave, patriotic individuals, independent, self reliant, relied upon one's own effects and abilities. They also were adventurers.

By 1810 this large county had a population of little more than 3,000. What was in this frontier valley? Natural resources, rich soil, clear water, forests, stones, abundance of wild life, and by 1808 a county government and a state militia.

xx

PIKEVILLE, TENNESSEE

Pikeville, the county seat of Bledsoe County, is the only incorporated town in the county at the present time.

Pikeville became the seat of justice after the War of 1812 when the county seat was moved from Madison. Pikeville was a frontier village, which had grown up around a large spring, on the western bank of the Sequatchie River. It was first known as Thurman, located on a plateau safe from flooding.

Thirty acres of land was purchased from Charles Love of Virginia in 1816 for the new county seat. The purchase price was $110.25, the land being located in Lot No. VIII which took in the "frontier village." The first commissioners of the town were Adam Sherrell, Aquilla Johnson, Joseph Peters and Eli Thurman.

By the 1830s Pikeville was an incorporated town with a population of one hundred and fifty. The town was on the stage route from Knoxville to Huntsville, Alabama and could also boast of a hotel, courthouse and being a United States Post Office in addition to having the Lafayette Academy in operation.

During the 1850s, members of four religious denominations, Methodist Episcopal, South, Baptists, Presbyterians, and Christian built a church in Pikeville.

The Bledsoe County Court voted $100.00 for building a bridge across the Sequatchie River where the old Thurman bridge once stood, voted for $1,500.00 for a new jail to be built of brick, and for the town spring, Pikeville's main source of water, to be taken over by the county.

By 1860 on the eve of the Civil War, Pikeville had a population of two hundred with two hotels. Several companies of Confederate soldiers were organized and left Pikeville in the early days of the war. Pikeville was occupied by the Federal Troops in June 1863.

By the 1870s, Pikeville was recovering from the war. The St. Elmo Lodge of the Masons was chartered and Peoples College was in operation.

In 1880, Pikeville was in the Sixth Civil District with a total of twenty-six households, three merchants, three doctors, one dentist, two hotels, two lawyers, two blacksmiths, two shoemakers, two mail carriers, one wagon maker, one minister, and two prisoners in jail.

In the 1890s Pikeville became a railroad terminal. A line of the Nashville-Chattanooga-St. Louis Railroad was being extended to Pikeville. Telephones were also being introduced in the town. The **Pikeville Banner**, a weekly newspaper, was being published. The People and Citizen Banks were in operation.

By the early 1900s, Pikeville had been incorporated again, the corporation had been abolished in the 1870s during Reconstruction. Pikeville had two banks, a new courthouse, and several new homes had been built on Cumberland and College streets.

By the second decade of the twentieth century electric power had been extended to Pikeville. A new Bledsoe County High School had been built on the site of Peoples College. Several automobiles were owned by the citizens of Pikeville.

Pikeville City Cemetery

Marker for sixteen unknown Confederate soldiers.

NAMING CHILDREN

The Scottish Tradition for Naming Children

Eldest Son - named for paternal grandfather.

Second Son - named for maternal grandfather.

Eldest daughter - named for maternal grandmother.

Second daughter - named for paternal grandmother.

This custom or tradition was very true in the first families of Bledsoe. The custom of using the mother's maiden name as the middle name for her sons was a common practice in the early families in Sequatchie Valley.

ACUFF

The Acuff family was in the American colony of Virginia in the early 1700s. The U.S. Census of 1790 shows Michael Acuff in Pennsylvania. Timothy Acuff born 1735 in Virginia, a Revolutionary War soldier died in 1823. He married Anna Leigh.

John Acuff was in Tennessee before Tennessee became a state. He was born ca. 1730 in Ireland. He received a land grant in Sullivan County in 1787. He died in Knox County in 1821. Several Acuffs served in the East Tennessee Militia during the War of 1812. John Acuff received a land grant from the state of 100 acres, East Tennessee, in Grainger County.

In 1830 three Acuff families were in Bledsoe County. William, the oldest was listed as being between the ages of 40 and 50. He and Nicholas were living north of Pikeville. John was living near Pikeville. In January 1838 John bought from John Bridgman two town lots designated as lots number 15 and 16.

The 1840 Bledsoe Census lists four Acuff families: James, John H., Nicholas and Jonathan all living north of Pikeville in the Smyrna area. On the tax list for Bledsoe County 1837, 1838 and 1839: James, John H. and Nicholas were in District V; Jonathan in District IV and John in District VI.

In 1850 the following Acuff families were living in Bledsoe County: Andrew and Nancy; Robert and Rebecca; Jonathan and Eleanor; William and Sarah; Nicholas and Rebecca; Buster W. and Serena J.; John H. and his mother Nancy (Hutcheson) Acuff, widow of James Acuff.

Acuff, James, born 1790-95; died 1840-1850, married Nancy Hutcheson May 5, 1810 in Grainger County. Nancy was born 1786 and died 1850-60. Sometime in the 1830s they moved to Bledsoe County. James and Nancy became the parents of John H., William, Robert, David, Barton, Anna and Mary.

John H. married Matilda Billingsley; Anna married Isaiah Greer; William married Sallie Henderson; Mary married Jonas Clark; Robert married Beckie Rankin; David married Nancy Billingsley; and Barton married Serena Randolph.

Acuff, John H., the son of James and Nancy (Hutcheson) Acuff was born May 4, 1811. He married Matilda Emily Billingsley May 24, 1835. She was born December 6, 1812. Their children were Samuel Jackson, William L., Robert D., Jasper S., Darius M. and Nancy Ann Matilda. Matilda Emily died March 4, 1847. John H. married second Mary Jane Owing. John H. was living in Bledsoe in the 1840 and 1850 Census.

Acuff, William, born 1819-1820, Married Sallie Henderson born 1820-1821. They were living in the Smyrna area in 1850. His occupation was a blacksmith. They were the parents of nine children: Almire Caroline, James H., Martha, Angeline M., Mary E., John, Joseph, Ann, and William Jr. James married Mary Tennessee Millican; Martha married first Samuel Farmer, second Richard Clark; Angeline married Erasmus (Ras) Johnson; Mary E. married Cal Gentry; John D. married Elizabeth Grimsley; Joseph married Mamie Frailey; Ann married Robert Worthington; William J. married Attie Card. Sarah (Henderson) Acuff died 1870-1880, William died ca. 1890. The estate of William Acuff (deceased) was settled in 1892. Those named were James H., Martha Clark, Ann (Angeline) Johnson, John H., Annie J. Worthington, Mary E. Gentry, and Joseph R. In

1897 Joseph R. deeded to Mary E. Gentry 1/2 interest in 58 acres of land.

The Civil War divided the Acuff family.

John H. and Matilda Emily (Billingsley) Acuff had four sons to serve in this terrible conflict. Jasper Sylvester and Samuel Jackson served in the Confederate Army. Jasper Sylvester enlisted at Pikeville 1861 in the Tulloss Rangers with Captain John M. Bridgman. Robert D. and Darius M. served in the Union Army. Robert D. lost his life during this war in 1863.

James H. (Jim), son of William and Sarah (Henderson) Acuff served in the Confederate Army.

James J. Acuff, son of Jonathan and Eleanor Acuff, served in the Union Army in Captain Andrew Payne's Company.

John H. Acuff moved to Roane County after 1860 and established a church near Rockwood. Family tradition says, sometime after the war, "John H. had his three sons, come up, shake hands in front of the pulpit to show that they were over the war."

Acuff, James H., the son of William and Sarah (Sallie Henderson) Acuff was born January 5, 1845 and died October 30, 1921. He married Mary Tennessee (Tennie) Millican June 25, 1878 in Roane County. Mary Tennessee was born April 4, 1857 and died March 4, 1934. James and Mary are both buried in the Smyrna Cemetery.

James H. served in the Confederate Army, a private in company F. Ashby's Tn Cav. C.S.A. he enlisted November 24, 1862 at Pikeville. James H. and Mary T. were the parents of nine children: William B., J. Fred, Sarah (Sallie), Claude Harding, Mose Scott, John Spencer, Anna, Robert Bates, and Sidney. J. Fred married Donna Poore, Claude Harding married Bertha Stepp and John J. Spencer married Ann Swafford. He served in World War I.

Sources:

Bledsoe County Census, 1830,1840,1850,1860.
Bledsoe County 1836 Tennessee Civil Districts and Tax List by James L. Douthat.
County Court Records - Pikeville, Tennessee; Register's Office, Pikeville, Tennessee.
Family Information: Mr. E.B. Acuff Sr. Moultrie, Ga.
Ann Acuff Wolfe Tullahoma, TN
First Families of Tennessee, Tennessee Historical Society
Tennesseans in the War of 1812, by Sistler.

Smyrna Cemetery

ALLISON/ELLISON

The Allison/Ellison family was in the American colonies by 1620.

Robert Allison was the owner of a land grant in Virginia and a member of the House of Burgesses. Thomas Allison was in Maryland and a land owner in the 1600s. Several members Allison/Ellison served in the American Revolution from North and South Carolina.

Soon after the Revolutionary War, the Allison/Ellisons had crossed the mountains into the territory that later became Tennessee. Several members of this family served in the War of 1812 from Tennessee.

By 1820 the Allisons/Ellisons were in Roane County. By 1830 some members of the family were living in the Sequatchie Valley (Marion County).

In June 1846, Robert B. Ellison enlisted at Washington, Rhea County, for service in the Mexican War. He served as a private, Company H., 1st Regiment, Tennessee Cavalry. He saw action in the Battle of Vera Cruz, Mexico. After the battle, Robert became ill with fever and was sick in camp for "fifteen or twenty days." Some time later his company was sent back to New Orleans. He was discharged at New Orleans May 1847.

Robert B. Ellison was in Pikeville in 1850. In 1856-57 he married Melvine Pendergrass, the daughter of Matthew Pendergrass.

Melvine was born ca. 1833.

Foss Mercer, Bledsoe County Court Clerk, made the statement on Melvine's widow pension application, that the marriage records were "lost or destroyed" during the Civil War.

Robert B. was born ca. 1822 in Roane County. His occupation was a "shoe-maker". In 1860 he was also the jailor in Pikeville.

Robert and Melvine Ellison's children, Frances, James, Mary, Derick, Dorah, Attie, Margaret, David, Ider and Ellen.

In 1870 Robert filed for a pension on his disability he had suffered during his service in the war. Dr. James A. Ross was his doctor. Robert died September 17, 1879. He has a government marker in the Pikeville City Cemetery. Melvine filed for a widow's pension in 1888. She drew $12.00 a month. She died March 9, 1911.

Sources:

Membership Roster and Soldiers Tennessee Society Daughters of the American Revolution, Vol. 3, Vol. 4.

Military Records, Pension Records, Census Records, Bledsoe County, 1850, 1860, 1870

Tennesseans in the War of 1812, by Sistler

National Society Colonial Dames XVII Century Ancestor Roster 1915-2005

Pikeville City Cemetery

ANDERSON

The Anderson name is found in the early 1700s in the American colonies. John Anderson Sr. and wife Rebecca (Maxwell) Anderson were in Washington County, Virginia in the late 1700s. John was born 1750 and died 1817. He married Rebecca in 1775. John served in the American Revolution. He was Captain of the county militia and was known as "Captain John Anderson Sr."

By 1796 the Andersons were in Tennessee. By early 1800 the Andersons were in Sequatchie Valley. Children of John and Rebecca that settled in Bledsoe County were: William born 1776; John Jr. born 1778; Mary born 1781 and Jane born 1791.

John Anderson Jr. signed a petition in 1807 to be presented to the Roane County Court to grant George Skillern the right to erect a grist mill in "Sequatcha Valley."

William Anderson, son of John Anderson Sr. and Rebecca Maxwell, was born October 31, 1776. He married Rebecca Skillern May 5, 1799. Rebecca, born February 1, 1773 in Virginia was the daughter of William and Mary (Anderson) Skillern.

William Anderson received over 5,000 acres of land by grants in Bledsoe County.

William and Rebecca (Skillern) Anderson became the parents of John, Louise, Audley M., Virginia, Josiah S., Martha and William.

In 1850 William and wife, Rebecca (Skillern) Anderson, were living near Elizabeth (McNair) Anderson Thurman Loyd, his sister-in-law. The Anderson family had a strong interest in land ownership, military service, and public office.

John Anderson Jr. born October 5, 1778, in Virginia, married Elizabeth McNair in Knox County, November 12, 1805. Elizabeth was born March 31, 1785, the daughter of James McNair. Soon after their marriage this young couple moved to the frontier area of Sequatchie Valley, which was in the southern part of Roane County. John Anderson received a land grant for 200 acres on the south side of the Sequatchie River in 1807, that was surveyed by A. Higganbotham.

In 1808 John Anderson was captain of the Bledsoe Militia and in 1810 he was serving as Lieutenant Colonel in the 31st militia.

In 1810 John Anderson was granted two land grants of 200 acres each by the state. He was serving as a county commissioner in 1811. During the War of 1812, he received an appointment of Lieutenant Colonel to serve in the 3rd Regiment East Tennessee Militia under Colonel William Johnson. He reported to serve in September 1814. He died October 27, 1814 while on the march with the army to New Orleans at Fort Strother, Alabama, the main headquarters for Andrew Jackson. His will mentioned his wife Betsy and brother Audley. He made a request for his children's education, "learning sufficient to do common business." Several other Andersons served in this war. Elizabeth was left with four small children and just before the youngest was born in December 1814.

Childen of John Anderson Jr. and Elizabeth (McNair) Anderson: Louise Maxwell born September 9, 1806. She is said to be "first white child" born in Sequatchie Valley. She married Allen Kirkland June 8, 1826. Allen born July 30, 1798 and died August 6,

1852. Louise died July 30, 1876. They were both buried Chapel Hill
Cemetery, Sequatchie County; Josiah McNair, born November 29,
1807, married Nancy Lamb. James Madison, born February 25,
1809, married Jane Lamb; and second Sarah Hixson. Elizabeth Ann,
born April 1, 1811, married Hugh Lamb; John, born December 2,
1814, married a Miss Allen, second Purlymly Luttrell.

Elizabeth (McNair) Anderson married James Thurman in
1816, the son of Phillip Thurman. James was born 1786 in South
Carolina and died in 1818 in Bledsoe County.

Elizabeth and James became the parents of Sophia Thurman
born February 27, 1817. Sophia married William Thomas and later
married George W. York.

In the early 1820s, Elizabeth (McNair) Anderson Thurman
married as her third husband, James Loyd. They became the parents
of Jane, married Dr. Thomas Mauzy; Albert married Frances
Swafford; Martha married James A. Tulloss and Roland Peterson
married Margaret Henninger. James Loyd died between 1840 and
1850.

In 1850 Bledsoe Census, Elizabeth Loyd age 64 was living
with her youngest son, Roland and his wife Margaret and young son
James, southeast of Pikeville.

Elizabeth/Betsy (McNair) Anderson Thurman Loyd died
August 13, 1859 and was buried near her home in the Wesley Chapel
Church Cemetery.

Mary Anderson, daughter of John Sr. and Rebecca, born
February 15, 1781, married John A. Skillern August 6, 1798. John

was born 1770.

John A. and Mary were in Sequatchie Valley in 1805. They became the parents of James Andrew, John Anderson, Anderson Campbell, Rebecca Maxwell, Mary Ann, Jane Anderson, Josiah Crawford, Audley, Martha LeVert, and William. John A. died 1846, and Mary died 1842, both buried at Skillern Cemetery.

Jane Anderson, youngest child of John Sr. and Rebecca was born January 20, 1791 and married November 14, 1815 the Rev. John Henninger.

The Rev. Henninger became a well known Methodist minister in Sequatchie Valley. He was born 1780 in Washington County, Virginia. He was in the Methodist conference as early as 1811 and in the Holston conference by 1824. Jane and the Rev. John became the parents of eight children: Eliza married Joseph Hixson, a farmer of Bledsoe County; Marcissa married John Stark moved to Missouri; Asbury married Elba Johnson of Bledsoe County; Emily married R.H. Hudson, lived near Pikeville; Margaret married Judge R.P. Loyd of Bledsoe County; Mary married Jefferson Sawyer of Hamilton County; Sarah married Frank Skillern and second William Skillern of Bledsoe County. John S. moved to Missouri.

The Rev. John Henninger died 1838 in Bradley County, a few days after his wife's death.

Sources:

Tennesseans in the War of 1812, by Sistler.

Bledsoe County Census, 1830, 1840, 1850.

****

Register of Deed Office, Pikeville, Tennessee.

Leaves From the Family Tree, by P.J. Allen.

Tennessee Society of Daughters of the American Revolution Members and Patriot, Vol IV, 1985-2001.

Skillern Family History and Genealogy, by Darlene R. Appell and Ethelmae E. Carter.

Wesley's Chapel Cemetery

ANNIS

Charles Annis, born 1638 in Ireland, was in the American colonies by 1666 when he married Sarah Chase. He was listed as a land owner. Charles died December 19, 1717.

John Annis, born July 20, 1732, married Mary Meloney in Massachusetts. He served as a Captain of a sloop. He and his crew raided commercial British vessels along the coast of New England during the American Revolution. He died of wounds received during a navel engagement 1783 in Massachusetts.

Robert Annis, born ca. 1815 in Tennessee, married Martha Love born ca. 1820. As a young man, Robert became a stage driver. He followed this occupation for over forty years. He lived in Roane County and later in White County. Robert and Martha became the parents of: William F., John R., Fannie E., Daniel C., Henry, Elizabeth, George and Sam. Two sons William F. and Henry served in the Union Army during the Civil War.

In 1828 Robert received from the state of Tennessee land grants of 200 acres in White County, in 1837 a grant of 500 acres in mountain District White County.

Robert died in 1865 in White County.

John R. Annis, was born August 8, 1850 in Roane County. He was the son of Robert R. and Martha (Love) Annis. John spent much of his younger years traveling with his father on the stage route. John was in Bledsoe County in 1880 a boarder in the home of Mrs.

Sarah Thompson in Pikeville.

On August 12, 1885, John married Laura White, daughter of William White. Laura was born ca. 1864.

John R. became a stage driver like his father and followed that occupation for several years traveling from Kingston to Sparta over the Cumberland Mountains. John R. also traveled to the states of Indiana, Arkansas and Texas. In later years he operated the County House in Bledsoe County.

John and Laura became the parents of Robert R., Alfred H., Martha, Ethel, Vida and Dewey.

John R. Annis died 1900-1910 and Laura (White) Annis died after 1930.

Sources:

Bledsoe County Census, 1880, 1900, 1910, 1920, 1930.

Compendium of Local Biography Part II Cumberland Region of Tennessee, 1898 by Geo A. Ogle & Co.

Tennessee Society Daughters of the American Revolution, Vol. 4, 1985-2001.

National Society of Colonial Dames XVII Century.

AULT

The Ault/Alt name is found in Pennsylvania as early as 1774. Michael Ault Sr., born ca. 1750 in Germany, was in Pennsylvania during the American Revolution. He served as a private in the Northumberland County Militia.

In the 1790 census, Michael Ault's family was still in Pennsylvania. Sometime before 1796 this family moved southwest to Tennessee. In 1796 Michael Ault was in Knox County, Tennessee.

Michael Ault died sometime before April 1827 in Knox County, as his will was probated in the April Session. His will named his wife, as Mary. His children were Catherine, George, Eve, Charity, Ann, Jacob, Conrad, Fredrick, Nellie and John.

Michael Ault received from the state of Tennessee a land grant of 100 acres in 1809 in Knox County. In 1834 he received 30 acres, Knox County Eastern District.

Conrad Ault, son of Michael Ault was born February 22, 1783, in Pennsylvania. By 1809 Conrad was in Knox County.

He married Susanna Newman who was born July 22, 1789. Conrad was a prominent citizen in Knox County, serving a juror several times; buying and selling property.

The 1830 census shows Conrad Ault's family in Roane County. He continued to invest in land and take an active part in the local government.

The children of Conrad Ault and Susanna (Newman) Ault: Thomas, George Washington, Margaret Ann, Charles Wesley, Henry, Jacob, and Wiley Newman.

In 1839 Conrad Ault purchased 160 acres of land from Richard G. Waterhouse in Rhea County for $300.00. By 1840 Conrad Ault had moved again, this time to Rhea County. He purchased 20 acres of land from Waterhouse for $400.00.

Conrad Ault died February 1, 1848 and Susanna died December 9, 1859. They are both buried at the Smith - Wilkey Cemetery in Rhea County.

Charles Wesley Ault, son of Conrad and Susanna (Newman) Ault, was born January 10, 1824 in Knox County. He married August 1, 1844 Leah Smith.

They were the parents of Albion, Mary J., George Washington, Olinda, William L. and Charles W.

Sometime after 1860, Leah Smith Ault died. Charles Wesley married second Minerva T. Frazier before 1870.

George Washington Ault, the son of Charles Wesley and Leah (Smith) Ault was born May 6, 1849 in Rhea County.

George W. Ault married Vesta A. Darwin May 3, 1876 in Rhea County. Vesta A. was born May 3, 1849. This family was in Bledsoe in 1880 census. George W. was a merchant living in District 2, northern Bledsoe, Litton Community.

George and Vesta became the parents of Gertrude b. Mar.

1878; Emma b. Nov. 1880; Lola b. Aug. 1882; Clinton b. Feb. 1884; Ethel b. Feb. 1886; Thomas b. May 1888 and Otto b. Oct. 1892.

In 1900 this family was living in the 6th District, Pikeville.

George Washington Ault died March 12, 1903. Vesta A. (Darwin) Ault died February 2, 1936. They were buried at the Pikeville City Cemetery.

Wiley Newman Ault, born September 29, 1828 in Rhea County was the son of Conrad and Susanna (Newman) Ault. He married Ruth Howard July 24, 1855. Ruth was born February 13, 1836. They became the parents of William Henry, James Franklin, Margaret Ann and Wiley Allison Ault. Ruth Howard Ault died February 2, 1865.

Wiley Newman Ault married second Margaret Adaline Able born 1846, died 1916. Wiley Newman Ault died June 25, 1897. In 1870 Wiley Newman was in Bledsoe County, living in District 3, post office was Ormes Store. He was a merchant in northern part of Sequatchie Valley. His wife Margaret A. and his children were: William Henry born 1857, James Franklin 1859, Margaret Ann 1861, Wiley Allison 1863, Perry W. 1866, Sam Wesley 1868, Versailles 1870, Mary Emma 1873, Suanna Adaline 1875, Icie Delle 1879, Ida Latitia 1881, and Lorinda Jane 1883.

William Henry Ault, son of Wiley Newman and Ruth (Howard) Ault, was born in Rhea County, December 1, 1856.

He was living with his family in Bledsoe County in 1870 in the Litton Community.

Sometime before 1900 William Henry married Syrene Tollett, the daughter of Elijah Gore and Nancy (Sherrill) Tollett. Syrene was born in 1862, near the Tollett Mill.

William Henry known as "Doctor Ault" was a farmer and a country doctor, served the rural areas of northern Sequatchie Valley and Walden Ridge in the early 1900s.

Sources:

Members and Patriots The Tennessee Society Daughters of the American Revolution, Vol. 4, 1985-2001.

Michael Ault and Son Conrad Ault Families by Mrs. Francis E. Pray.

Bledsoe U.S. Census Records, 1870, 1880, 1900.

First Families of Tennessee, Tennessee Historical Association.

BEATTY/BEATY

The name Beatty/Beaty is found in the American colonies of New York, Pennsylvania and North Carolina in the 1700s. Several served in the America Revolution from Pennsylvania and North Carolina.

The Beatty/Beaty family was in Tennessee by the late 1700s, when Tennessee became a state in 1796. Several served in the War of 1812 from Tennessee.

Hugh Beaty was in Bledsoe County in the 1820s. He was a member of the Vale Temple Lodge in Pikeville in 1825, the first lodge organized in Pikeville. Between the years of 1825 to 1836, he received over 600 acres in land grants from the state.

Hugh Beaty was born ca. 1774 in Ireland. He married Jane Miller born ca. 1785 also in Ireland. They were married in Knox County, Tennessee.

Hugh and Jane settled about eight miles north of Pikeville on the western side of Walden Ridge in a cove which became known as "Beaty Cove". Hugh and Jane became the parents of John M., Edward, Nancy, Isabella and Margaret.

John M. and Edward were on the Tax List in District IV Bledsoe County 1837, 1838, 1839.

This family was interested and believed in education. Miss Nancy McCall, a teacher age 48 was living in the Beaty home in

1850. In 1860 she was in the home of Margaret Beaty and John Swafford. Hugh and Jane Beaty both died after 1850 and before 1860 and were buried in the Beaty Cemetery.

John M./J.M. was in Jasper, Tennessee in February 1827 as he wrote his sisters Nancy and Isabella a letter. It was a two page, double sheet of paper, being folded without an envelope. He encouraged and advised his sisters to listen to their mother, to read newspapers and good books at night and their leisure time. He will subscribed for them a paper printed in Philadelphia for young ladies containing many useful lessons for history, geography and poetry. The letter is signed "I am Dear Sisters your Affectional Brother J.M. Beaty."

John M. served as county commissioner of Bledsoe County in the late 1830s and early 1840s.

Isabella Hood born 1809, Knox County married James Stephens June 28, 1831. They became the parents of Anna J. born 1832, Isaac Hugh 1834, Martha E. 1837, William E. 1840, John Beaty 1842, Margaret 1845, and James Mark 1848. James Stephens and Isabella moved to Honey Grove, Texas sometime before 1860. Isabella died 1872 and buried in Honey Grove.

Margaret Beaty, born October 20, 1828, married John Swafford. John was born December 8, 1828. He served in the Confederate Army during the Civil War. He was known and called "Beaty John" to distinguish him from other John Swaffords in the area. John and Margaret lived in the Beaty Cove. Margaret died August 8, 1896 and John died July 30, 1911. They were both buried in the Beaty Cemetery.

John and Margaret Swafford became the parents of Martha Jane born 1852, Hugh B. born 1855, John Edward born 1857, and Jesse born ca. 1860, died young. John Edward Swafford married Julia Pollard.

Martha Jane married John A. Patton. Martha Jane known as "Mattie" when a student at Sequatchie College in 1869. She used a *McGuffey's New School Reader.*

Beaty John Swafford

Sources:

National Society, Colonial Dames XVII Century, Ancestor Roster, 1915-2005.

The Tennessee Society Daughters of the American Revolution Members and Patriots, Vol. 4, 1985-2001.

First Families of Tennessee.

Tennesseans in the War of 1812, by Sistler.

Bledsoe County, Tennessee, A History, by Elizabeth Parham Robnett.

Bledsoe County Census, 1830, 1840, 1850.

Descendants of Solomon Stephens and Milly Britt/Stephens, Stephens Book I, V.

BILLINGSLEY

The name Billingsley is found in the American colonies of Maryland and Virginia in the 1600s. Francis Billingsley was in Maryland in the 1680s. He was a planter and owned a sloop.

Several Billingsleys came to the English colonies as "Transportee", and later served in the American Revolution. Samuel Billingsley was born 1747 in St. Mary's County, Maryland. During the Revolution he lived in North Carolina. He served as a private in Lighthorse Regiment under Captain George Sharp and Colonel Francis Locke.

He married Mary Griffith. She was born September 1, 1743 in North Carolina. They became the parents of eleven children: James, Mary, Samuel, William, Jephtha, Sarah, John, Thomas, Amanda, Elijah and Nancy.

Samuel Billingsley was in Sullivan County, Tennessee when it was still part of North Caroline.
The Billingsleys were in Sequatchie Valley, Bledsoe County, by 1808.

John Billingsley held by "a right of improvement and occupancy and preemption" 126 acres on Sequachey Creek," 1808 Bledsoe County.

Samuel Billingsley held by "right of improvement occupancy

Billingsley

and preemption 120 acres on Sequachey Creek, joining line with John Billingsley."

In 1815 John Billingsley and Samuel Billingsley Jr. signed the Petition "to delay enactment of the Land Law" during the War Between the United States and Great Britain.

Samuel was a member of the Missionary Baptist Church and a charter member of the first Masonic Lodge in the county.

In the 1830 Bledsoe Census, five Billingsley families were

listed. In the 1840 census there were seven heads of families. In 1850 census on the eve of the Civil War, showed seven heads of families by the name of Billingsley, however three were listed "free blacks".

John Billingsley, the son of Samuel, born September 10, 1781 in Onslow County, North Carolina. He served as a member of the Bledsoe County court for many years and as chairman several times.

He served in the 15th Tennessee General Assembly, Senate, 1823-25, representing Bledsoe, Anderson, Morgan, Roane, Rhea, Marion, Hamilton and McMinn counties.

In 1830 he built and finished his twelve room brick house that was in District V. John at the time of his death owned forty slaves, twenty-three males and seventeen females, and owned 1,500 acres of valley land and 7,000 acres of mountain land.

John Billingsley married Martha Blackwood October 10, 1802. Martha was born March 12, 1786 in North Carolina. They became the parents of ten children: Samuel born 1803, married Almire Tennessee Whitesides; William born 1805, died 1811; Nancy born 1807, married John Hutcheson; Mary born 1809, died 1828, married James Griffith; John Calvin born 1812; Andrew Blackwood born 1814, married Susan Jane Myers; Mahala born 1816, married John Munsey; John Davis born 1819; Martha Jane born 1822, married Thomas S. Myers; Elizabeth E. born 1824, married James Rankins. Martha (Blackwood) Billingsley died March 11, 1829.

John Billingsley married second September 15, 1831, Jane Hoodenpyle, the daughter of Phillip Hoodenpyle. She was born April 12, 1812 in North Carolina.

They became the parents of nine children. Mary Theola born 1832, married Reuban Rankins; Phillip Marshall born 1834, married Mary M. Smith; Amanda born 1836, married John L. Rankin; Hixie O. born 1838, married Jesse Hall; Viola C. born 1841, married William W. Farmer; Leander Travis born 1843; Satune born 1845, married Tullos A. Reynolds; Sarah Flora born 1847, married Frank Hutcheson; Evalista Jane born 1853, married John L. Swafford.

John Billingsley died May 25, 1856 and Jane, his wife died September 3, 1894. They were buried in the Billingsley Family Cemetery, in the Smyrna area of Bledsoe County.

Leander Travis (Lee), youngest son of John and Jane (Hoodenpyle) Billingsley enlisted in the Confederate Army June 1861. He was 1st Corporal in the famous "Tullos Rangers" from Sequatchie Valley. After the war Lee attended Sequatchie College for eight months.

On December 23, 1873, he married Mary F. Worthington daughter of James Worthington. She was born May 27, 1849 and died April 1, 1890.

In 1898, he married his second wife Lucy Houston. Lee served as justice of peace for many years, and supported the Democratic Party. Lee Billingsley died June 12, 1927 and was buried in the Worthington Cemetery.

Samuel Billingsley, son of Samuel Sr. and Mary Griffith born April 9, 1775 in North Carolina married Nancy Mulkey April 9, 1798, the daughter of Jonathan Mulkey. Nancy was born March 9, 1780 in North Carolina.

Samuel Billingsley was in Kentucky in early 1800. However, in Bledsoe in 1830 and 1840 census. In 1850 he was 75 and Nancy was 70, both living in household of their youngest son, Jonathan in the Smyrna area.

Nancy died September 2, 1850 and Samuel died May 29, 1857, both buried in Smyrna Cemetery.

Children of Samuel Jr. and Nancy (Mulkey) Billingsley: Mary born 1800, married John Freiley; Sallie born 1802, married Robert Lowery; Rebecca born 1804, married Nicholas Acuff; John M. born 1805, married Hannah D. Myers, a son William Newton Billingsley served for many years as President of Burritt College; Elizabeth born 1807, married William D. Carnes who served as President of Burritt College at Spencer; Jonathan born 1810 in Kentucky, married Hannah Ogle; Matilda born 1812, married John H. Acuff; Joseph B. born and died 1814.

Sources:

The Tennessee Society Daughters of the American Revolution Members and Patriots, Vol. 4, 1985-2001.

Ancestor Roster National Society, Colonial Dames XVII Century, Ancestor Roster XVII Century 1915-2005.

First Families of Tennessee East Tennessee Historical Society 2000.

Biographical Directory of the Tennessee General Assembly, Vol. 1, 1796-1861.

Tennessee Homesteaders and Landowners 4th Surveyors District Survey Book 1808-1810, Entry Book 1814-1815.

Compendium of Local Biography Cumberland Region of Tennessee, Geo. A. Ogle & Co. 1898.

Tennessee Historical Committee Civil War Questionnaires.

Bridgman

The Bridgman name is found in the American colonies of Massachusetts and Pennsylvania as early as 1640. By 1800 the Bridgmans were in Wythe County, Virginia. In the 1810 Wythe County Census, Franklin Bridgman is head of a house. He is over 45 years of age, one male between the ages of 16 - 26.

John Bridgman was born November 14, 1789 in Virginia. He married Lavina Cox, who was born in Tennessee, March 27, 1796.

On January 10, 1814, John joined the East Tennessee Militia at Washington in Rhea County, to serve in the War of 1812. He was a sergeant in Captain John Inglish Company, East Tennessee. He was discharged May 14, 1814 at Washington, Rhea County.

December 1815 John gave power of attorney in Campbell County to collect payment due him for his military service. He had served four months and eleven days. His pay $47.90. He was allowed six days travel time.

John Bridgman was in Bledsoe County in 1818, as he was serving as a commissioner for the new county seat, Pikeville.

After moving to Bledsoe County, John began investing in real estate and farm land. He became a well-known citizen of the county. He was a merchant, farmer, land owner, slave holder, civil servant, policital leader in the Whig Party. He served in the 13th General Assembly as a member of the House 1819-1821, representing Bledsoe and Marion counties. The capital of Tennessee at this time was at Murfreesboro.

Revolutionary War veterans living in the county, often gave his name as reference in applying for their pensions in the 1830s.

In 1828 John purchased the "Eastern part of Lot number 28 in the town of Pikeville." This is where he built the two story Federal style brick house in about 1830.

John was a community leader. In 1826 he sold "one-half acre" joining the town on the northwest corner, "for an academy". This school was later known as Lafayette Academy. This was the first school of any significance in the county. He served on the board of trustees.

**The John Bridgman House
built ca 1830**

In 1836 John deeded four town lots to his daughter Eliza C. and her husband, Samuel W. Roberson, lots number 48, 49, 50 and Lot 38, the "Whiteside brick", where she now lives.

In 1842 John Bridgman, Adam Lamb and James L. Schoolfield were appointed commissioners for the purpose of receiving $2,000.00 appropriated to be used, "expended" upon Sequachee River within the limits of Bledsoe County.

John died October 19, 1847. Lavina survived the Civil War by two years and died March 13, 1867. She was buried in the Pikeville City Cemetery with her husband and four young children.

John and Lavina became the parents of nine children: Benjamin F., James, Eliza C., Sampson D., Tilford P., Martha E., Rufus K., John M., and Calvin.

Benjamin Franklin, (B.F.) (Frank), oldest son of John and Lavina born September 25, 1813 and died September 24, 1873 (Pikeville City Cemetery marker). (This Bridgman has two places of burial), Benjamin Franklin Bridgman born September 15, 1812 and died April 23, 1875 (Little White Church Cemetery marker), Marion County.

Benjamin Franklin enlisted in the service of the United States (Cherokee War 1836-38). This was the removal of the Indians from East Tennessee to Indian Territory west of the Mississippi.

Benjamin Franklin married first Narcissa Frances Massingale. This marriage ended in divorce. He married second Martha in Marion County.

Benjamin Franklin like his father was a merchant, owned much property in Pikeville as well as land in the valley.

He was listed in Marion County in the 1840 census. In 1850 and 1860 Benjamin Franklin was listed as head of household in both Bledsoe and Marion counties. The 1860 Marion County census, Benjamin and wife Martha's children were Mary Ann, Josephine, Eliza J., Elizabeth and John D.

In 1857 the Tennessee State Legislature detached the Tenth Civil District from Bledsoe County and added it to Hamilton County. At the same time, detached the First and Second Civil District from Marion County. The former Bledsoe Tenth and the First and Second District became Sequatchie County.

In 1858 Benjamin Franklin Bridgman, "a prominent citizen of Bledsoe filed suit in his individual rights and a citizen of Bledsoe on behalf of the justice in Chancery Court against Sequatchie County." This began the well-known "law suit between Bledsoe and Sequatchie County."

In the 1870s Benjamin Franklin was age 56, a merchant in Pikeville, a boarder at the Hotel. Records show he sold two blankets to the county jail. In 1871 he sold eleven acres of land for Peoples College.

James, second son of John and Lavina, born August 8, 1815, died March 21, 1831. A Nashville newspaper reported his death at age of 15. He was buried in the Pikeville City Cemetery.

Eliza C. Bridgman, oldest daughter of John and Lavina, born August 1, 1817 and died February 19, 1891. She married Samuel W.

Roberson. She is buried in the Little Hopewell Baptist Church Cemetery in Sequatchie County.

In 1851, a deed, for the south part of Lot number 18, was made to Bledsoe County for the new jail for $100.00. The deed was made by Eliza C. Bridgman Roberson and husband, Samuel W. Roberson heirs of John Bridgman.

Telford P. born February 24, 1822, died November 5, 1823. He was the first person buried in the Pikeville City Cemetery. This land owned by the Bridgman family was later donated to the city.

Sampson D. born ca. 1823, married Pricilla, born ca. 1825. Sampson D. served as Clerk of the County Court, Clerk and Master of the Chancery Court and Register of Deeds. In 1856 Sampson D. was paid $130.00 "to cover the courthouse."

In 1860 Sampson D. and Pricilla were living in Pikeville. This family moved from Tennessee to Georgia and back to Tennessee several times before 1870. Sampson D. died after 1869.

In 1860 Sampson D. gave his occupation as a "distiller". His wife Pricilla was born in Georgia. The children were Sarah, John L., Ben F., James, Lavina, Martha J., and Sampson D.

Martha E. Bridgman born June 21, 1824 and died April 15, 1900. She married David Cleage. They lived at Athens, McMinn County.

In 1880 McMinn County Census, David Cleage was 73 and Martha was 54. Other members in the household were Samuel 21, David 27, Mary 15, Eliza 20, and Sallie 16.

Rufus K. Bridgman born March 8, 1826 and died July 7, 1826. He was buried in the Pikeville City Cemetery.

John M. Bridgman born November 20, 1827 and died March 2, 1872. He married Naomi Pendergrass. He was buried in the Pikeville City Cemetery. He served as Captain in the Tulloss Rangers, Confederate Army. This company was raised in Pikeville, July 1861. He served as postmaster at the Pikeville post office and Circuit Court Clerk for the county.

In December 1863, the Union soldiers were in control of Pikeville and Sequatchie Valley. This was after the battles around Chattanooga. As one Union soldier put it, "our work was lighter, our thoughts turned to pleasure and a party, December 24 at Colonel Bridgman's house." This was the Bridgman brick.

Calvin L. Bridgman born February 5, 1836 and died July 3, 1839. He was buried in the Pikeville City Cemetery.

Sources:

The History of the William T. Bridgman Family, by Lonnie & Alma Hazel Bridgman, Katherine Bridgman McClure, 1990.

Bledsoe County Census, 1830, 1840, 1850, 1860, 1870.

Pikeville City Cemetery.

National Archives, Washington D.C.

Bledsoe County, Tennessee, a History, by Elizabeth Robnett, 1993.

Brown

The name Brown is found in early 1600s and 1700s in the New England colonies. It is also found in New York, Pennsylvania, New Jersey and Maryland.

By the time of the American Revolution, Browns were in the South, Virginia, North and South Carolina. Several served in the American Revolution.

Jesse Brown, born June 12, 1793 in Virginia was in Bledsoe County in 1814. He married Cary Wilson, daughter of Greenbury Wilson on August 13, 1814. Cary (Kary) was born February 20, 1794 in North Carolina.

By October 1814, Jessee was buying land on the "bench of the Cumberland Mountains" and "on the waters of Sequatchie Creek." Witnesses to the deeds were James Ormes, Johnson Parham, Benjamin Hamilton and William Nail.

In 1840 Jesse Brown's family was living in District II of Bledsoe County. He and Cary had five daughters and six sons.

Jesse and Cary (Wilson) Brown became the parents of: Elizabeth (Betty), born June 11, 1815, married John Parham, died July 28, 1913; Greenbury W. born March 7, 1817, died September 1818; Temperance B. born March 27, 1819, married Jesse Worthington, died April 25, 1864; Stephen born August 21, 1821, died after 1840; William S. born June 12, 1822, married Mahaley Cordell; Joseph W. born September 24, 1824, died after 1840; Sarah (Sally) born February 28, 1827, married William (Bill) Parham, died

The Home of Jesse and Carrie (Wilson) Brown
Brown Ridge ca 1957

May 1, 1872; Jesse Walker born March 19, 1830, married Emily Miller; Charles Crockett born 1832, drown December 11, 1856 in White Creek, returning from a trip to Kentucky with his aunt Polly Ormes, to get salt. They were traveling in an "ox wagon"; Carrie Emaline born November 22, 1833, married A. Zariah Dorton, died February 10, 1902; Mary Jane born February 28, 1835, married J.M. Miller; John LaFayette (Fate) born July 24, 1837, died Andersonville Prison, Georgia during Civil War.

Jesse Brown died May 29, 1861, Cary (Wilson) Brown died September 22, 1875.

Jesse Walker Brown and Emily (Miller) Brown were the parents of Cary Frances, Mary A., Sarah, Catherine, Amanda E.,

Martha, Tennie, James L., Luther, Laura and William. Jesse Walker was a farmer.

William and Mahala (Cordell) Brown were the parents of Darius, Horace, LaFayette (Fate), Flora and Allie. William was a farmer and a blacksmith. Both Jesse Walker and William lived near their birthplace.

The Fate Brown Story, by Elizabeth Robnett, Bledsoe County Historian

This story was told by Mrs. Elizabeth "Betty" (Brown) Parham to her granddaughter, Mrs. Addie (Swafford) Robnett, mother of Elizabeth Robnett, sometime before 1913.

"Fate" LaFayette Brown was the son of Jesse and Cary (Wilson) Brown and a brother of Elizabeth (Brown) Parham. Fate lived with his parents at the Brown home on top of the mountain, Cumberland Plateau, on the Brown Gap Road overlooking the Sequatchie Valley. The Brown family had no sons on either side of the Civil War, but a grandson was in the Union Army. They were poor pioneers living a truly frontier life to the point of being almost self-sufficient. These people, like the majority in the East Tennessee mountains, had no connections with slavery but were Union sympathizers.

One day, as the story goes, Fate decided to take his money and gun and bury them for safekeeping. Fate was about 25 years of age, the youngest son. Soldiers of both armies were being seen or heard of more frequently in and around the Sequatchie Valley. Even this remote place on the Brown Gap road was not safe. The guerillas also were being heard of.

No member of the family knew Fate's secret hiding place. Several days later, he told his family he was going to take his horse to a back pasture, also for safekeeping. This was the last time they saw Fate. Several weeks later, the Brown family got news of a band of guerillas passing through the area. No word was ever heard from this son again.

After the war was over, a stranger appeared at the Brown's gate. This man told Mrs. Brown that he had been in prison with her son, Fate, and that both made a vow: if either one survived, they would go to the other's home and tell his mother what had happened. Fate had not survived Andersonville. The stranger told the story of Fate and that his gun and money would be found buried in a certain place.

The Brown family knew this was a true story because the small but worldly possessions of this innocent civilian were found as directed.

Sources:

Jesse Brown's Bible.

Bledsoe County U.S. Census.

Register of Deeds, Bledsoe County Courthouse.

Cumberland County Census.

Reuben Brown born May 18, 1781 in North Carolina, married Sarah (Sallie) Worthington, daughter of Samuel Worthington. Sarah was born June 10, 1784 in Virginia.

Reuben was in Tennessee, Anderson County, on the Tax list in 1805. In May 1808 Reuben was in Bledsoe County.

Reuben is said to have brought the first wagon into Sequatchie Valley. It being separated into two, "two wheel carts".

In 1813 he signed a petition for Peter Hoodenpyle to "improve at his own expense a certain wagon road that crossed the Cumberland Mountains from Bledsoe County to White and Warren counties, along the Kioky Trace - on completion of the work, Hoodenpyle requests permission to erect a toll gate."

He served as a county commissioner very early in the county. He was appointed commissioner to select a new county seat in 1813. Madison was the county seat located near the Indian boundary line.

The 1830 Bledsoe Census shows Reuben and Sarah Brown's family consisted of eight children. The 1840 census shows this family living in the IV Civil District. He was on the tax list in District IV in 1837, 1838, 1839.

He became a prominent citizen, large land owner and slave holder in the county. Sometime in the 1840s Reuben built his "brick house", that stood to the late 1920s.

Reuben and Sarah were members of the Cumberland Presbyterian Church. He died in October 1850 and was buried on his land "The old Brown Cemetery". Sarah died in December 1873.

Reuben and Sarah became the parents of: Nancy, married Samuel Close; Dicey, married Samuel Rankin; Margaret (Peggy) married William (Big Spring Bill) Worthington, a cousin; Elizabeth (Betsy) born September 19, 1809, died January 16, 1876, married William (Creek Billy) Brown, a cousin.

In 1833 Reuben Brown gave to his daughter Betsy and her husband a 110 acre farm on Sequatchie Creek "for the love and affection where they now live". William died September 2, 1870. He and Betsy and almost all their family are buried in the Creek Billy Brown Cemetery. On William's grave marker, "moved to this place December 16, 1831."

Frances (Fannie) born ca. 1811 married Jeremiah Dorsey. Sometime before 1870 this family moved to Mississippi; Sarah (Sally) born February 14, 1813, died June 5, 1891, married Phillip Hutcheson; Jesse born May 31, 1815 died May 3, 1876, married Sarah Jane Swafford; James R. born October 1, 1820, died March 12, 1884 married Lodemie Worthington, married second Minerva Swafford; Minerva born April 13, 1826, died May 11, 1892, married James Worthington, married second Isaac Easterly Swafford.

Sources:

Bledsoe County Census, 1830, 1840, 1850.

Bledsoe County, Tennessee 1836 Tennessee Civil Districts and Tax List, by James L. Douthat.

Tennessee Homesteaders and Landowners, 4th Surveyors District, by Willis Hutcherson.

Early Tax List, Anderson County, by Curtis.

Cemetery Records.

Compendium of Biography Cumberland Region of Tennessee, 1898, Geo. A. Ogle & Company.

William Lilly Brown, born in 1792 in Virginia, was the son of John Brown who had helped the nation gain its independence by fighting in the American Revolution. In June 1812, the young nation became involved in war with England. In August 1814, William Lilly enlisted as a private in the 7th Virginia Militia in Captain Ford's Company. He had not yet reached his 22nd birthday. This young soldier was described as being 6 ft. 2 in. tall, hair light, eyes blue, and complexion fair.

This was a dark time for the nation and the young soldier. The British had landed soldiers on the coast of Maryland and marched to Washington, set fire to the capitol, the president's house and other public buildings. William L. Brown was discharged in February 1815 at Camp Carter which was located twelve miles south of Richmond. He was allowed three days travel time with pay to travel the sixty miles to his home. His pay was $8.00 per month.

On September 14, 1816 he married Nancy Humphrey in Fluvanna County, Virginia. Nancy was born in 1798 the daughter of William Humphrey. Sometime between 1823 - 1825, William with his wife and three children, he moved from Virginia to East Tennessee.

This was the general pattern of migration in a southwest direction. This family lived in Roane County a few years, but by 1830 they had made their last move to Bledsoe County in Sequatchie Valley.

In 1852 William Lilly Brown made an application for bounty land for his service in the War of 1812. His address was Foster Cross Roads. This was a small rural post office southeast of Pikeville. A letter written in 1853 to his son, Thomas G., a student at Emory and

Henry in Virginia, was headed River Bend, which was probably the

**Descendants of William Lilly Brown
Marking his grave 1981**

name of his farm. William Lilly Brown died February 1859 and was buried in the Oak Grove Cemetery in Bledsoe County.

In 1878 Nancy Brown was 80 years old when she made application for a land warrant on her husband's service. She did not sign the application, but made her mark which was witnessed by William A. Schoolfield and her grandson, Robert Brown Schoolfield. In 1870 Nancy was living with her daughter's family Mary Schoolfield in District VI. In 1880 Nancy was living with her son Elijah and family near Pikeville and reported she was born in Virginia, also her parents were born in Virginia. Nancy died in January 1881 and was buried in the Oak Grove Cemetery.

William Lilly and Nancy (Humphrey) Brown had the

following children: Thinza, married John Stout; Sarah married Isaac Anderson; Adaline married the Union General James G. Spears and later Col. William T. Gass of the Confederate Army; Mary, married William H. Schoolfield; Sammie married James Foster; Thomas G. a dentist never married; Virginia married Rowland F. McDonald; William L. Jr., married Elizabeth; Elijah H. married Charlotte Grafton; Julia; and Rufus K. married Kate Thomas. Rufus K. was a member of the faculty of Sequatchie College in 1874. The first three children of this family were born in Virginia.

In October 1981 members of the Volunteer Wauhatchie Chapter U.S.D. 1812 dedicated an official marker at the grave of William Lilly Brown in the Oak Grove Cemetery located southeast of Pikeville. Several descendants attended.

Sources:

Bledsoe County Census Records.

Schoolfields, by Cleopatra Doss Schoolfield.

William Lilly Brown's military Record, land Warrent applications.

CARNES

The Carnes family was in Mecklenberg County, North Carolina in the late 1700s. In early 1800, Alexander and Mary (Davis) Carnes were in South Carolina.

William Davis Carnes born October 23, 1805, in Lancaster County, South Carolina, was the oldest son of Alexander and Mary (Davis) Carnes. This family was in Tennessee, Warren County, by 1809.

William Davis entered the ministry of the Christian Church at the age of nineteen. At the age of twenty he agreed to assist an evangelist on a missionary tour across the Cumberland Mountian into Sequatchie Valley. By the 1820s he was in Bledsoe County, in the community of Smyrna. William Davis met Elizabeth Billingsley, daughter of Samuel Billingsley. He was invited to hold services at the church. Elizabeth became one of his first converts. William D. and Elizabeth were married June 1, 1825.

William D. purchased a farm in the Smyrna area and became a successful farmer and business man, operating a grist mill and a saw mill. He also ministered at the Smyrna Church and taught at the Lafayette Academy, Pikeville.

However, realizing the need for more education, he moved his family to Knoxville and enrolled at the University of East Tennessee. As he was older than the other students, he acquired the name "pap Carnes".

By 1830, Mary Carnes had moved her family from Warren County to Bledsoe to be near her oldest son, William D. In 1837 William D. and A.B. Carnes were on the tax list in the V District as land owners.

William Davis and Elizabeth (Billingsley) Carnes became the parents of eight children, Mary M. born May 4, 1827 in Bledsoe County. She graduated from Burritt College with a Mistress of Art Degree. She married William Jasper Hill, July 18, 1854 in Van Buren County. He was born December 12, 1827. He enlisted in the Confederate Army and died March 15, 1862. Mary was a long time teacher and was engaged in teaching at the time of her death December 12, 1901, age 75 years. She was buried at the Billingsley family Cemetery, Smyrna, beside her husband, Alexander Campbell, born March 1, 1829 in Bledsoe County. He became a teacher at Burritt College. Nancy Amanda born June 1831 married George W. Rogers, a merchant in Pikeville. She graduated from Burritt College with a Mistress of Art Degree. Amanda died ca. 1858. In 1860 George Rogers and Amanda's only daughter, Ida, was living in the household of William J. Hill and Mary Carnes Hill. In 1866, George Rogers was president of Sequatchie College. Ida Rogers served as a teacher at Sequatchie College for many years. Alva, born 1833 in Bledsoe County, died at age of six years; Samuel Erasmus born August 7, 1835 in Bledsoe County. He became a lawyer. Joseph M. born 1840 in Bledsoe County, served in the Confederate Army. He later served as president of Sequatchie College; William D. Jr. born April 13, 1845 Knoxville, University of East Tennessee Campus. He enlisted in the Confederate Army and died March 1865 at Camp Douglas near Chicago, Illinois; Elizabeth Annette born July 15, 1848.

Elizabeth (Billingsley) Carnes died 1859 and was buried at the Billingsley family cemetery Smyrna. William Davis Carnes married his second wife Mrs. Mary Morgan, April 12, 1865.

In 1850 Van Buren County census, the Carnes family lived at Spencer. William Davis was listed as a college teacher; his daughter Mary was also listed as a teacher. Others in his family were his wife Elizabeth, children Alexander C., Nancy A., Samuel E., Joseph M., William D. and Elizabeth A. Also in the household was his mother Mary Carnes, age 77, and James A. Garvin, a young student son of his good professor Garvin.

William Davis Carnes was a well-known educator, having taught in the rural school, Smyrna; Lafayette Academy, Pikeville; teacher of English at the University of East Tennessee, Knoxville; Principal of the Preparatory Department at the University of East Tennessee, President of the University of East Tennessee, President of Franklin College, President of Burritt College 1850-1858 and from 1872-1878, and President of Waters and Walling College, McMinnville.

The great pioneer teacher and educator died November 20, 1879 and was buried in the city cemetery, Spencer. The students of Burritt erected a marble shaft over his grave.

The following account gives what a prominent citizen, well-known minister and educator that President Carnes was in Pikeville during the Civil War. When advancing lines of the Federal Army reached Pikeville, President Carnes among others, who had supported the cause of the South was arrested on charges of disloyalty to the United States government. When he was arraigned for trial he was informed that he was not charged with an overt act, only with giving aid and comfort to the enemy and if he would take the oath and give bond he would be released. The alternative was to be sent to one of the camps for citizen prisoners in the northern states. He asked to have the oath read, after hearing it, he said "I am willing to swear that I will not take up arms against the United States, but I have friends, including three sons and one son-in-law in the Confederate Army. It is not probable that I shall have an opportunity to give what you call aid or comfort to them, but it is possible, and I refuse to swear that I will not." "Then you go North", explained the Provost Marshal.

At this critical moment, Judge Thomas N. Frazier, the most influential Union man in Sequatchie Valley, in advancing and confronting the provost marshal, explained in positive tone: "I demand the unconditional release of President Carnes." Several other prominent Union men who were present, by Judge Frazier's request, seconded his demand pledging their word and honor that President Carnes would do no harm to the Union cause and threatening to appeal to President Lincoln. The provost marshal gracefully accepted the situation and congratulated the discharged prisoner on having so good personal friends among political enemies.

Much of the success of Burritt College 1849-1939 was due to President Carnes. His investment in stock of the college (from sale of his property in Sequatchie Valley), co-education, his work to get the state legislature to pass the first statewide prohibition ordinance in Tennessee, his standards in intellectual, moral and religion.

Sources:
Bledsoe County Census, 1830, 1840, 1860

Van Buren County Census 1850

The Chattanooga Sunday Times, Magazine section, March 18 & 25, 1934 by Raymond Hyde

A History of Christian Colleges, Burritt College Centennial Celebration 1948, by Charles Lee Lewis, Class of 1903.

CLARK

The name Clark is found in the American colonies of Virginia in early 1700s. Several served in the American Revolution.

The Clarks were in Tennessee before Tennessee became a state.

Charles Clark, son of Norris Clark, a native of Ireland, was born March 10, 1784 in Greene County. He married Hannah Denton in Sevier County. Hannah was born September 16, 1794.

Charles was in Bledsoe in 1809, as he was serving as Lieutenant in the 31st Regiment, Tennessee State Militia. In 1814 Charles was an ensign in the 31st Regiment. The Clark name was well represented in the War of 1812 from Tennessee.

In 1821 Charles Clark purchased eighty-five acres of land on the south side of Sequatchie Creek, "including part of the premises and improvements where he lives". Two years later 1823, he purchased 146 acres for $500.00 from Mrs. Mary Billingsley in Lot V "including the plantation and improvements."

By 1836 Charles owned a total of almost five hundred acres in Lots IV and V. He was on the Bledsoe Tax List District 4 and 5 in 1837, 1838, 1839. Charles was a blacksmith and several of his sons followed the same occupation.

Charles Clark died November 18, 1853. Hannah died September 12, 1858. Both were buried in the Smyrna Cemetery.

Children of Charles and Hannah Clark: Jonathan born March 10, 1810, a large land owner, married Nancy (Brown) Close and second Matilda Mitts. He lived in the area of Swafford Chapel Church. He died in February 1860 and was buried on his land. Tabitha born December 29, 1812 married, moved West; Clarissa born October 16, 1814, married James Clendenen, died January 25, 1879 in Van Buren County; Jonah born February 21, 1819. He married Mary B. Acuff, daughter of James Acuff. In 1860 he was living in the Smyrna area. His occupation, a gun smith. At this time he was the only gun smith listed in the county. In his household is listed two young men, "apprentice gun smiths". By 1870, he had moved to the southern part of the county. In 1886 Jonah was postmaster at Pailo, he died in 1906. William born November 3, 1821 moved to Missouri; Isaac Newton, born February 8, 1824, married Martha A. Roberts July 30, 1851. She was born August 19, 1825. Isaac Newton died January 18, 1887, buried Clark Cemetery, Pailo Community. James Jr. born February 27, 1826. He lived on Walden Ridge and was postmaster at Flag Stone and later after Flag Stone became postmaster at Tan Bark. Francis M. born February 27, 1828; he lived in Warren County. Nancy born November 7, 1830, married Larkin Swafford and second John McKinney, lived on Walden Ridge; Bird born February 1832, a twin married Sarah Williams, died in Van Buren County February 22, 1907; Jacob, a twin to Bird, born February 1832, married Mary Ann Romines, daughter of Thomas Romines and a brother of Jobe Romines, a soldier in the Mexican War. Jacob attended the district school at Smyrna. Jacob was a blacksmith and operated a wagon shop. In 1898 he lived on the side of Walden Ridge overlooking Sequatchie Valley. He was owner of the large Clark Apple Orchard. Jacob died February 2, 1923; Jerusha born February 2, 1840 and died September 17, 1858. Several members of this Clark family are buried in the Smyrna Cemetery.

Sources:

Tennessee Society Daughters of the American Revolution, Vol. III & IV, 1985-2001.

First Families of Tennessee, The East Tennessee Historical Society 2000.

Tennesseans in the War of 1812, Sistler 1992.

Record of Commissions of Officers in the Tennessee Militia, 1796 - 1815, compiled by Mrs. John T. Moore.

Bledsoe County Register of Deed Office, Pikeville, Tennessee.

Bledsoe County, Tennessee 1836 Tennessee Tax Lists, by James L. Douthat.

Clark Family History, by Sara Agee Goins.

Compendium of Local Biography, Part II Cumberland Region of Tennessee, 1898.

Bledsoe County Census 1860.

COULTER

Alexander Coulter Sr. born ca. 1740 lived during the American Revolution in North Carolina. He rendered both patriotic and civil service during this time in Tryon County. He married Mrs. Mary Moore, the widow of William Moore.

Sometime before 1796, Alexander Sr. and his three sons James, Thomas and Alexander Jr. moved to what is now East Tennessee. The Coulters were in Roane County in 1801. Alexander Sr. died in 1807 in Knox County. By 1808 the Coulters were in Sequatchie Valley.

James Coulter, son of Alexander Coulter Sr., born April 1, 1772 North Carolina, married Catherine Tunnell July 6, 1792. Catherine was born January 31, 1777, the daughter of William Tunnell. This family settled in Rhea County. In 1830 James Coulter is in Rhea County census. However, later James Coulter and all his family except Thomas moved to Arkansas where James died in 1849. Children of James and Catherine Coulter: Thomas, Polly, James Jr., Elizabeth, Ann, Lavinia, Margaret, Marian, Ruth, Alexander, Letitia, Rebecca and Jemima.

Thomas Coulter, son of Alexander Coulter Sr., born October 20, 1777, married Louise Johnson January 27, 1800 in Knox County.

In 1808 Thomas was in Bledsoe County. He was Lieutenant Colonel, 31st Regiment, State Militia. In 1809, Thomas signed a petition asking for some provisions be made to those who settled below the Indian Boundary line, before it was run. Those settlers that had left their improvements.

In 1810 Thomas was a Brigadier General of the 8th Brigade in the Tennessee Militia. In 1811 he was serving as one of the county commissioners. Thomas served in the War of 1812 as Brigadier General, Division of Major General William Carroll.

Thomas signed the petition in 1815 in Bledsoe County to delay the land laws during the War of 1812. Thomas died 1826 in Bledsoe County.

Children of Thomas and Louise (Johnson) Coulter: Alexander H., Matilda, William S., Hudson J., Pleasant M., Thomas H., and William J.

In 1830 census, Louise Coulter and children are still in Bledsoe, living next to the oldest son Thomas' household. Sometime before 1840 Louise Coulter and family left Bledsoe County. In 1850 Louise filed for Bounty land for service on her husband's service in the military. She was living in Newton County, Missouri.

Alexander Coulter Jr., son of Alexander Sr. and Mary Coulter, born August 16, 1775 in North Carolina, married Margaret McReynolds, daughter of Samuel McReynolds in 1804 in Roane County. Margaret was born April 22, 1786 in Washington County, Virginia.

In 1807 Alexander signed a petition for a grist mill to be erected in "Sequacha" Valley where the Kuika Trace crosses the mountains from the Tennessee Valley.

Alexander was in Bledsoe in 1809, as he signed a petition as a citizen of the county, "for some provisions to be made for the settlers who settled below the Indian Boundary line, before it was run, for property and improvements left behind by the settlers."

In 1810 Alexander received land grants for over 500 acres in Bledsoe from the state. In 1811 Alexander deeded to the county commissioners John Anderson, John Narramore, John Tollett, Michael Rawlings, William Roberson, James Standefer and Thomas Coulter, forty acres of land "in consideration of the good will and general disposition he bears toward the accommodate of the county." This forty acres was from part of the grant and from the farm where he lived, this was for Madison, first county seat; after 1815 the county seat was moved to Pikeville.

Alexander served in the War of 1812 as an ensign under Captain James Standifer, East Tennessee Militia and with Brigadier General Thomas Coulter, East Tennessee Militia.

By 1830 Alexander Coulter was in Marion County. Later the Coulter family moved to Walker County, Georgia. Alexander died in 1853 and Margaret died 1870 in Walker County.

The children of Alexander and Margaret: Delila J., born May 1809; Samuel Woods, April 1811; Alexander W., October 1813; James Jefferson, January 1815; Thomas Monroe, July 1818 and William Mitchell, October 1823.

Sources:

History of Rhea County Tennessee, Rhea County Historical and Genealogical Society, 1991.

Tennessee Society Daughters of the American Revolution, Vol. IV, 1985-2001.

Family Records, by Doris Hetzler, Kensington, Ga.

Coulter Family, by John Wilson, Chattanooga Free Press staff writer.

Coulter Family, by Ralph Coulter, Southhaven, Miss.

Record of Commissions of Officers in the Tennessee Militia, 1796 - 1815, compiled by Mrs. John T. Moore.

Bledsoe County Register of Deed Office, Pikeville, Tennessee.

Dwiggins

John Dwiggins was in Anderson County in 1805. He was in Bledsoe County in 1815. He married Nancy Brown. They became the parents of Robert, Tabitha and Charotty. John Dwiggins died before 1830. Nancy (Brown) Dwiggins married second George Washington Ballard. This family moved to Georgia. There tragedy struck, both parents died leaving four children, Samuel, William, Joseph and Nancy.

Robert Dwiggins born ca. 1812, the son of John and Nancy (Brown) Dwiggins, became a well-known citizen in the IV Civil District. He was on the tax list in 1838, and 1839. He served in the Cherokee and Seminole Indian War 1836-1838 under Captain Scott Terry.

In 1841 he was appointed by the county court to enumerate the free white males age 21 and older in the county. His list of 859 citizens hand written and tied with a green ribbon was found in the State Library. This listing was for military use. Robert served as deputy sheriff for a number of years. In 1851 he was appointed guardian for the "orphans Ballard children," his half brothers and sister. Robert was living in the home of his uncle Reuben Brown in 1850.

Sometime before 1850 the Ballard children were brought back to Bledsoe County. Family tradition is that, "friends Jesse and Elizabeth (Swafford) Day carried the children on "horse back" back to their Brown relatives. The children, Samuel, William, Joseph and Nancy lived with William Brown, an uncle.

In about 1851 Robert married a widow, Susan (Loyd) Sampson, with three children. Susan was the widow of William Sampson. Susan was born ca. 1822. The three Sampson children were Emaline, John and James. Susan was a sister of Benjamin Loyd who was a Confederate soldier.

Robert and Susan (Loyd) Sampson Dwiggins became the parents of thirteen children: LeVander, Mary, Benjamin, Tencey, Matilda, Hester Ann, Reuban, Samuel, Tiltha, Margaret, Robert, Susan and William B. Robert was a farmer and lived in the Beaty Cove area.

Sometime after 1870 Robert Dwiggins and family, all except Mary, who had married Polk Gentry, moved to Arkansas. Robert died 1876 in Arkansas and Susan died in 1880 in Texas.

Sources:

1805 Anderson County Tax List.

1815 Bledsoe County Petition to Delay Land Laws.

Bledsoe County Tennessee Civil District Tax List.

Bledsoe Census, 1850, 1860, 1870.

Dwiggins Family History, by W.B. Dwiggins, 1950, Everman, Texas.

EVITT

The Evitt family is in Bledsoe County in 1830. John Evitt and his wife were both between the ages of 50 and 60 in the 1830 Bledsoe County Census. Also in the county was William Evitt and wife between the ages of 20 and 30.

William Evitt Sr. received a land grant from the state of Tennessee in 1832 for 200 acres in the Mountain District.

The county Tax List of 1837, 1838, 1839 shows the following John Sr., Henry, Nehemiah and William Evitt in Districts IV and V. In 1840 William Evitt was living in District IV.

In the July 1845 session of Bledsoe County Court, Joel Segraves was appointed administrator of the estate of William Evitt, deceased.

In 1850 Suzanne Evitt age 54 born in Virginia was living in household of Joel Segraves.

William Evitt born ca. 1815 and died 1841 in Bledsoe County, Suzanne died after 1850. William and Suzanne Evitt were the parents of Nancy Jane Evitt born ca. 1836, married "Curley" John Thurman, son of John and Cloe (Rector) Thurman.

Thomas Evitt born ca. 1836 married Mary Ann Capps. They lived in Bledsoe County, Walden Ridge, their post office was Tanbark. This family moved to Crawford County, Missouri after 1860.

William Evitt Jr. or II, born October 22, 1841, married Catherine Victery. She died in 1875, near Little Rock, Arkansas.

William and Catherine became the parents of one daughter, Virginia Victoria "Vic". Victoria was born June 1873, she married Adam Watson ca. 1892 and moved "west" after 1900.

William Evitt Jr. married second Missouri Johnson, August 1880 in Nashville. Missouri was born December 19, 1849. William Jr. died January 29, 1911; Missouri died December 8, 1908. They were the parents of William III, John, Mattie, Thomas, Maggie, Maude and Ida.

From William Evitt's military record, he was born in Bledsoe County, enlisted November 18, 1863 at Bloomington, Indiana in the Union Army. He served as a private in Company I, 10th Regiment Indiana Cavalry.

He was described as being 5 ft. 8 in., complexion sandy, eyes hazel, hair sandy, occupation farmer. William was discharged August 31, 1865 Vicksburg, Mississippi. Later the date was given as September 2, 1865, Indianapolis, Indiana.

In 1892 William was living on Walden Ridge, his post office was Tan Bark. He was 53 years of age, unable to work. He was making application for Civil War Pension. G.W. Birditt was the Justice of the Peace. Sam Birditt and Jacob Garrison witnessed William's mark.

In 1900 William lived in the Luminary Community. Another application states William was suffering from rheumatism and liver complaint. In 1907 his post office was Milo, his pension was $12.00

a month.

Missouri, born December 19, 1849, died 1908. William died January 29, 1911. Both buried in Winnie Cemetery.

Sources:

Bledsoe County Census, 1830, 1840, 1850, 1900.

National Archives, Military Records, Washington, D.C.

Personal Interview with John Evitt, son of William Evitt II, January 1976.

Wilkinson, Johnson and Related Families, by A.T. Wilkinson, 1967.

FARMER

The name Farmer is found in the American colonies of Virginia and Maryland in the 1600s. They were land owners. One Thomas F. Farmer was a member of the house of Burgesses in Virginia 1629-1630.

A Nathan Farmer served in the American Revolution from Virginia.

Farmers were in Tennessee, Anderson and Roane counties in early 1800s. Several served in the War of 1812 from Tennessee. A Nathan Farmer was an officer (Captain) during the war.

In 1815 Aquilla and William Farmer were in Bledsoe County. They signed the petition to delay the land laws during the War of 1812.

The Bledsoe County 1830 census list Aquilla Farmer age 60-70, and William age 20-30.

Aquilla Farmer, the son of William Farmer, was born ca. 1775. He married Mary Elizabeth Nail. A son William Nail Farmer was born in 1805 in Georgia. The Nail family lived in Lincoln County, Georgia.

Between the years 1825 and 1828, Aquilla Farmer Sr., received land grants of a total of 250 acres from the state. In 1826 Aquilla Farmer and Thomas Nail received a 300 acre grant from the state.

The Bledsoe County tax list gives William Farmer, Robert F. Farmer, and Samuel Farmer in District V in the years 1837, 1838 and 1839.

The 1840 Bledsoe census list Elizabeth Farmer and William Farmer heads of household in District V and Thomas Farmer and wife both 70-80 (ages), in District VI.

Aquilla Farmer died 1830/1840. Elizabeth Farmer died 1840/1850. William N. Farmer born March 18, 1805 in Georgia, married Martha Ann Jones, daughter of Gabriel and Isabella McDowell Jones. Martha Ann was born September 11, 1808 in North Carolina. William N. and Martha became the parents of: Aquilla, married Mary Ann Hall; Mary Lillie, married Burton Clark; Isabella, married James Smith; William W., married Viola Billingsley; Sarah, married William Dyer; Martin, married second Vester Clark; Thomas, married Crocia Billingsley; Samuel, married Martha Pendergrass; Elizabeth died unmarried.

William N. Farmer received land grants in the late 1840s from the state for 500 acres.

He served as sheriff and was killed in the line of duty September 30, 1861. He was buried in the Smyrna Cemetery. Martha (Jones) Farmer died September 2, 1881 and was buried in the Farmer Cemetery.

Aquilla Farmer, oldest son of William N. and Martha (Jones) Farmer, was born June 14, 1829 in Tennessee. He married Mary Ann Hall, daughter of Benjamin Hall. She was born July 6, 1829 in Tennessee. They became the parents of: Alexander F. born 1849, married Louise Frazier; Kossuth H. born ca. 1851; William T. born ca 1855; John M. born ca. 1856, married Violet Dugger; Martin L. born 1858, married Laura Greer, daughter of Isaac S. Greer; Mary J. born ca. 1860, married Joe Johnson; James C. born ca. 1863; Martha E. born ca. 1865, married L.C. Johnson; Permelia born ca. 1867, married Henry Clay Greer; Lula A. born ca. 1870; Erastus H. born ca. 1873, married Maggie Norwood.

Aquilla Farmer died June 2, 1900, Mary Ann (Polly) died March 14, 1904. Both buried Farmer Cemetery.

William Worthington Farmer, second son of William N. and Martha (Jones) Farmer, was born September 15, 1835. He married Viola Billingsley, daughter of John Billingsley. She was born May 15, 1841. They became the parents of Nina Jane born 1863, married John W. Greer; Rhoda born 1865, married Riley Hoge; Loucretia born 1867, married Dr. W.H. Harris; Thomas A. born 1870, married Lena Billingsley; Wade Marshall born 1872; Lizzie born 1875, married A.C. Hutcheson; Ruby born 1881, married Lee Henson.

William W. Farmer died March 16, 1889. Viola (Billingsley) Farmer died April 18, 1921. Both were buried at Smryna Cemetery.

Five Farmers served as sheriffs in Bledsoe County. William N. Farmer served as sheriff in the early 1860s. After his death, Governor William G. Brownlow appointed his son William W. Farmer to serve during the days of Reconstruction. He was later elected and served in the 1870s and 1880s.

John Farmer, grandson of William N. Farmer served as sheriff in the late 1890s. Thomas Farmer, grandson of William N. Farmer served as sheriff in the early 1900s. Willie N. Farmer, son of Samuel and grandson of William N. Farmer served as sheriff during the first decade of the 1900s.

Sources:

Bledsoe Census, 1830, 1840, 1850.

Farmer Family Cemetery.

Smyrna Cemetery.

Bledsoe County, Tennessee 1836 Tennessee Civil Districts and Tax List.

Tennesseans in the War of 1812, by Sistler 1992.

Family Information

National Society Colonial Dames XVII Century Ancestor Roster, 1915, 2005.

Daughters of the American Revolution Roster, Vol I.

FERGUSON/FORGUSON

The name is found in the New England colonies in the 1600s and also in Virginia and North and South Carolina. Some came to the American colonies as transportee. Several served in the American Revolution.

The Fergusons were in East Tennessee before Tennessee became a state in 1796. Alexander Ferguson and Ellis Ferguson were in Rhea County in 1808.

Several Ferguson from Tennessee served in the War of 1812.

Thomas and Warner Ferguson were on the Tax list in Bledsoe County in 1838 and 1839.

Abner and Warner Ferguson were on the 1840 census of Bledsoe County.

In 1850 Mahaly Ferguson, born in North Carolina in 1795 and Thomas L. Ferguson age 35, a farmer also was born in North Carolina, were living in Bledsoe County.

Frank S. Ferguson born 1868-69 in Bledsoe County, the son of James and Elizabeth Ferguson, served as sheriff, chairman of the county court and was clerk and master of the Chancery Court for many years.

Sources:

Tennessee Homesteaders and Landowners, Fourth Surveyors District, compiled by Willis Hutcherson 1864.

Bledsoe County, Tennessee 1836 Tennessee Civil Districts and Tax Lists, by James L. Douthat 1993.

First Families of Tennessee, East Tennessee Historical Society 2000.

National Society Colonial Dames XVII Century Ancester Roster 1915-2001.

The Tennessee Society Daughters of the American Revolution, Vol. IV, 1985-2001.

FORD

The name Ford is found in the American colonies in the 1600s; most were listed as land owners.

The Fords were in Tennessee, Hawkins County, in the late 1700s. Several served in the American Revolution. After the War, John Ford was one of the many veterans that moved southwest. John Ford was born November 13, 1764 in Albermarle County, Virginia. He enlisted in the Virginia militia from Fluvanna County. His service was guarding British prisoners at the Albermarle Barracks. John enlisted again and "marched to Richmond then to Williamsburg, New Castle, Little Youk, back to Williamsburg and to Shirley Hundred, 16 miles below Richmond where he was discharged." He reported, shortly before his discharge he saw Marquis de Lafayette (General Lafayette), who came from France to help the American cause.

John Ford married Elizabeth England April 12, 1785 in Fluvanna County, Virginia. By the late 1700s (1797) he was in Tennessee; after living in Roane County he moved to Bledsoe County in the early 1800s.

Several soldiers by the name of Ford, served in the War of 1812, from Tennessee.

John Ford and Elizabeth (England) Ford became the parents of: Jane born 1786, married Richard Mathias; Sarah born 1789, married Nathaniel Bristow; John Jr. born 1796, married Nancy Lowden; Nancy born 1798, married William Lowden; Mary born 1803, married William Renfro; and Reuban born 1806.

John Ford applied for Revolutionary War Veteran pension in February 1833 while living in Bledsoe County.

Bledsoe 1830 census list John Ford Sr., Reuban Ford, John Ford Jr., and Nathaniel Bristoe as heads of families. The 1840 Bledsoe census list John Ford Sr., and sons John Jr., and Reuban and sons-in-law Nathaniel Bristoe, Richard Mathias and William Lowden all living in District II (Grassy Cove), William Renfro was living in District I.

John Ford died August 28, 1844. Elizabeth Ford died September 30, 1845, both are buried in Grassy Cove Methodist Cemetery.

Sources:

Bledsoe County Census 1830, 1840

John Ford's Pension Records

Cumberland County First hundred Years, by H. B. And J. M. Krechniak, 1956

Membership Roster and Soldier - The Tennessee Society of the Daughters of the American Revolution, 1970-1984, Volume III.

Tennesseans in the War of 1812, by Sistler, 1992.

FRAZIER/FRAZER

Samuel Frazier born April 10, 1749 in North Carolina, married Rebecca Julian who was born March 17, 1748 in Virginia. Samuel served in the American Revolution while living in North Carolina. He took part in the battles of King's Mountain and Guilford Courthouse.

By 1789 Samuel had moved his family over the mountains to Greene County, Tennessee. In Greene County he became a political leader. He served as a delegate to Tennessee First Constitutional Convention. Later this family moved to Knox County.

Children of Samuel and Rebecca (Julian) Frazier: Abner born April 18, 1772, died May 17, 1843; Samuel born ca. 1774, died December 3, 1826; Beriah born May 4, 1776, died October 28, 1858; Rebecca born June 3, 1779, died young; Julian born November 7, 1781, died December 16, 1848; Thomas born December 25, 1783, died after 1850; Barbara born August 23, 1787, died April 7, 1859.

Samuel died April 10, 1838. Rebecca died August 23, 1838.

By the 1830s the Fraziers were in Rhea and Bledsoe County. Thomas Neal Frazier was on the Bledsoe Tax List District VI in 1839.

Abner Frazier born April 18, 1772, married Mary Edmonson April 29, 1801 in Greene County. Mary was born September 11, 1768. Abner died May 17, 1843. Mary died May 19, 1847.

Children of Abner and Mary (Edmonson) Frazier: Samuel

born March 2, 1802 and died May 13, 1845, Rhea County; Rebecca born June 17, 1804, died after 1850; Abner Jr. born December 2, 1806, died December 3, 1853; Thomas Neal born May 24, 1810 and died 1887; Beriah born September 22, 1812, died October 1, 1886.

Several Fraziers served in the War of 1812 from Tennessee.

Thomas Neal Frazier, born May 24, 1810, the son of Abner and Mary (Edmonson) Frazier, was educated at Greenville College. He later came to Washington in Rhea County to study law under his brother, Samuel, Attorney General for the Southeastern Tennessee district. Thomas N. was admitted to the Bar in 1836.

By 1840 Thomas N. is in Bledsoe County. On September 20, 1839 he married Margaret A. Springs, the daughter of John Springs. Margaret was born August 11, 1820 and died November 16, 1840. She was buried in the Pikeville City Cemetery.

Thomas N. and Margaret were the parents of Mary Ellen born 1840, she married Major George S. Deakins on December 9, 1862. Mary Ellen died September 27, 1863. She was buried in the Pikeville City Cemetery.

Thomas Neal Frazier married second Margaret M. McReynolds, daughter of Samuel McReynolds, April 10, 1845. Margaret was born November 8, 1824. They became the parents of Samuel J. born 1846, Sarah J.M. born 1849, Rebecca, Tom and James B. born October 18, 1856 in Pikeville.

James B. was elected governor of Tennessee in 1902 and re-elected in 1904. In 1905, after the death of United States Senator William B. Bates, he was elected to serve as Senator Bates' replacement. James B. Frazier died March 30, 1937 in Chattanooga, Tennessee.

Thomas Neal Frazier lived in Bledsoe County, Pikeville from the late 1830s to the mid 1860s. Known as "Judge Frazier", he was a "staunch Whig", a "Bridgman Whig" in the 1840s, a strong Union supporter, and a well-known lawyer. He served as clerk and master for Bledsoe Chancery Court. In 1860 Judge Frazier was on a committee to "supervise repair of the courthouse."

In 1858-1859 Judge Frazier deeded a lot to four religious denominations, the Methodist Episcopal Church South, the Presbyterian, Baptists and Christians. The churches were to use the first floor. The second floor was the Temperance Hall.

Citizens from throughout the county came to Pikeville to seek legal advice. Mrs. Elizabeth Brown Parham living near the head of Sequatchie Valley traveled some twenty miles on horse back to seek advice from Judge Frazier. From a letter dated April 30, 1855 it seems the Judge was not at home, when Mrs. Parham reached Pikeville, therefore he advised her by letter in details of her rights as head of a family.

According to tradition, when General Nathan B. Forrest and his troops were camped in Pikeville, near the Frazier home, General Forrest was a dinner guest of Judge Frazier.

Judge Frazier had acquired the beautiful two-story home of Scott Terry.

After the battles around Chattanooga, several companies of Union soldiers were in Pikeville, as one soldier reported a "Christmas

Party at Judge Frazier's house."

After moving from Pikeville to Rutherford County, he was appointed Judge of the criminal court for the counties of Davidson, Rutherford and Montgomery by Andrew Johnson, military governor of Tennessee. Judge Frazier died 1887.

Sources:

Bledsoe County census 1840, 1850.

Samuel Frazier of Tennessee and His Family, by Virginia Knight Nelson 1978.

Tennesseans in the War of 1812, by Sistler 1992.

Bledsoe County Tennessee, a History, by Elizabeth Parham Robnett 1993.

GENTRY

Gentrys were listed in Virginia as landowners in the 1600s. More than one served in the American Revolution. Several Gentrys were in the upper East Tennessee counties before 1796. Several Gentrys served in the War of 1812 from Tennessee.

Allen Gentry was in Bledsoe County in the 1830s. He was on the Bledsoe Tax List 1837, 1838, 1839 in District IV. He is on the 1840 Bledsoe Census.

In 1850 the following Gentrys were heads of households in Bledsoe County: Allen, John, Thomas H. and John A. Their occupations were blacksmiths and wagon makers; both occupations closely connected with farming at this time.

Allen born ca. 1791 in Georgia married Sarah (Fine) King who was born ca. 1802 in Tennessee. Their children were: Zelzy born ca. 1826; Amy Lou born ca. 1830; Sarah E. born ca. 1833, married T.F. Henderson; Eliza E. born ca. 1836; Joshua C. born ca. 1838, married Anna Acuff; James K. Polk born March 25, 1841, married Mary Dwiggins; and Francis Morgan born April 14, 1846, married Mary E. Roberts, died August 22, 1905 in Alabama. Allen Gentry died after 1850 and Sarah lived with her daughter Sarah (Gentry) Henderson and later with son, James K. She died July 1880.

Two sons, Joshua and James K., of Allen and Sarah served in the famous Tulloss Rangers, a company of Confederate soldiers, formed at Pikeville in 1861. Francis Morgan also served in the Confederate Army.

James K. Polk (J.P. or Polk) Gentry married Mary Dwiggins, daughter of Robert Dwiggins. They became the parents of Leroy (Lee), Anna J., Hugh, Lizzie, Josie, Cora and Flora. James Polk died April 27, 1899. Sometime before 1910, Mary married Terrell Marsh.

Leroy (Lee) R.L., oldest son of James K. and Mary (Dwiggins) Gentry, was living in Rhea County in 1925. His occupation was a farmer and a school teacher. He had graduated from the Grandview Normal Institute in 1902. He was known as "Professor Gentry". He lived two miles from Dayton on a 106 acre farm. As he was being examined as a potential juror by Clarence Darrow in the famous Scopes Evolution Trial, he explained, "taught school fall and winter, farmed spring and summer." Professor Gentry was the only school teacher to serve on the jury. However, the majority of the other members were farmers and Baptist church members, as was Professor Gentry.

Sources:

Tennesseans in the War of 1812, by Sistler 1992.

National Society Colonial Dames XVII Century Ancestor Roster, 1915-2005.

Bledsoe Census, 1840, 1850, 1860.

Gentry History, by Thom Rigsby, Carrollton, Texas.

Members and Patriots The Tennessee Society Daughters of the American Revolution, Vol. III, IV, 1985-2001.

First Families of Tennessee, East Tennessee Historical Society, 2000.

The World Most Famous Court Trial, Reprint Edition 1978.

GREER

The first member of this Greer family to migrate to the American colony, Maryland was the William Greer family. William and his wife Mary (Finch/Fitch) Greer came to America in ca. 1730, settled in Anne Arondel County, Maryland. They became the parents of eight sons and one daughter. Four of the oldest sons, William, James and John born in England remained neutral during the American Revolution. Shadrack served in the British Army. The three youngest sons, Walter Acquilla and Moses born in American Colonies, served in the American Army or became American Patriots.

Moses Greer Sr. born in 1744 in the colony of Maryland, was the son of William and Mary Greer, the immigrants. Moses Greer Sr. married Nancy Bailey and moved to Virginia. They became the parents of William, Moses Jr., Walter, John F., Thomas Bailey, Betsy, Nancy, Mollie, Sally, Nellie and Kitty. Several Greers served in the War of 1812 serving as officers as well as enlisted men from Tennessee.

John F. Greer, the fourth son of Moses Sr. and Nancy Greer was in Bledsoe County in 1830, 1840 census. He had received a land grant for the land in Grassy Cove. He was on the Bledsoe Tax List in 1838 in District II (Grassy Cove).

Weatherston Shelton Greer Sr. (W.S.), born 1800 in Franklin County, Virginia, the second son of Moses Greer Jr. and Susannah (Woods) Greer, was in Bledsoe County District II, Grassy Cove in the 1830s. He was serving as postmaster of the Grassy Cove post office in 1837. He was also listed on the Bledsoe Tax List in District I and II in 1838. Weatherston S. married Mary Kyle born 1803 in Ireland. In the 1840 Bledsoe census this family was living in District II. Weatherson S. became a large land owner and slave holder in the area of Grassy Cove.

During the Civil War, this Greer family were southern

sympathizers and supported the Confederate cause.

The children of Weatherston S. and Mary (Kyle) Greer: William Henry born 1821, married Mahala Hutcheson; Elizabeth Charlotte born ca. 1823, married Mark Stephens; Harriet Ann born 1825, married William Ormes, second married James Vernon; Emily Calloway born 1827, married Alexander H. McReynolds; Moses born 1829, married Orpha Foster; Weatherston S. Jr. born ca. 1832, served in the Confederate Army; Thomas born ca. 1835; Henry Clay born March 1, 1939, married Hortense Randals.

After the war, Weatherston S. Greer and Mary (Kyle) Greer moved to Sequatchie Valley near Pikeville and made their home with their daughter, Harriet Ann (Greer) Ormes Vernon. Weatherston S. died 1870, Mary (Kyle) died 1886.

Henry Clay enlisted in the Confederate Army in 1861 and served until the close of the war. After the war he served as county surveyor for many years. Henry Clay served in the Tennessee House of Representatives from 1901 to 1903 representing Bledsoe, Cumberland, Grundy, Sequatchie and Van Buren counties. Henry Clay Greer died 1914, Hortense (Randals) Greer died 1904.

Sources:

Leaves From the Family Tree, by Penelope J. Allen, 1933.

Biographical Directory of the Tennessee General Assembly, Vol. III, 1901-1931.

Bledsoe County Census, 1830, 1840.

GREER/GRIER

The name Greer/Grier is found in the colony of Maryland in the 1600s. By the time of the American Revolution, Greers were in Pennsylvania and the southern colonies of Virginia, North and South Carolina.

Greers were in the Watauga Settlement (North Carolina and later Tennessee). Several Greers served in the American Revolution. By 1800 Greers were in Sullivan County, Tennessee. Several served in the War of 1812 from Tennessee, some served as officers.

By the 1830s the Greers were in Bledsoe County. Isiah Stephens Greer was born April 13, 1813 in South Carolina. He was on the Bledsoe County Tax List in District V in 1839.

Isiah Greer married Anna Acuff, daughter of James and Nancy (Billingsley) Acuff. In the 1840 census, this family lived in District V. In 1850, Mary Ann Greer, the mother of Isiah, born in 1789 in North Carolina, was living in the household of her son Isiah.

Isiah Greer and Anna (Acuff) Greer became the parents of James L., Nancy, Matilda, Sarah Margaret, Mary Ann, Alexander Campbell, William Carnes, Louise Evaline, John Bartow, Laurilla and Jonah Clark Greer. Isiah Greer died August 1903 and Anna died before 1900.

James L. born in 1840, died while a prisoner during the Civil War, April 23, 1864 and was buried in Camp Chase Confederate Cemetery, Columbus, Ohio.

Nancy Matilda, oldest daughter of Isiah, born February 7, 1842, married Joseph Alexander Card in 1863, the son of Zimry Card and Catherine (Shoemate) Card.

Joseph A. served in the Confederate Army. He was captured and held a prisoner until May 1865. After he returned to Bledsoe County, he and Nancy moved across the Cumberland Mountains to Coffee County, later to Texas and finally to Oklahoma where he made an application to the Oklahoma Land Rush Homestead Act.

Sarah Margaret, third child of Isiah and Anna Acuff Greer, born September 15, 1843, married George Washington Walker, September 9, 1866. Sarah Margaret died in 1907 in Franklin County.

Mary Ann born 1846 married William LeQuire Standefer ca. 1873. Mary Ann (Greer) Standefer died 1913 in Marion County.

Alexander Campbell born August 9, 1848 married Rachel Isabell Walker, November 30, 1870. This family lived in Bledsoe County.

William Carnes, sixth child of Isiah and Anna Greer, was born Mary, 1850 and died 1929 in Hall County, Texas.

Louise Evaline born 1852 married James Jones Howard, March 21, 1878. She died September 23, 1929.

John Bartow, eighth child of Isiah and Anna (Acuff) Greer, was born May 9, 1854. He married Mattie Barker Ewbanks January 12, 1881. This family lived in Missouri, Oklahoma and Ohio. John Bartow died in 1937 in Ashtabula, Ohio.

Laurilla (Laura), youngest daughter of Isiah and Anna, was born September 9, 1856, married Martin Luther Farmer November 28, 1880. This family lived in Bledsoe County. Laura (Greer) Farmer died 1938 in Chattanooga, Tennessee.

Jonah Clark Greer, youngest son of Isiah and Anna, born November 19, 185,7 married Drucilla Rains. He died July 13, 1946 in Hamilton County.

Sources:

History of the Greer Family Isiah Greer, by Imo Greer Wood, Alice, Texas.

Bledsoe County Census, 1830, 1840, 1850.

Bledsoe County Tax List 1836, by James L. Douthat, 1993.

National Society of Colonial Dames XVII Century Ancestor Roster, 1915-2005.

Membership Roster and Soldiers The Tennessee Society of the Daughters of the American Revolution, Vol. III.

HALE/HAIL

The name Hale/Hail is found in the American colonies (New England) in the 1600s. The Hales were listed as land owners, taxpayers and transportees.

By the 1750s the Hales were in the southern colonies (Virginia). Several served in the American Revolution.

The Hales were in Tennessee before Tennessee became a state, 1796. Several served in the War of 1812 from Tennessee.

John Hale was born in Bedford County, Virginia in ca. 1753/54. He enlisted as a private in 1776 in Captain Harry Buford's Company. They marched west to the Cherokee country on the Holston River. There he took part in the Battle of Long Island. After six months he was discharged. His next enlistment was in 1777 under Captain Charles Watkins. He served three months, marched to Richmond and on to Norfolk. His third enlistment took him into North Carolina. He reported he served a total of twenty-four months. After the war John Hale moved to Wythe County, Virginia. He later moved to Greene, Washington and Blount counties before he moved to Bledsoe County in ca. 1813.

In the 1830 Bledsoe census, he is listed between the ages of 70 and 80 years, also his wife the same age.

On February 7, 1833 he applied for a pension based on his Revolutionary War service. He was living in Bledsoe County and was well-known as he gives as character witnesses by Rev. John Dalton, Eli Thurman, Elisha Kirklen and James A. Whitesides. His pension was approved and was to be $80.00 per annual. John Hale died March 4, 1838.

John T. Hale, son of John Hale, born 1787, married Martha Jane Tate, born 1787. John T. and Martha became the parents of: Thomas born 1811, married Jerusha Smith born 1813; William born 1813, married Susan P. Smith born 1815; Isham born 1819, married Nancy Tucker; John T. Jr. born 1824, married Mary Ann Hall; Hezekiah born 1824; King born 1826; Martha Jane born 1828, married Moses Morris Tucker; Aquilla born 1833, married Matilda Swafford.

Thomas Hale, son of John Hale, born ca. 1790, married Mary Ann. They became the parents of: Elijah born 1811, married Margaret Agee; John N. born 1814, married Mary Ann Nichols; Andrew Jackson born 1820, married Mary Wyatt and second Elizabeth J. Selby; Sarah born 1823, married John Rector; Arranzena born 1824, married Alfred Hyder; Elizabeth born 1828, married Luke Lay; Thomas Hale born 1829, married Sarah Ann Lowe, second Susan Evans; Mary Ann born 1832, married Richard Lay; Michael born 1838, married Suzannah.

Sources:

Tennesseans in the War of 1812, by Sistler, 1992.

National Society Colonial Dames XVII Century Ancestor Roster, 1915-2005.

First Families of Tennessee, East Tennessee Historical Society, 2000.

The Tennessee Society of Daughters of the American Revolution, Vol. IV, 1985-2001.

The Tennessee Society Daughters of the American Revolution, Membership Roster and Soldiers, Vol. III.

Pension Records.

Spanning the Centuries with the Hale Family, Muriel Nadine (Hale) Lynch, Independence, Missouri, 1990.

HAMILTON/HAMBLETON

The name Hamilton is found in the American Colony of Maryland in the 1600s. They were original land owners, planters and active in the local militia. Several Hamiltons were soldiers or patriots of the American Revolution while living in Virginia and North and South Carolina.

Hamiltons were in Tennessee in 1796. They were in the Sequatchie Valley by 1808. Abraham Hamilton signed the petition to delay of the Land Laws, during the War of 1812.

Early Hamiltons in Bledsoe County were: Abraham born 1776, married Dely Nail born 1778. Their children were Delilah born 1794, died 1860, married William Nail; Benjamin born 1796, married Mary Rankin, is buried in Hamilton Cemetery; Rachel born March 5, 1800, died August 20, 1871, married William Brown born August 20, 1800, died April 7, 1876, both buried at Brushy Cemetery. Mary died 1809, buried at Brushy Cemetery.

Several served in the War of 1812 as officers and enlisted men from Tennessee. The 1830 census gives a John and Harvey Hamilton as heads of households in Marion County. George and Benjamin Hamilton were heads of households in Bledsoe County. Benjamin and William Hamilton were on the Bledsoe County Tax List in District III in 1837, 1838, 1839. William and Benjamin were living in 1840 in District III as heads of households.

Benjamin Hamilton born October 5, 1796 in Sullivan County, married Mary Rankin born May 20, 1801 in South Carolina. They became the parents of: Delila born ca. 1818 in Tennessee; John born

May 6, 1820, married Margaret Worthington, John died June 2, 1904; James born ca. 1822, married Sarah; Abraham Jr. born ca. 1824, married Mary Nail; Isaac born ca. 1826, married Mary born ca. 1831 in North Carolina; Rachel born ca. 1828; Jacob born ca. 1830; Benjamin born ca. 1836; Mary A. born ca. 1838; Martha J. born ca. 1840, married December 10, 1871 Dr. Robert A.B. Moyers, a dentist born August 20, 1843; William E. born ca. 1842; Nancy E./Sarah E. born ca. 1846, married T.F. (Frank) Hale who was born 1843 and died 1910. Benjamin Hamilton died April 18, 1868; Mary, his wife, died June 5, 1892. Both were buried in Hamilton Cemetery.

Sources:

National Society Colonial Dames XVII Century Ancestor Roster, 1915-2005.

Membership Roster and Soldiers, Tennessee Society of the Daughters of the American Revolution, Vol. 3, Vol. 4.

First Families of Tennessee East Tennessee Historical Society, 2000.

Tennesseans in the War of 1812, by Sistler.

Census records Bledsoe County, 1830-1840.

Hamilton Cemetery Records.

HANKINS

The name Hankins is found in the colony of Virginia in the mid 1700s with names such as William, Richard and Absolem. William and Absolem took part in the American Revolution.

The Hankins family was in the counties of Hawkins and Grainger before Tennessee became a state. William Hankins received a land grant from the state of North Carolina for 400 acres in Hawkins County in 1793.

John Hankins born 1760-1765 in Hawkins County was the son of William Hankins and Jane (Sharp) Hankins. John Hankins married Sarah Gill, married second July 25, 1804 in Grainger County, Mary (Polly) Gallant, daughter of James Gallant I of North Carolina. Mary was born in 1772.

By 1805 John Hankins was in Roane County on the Tax List.

In 1807 John Hankins signed a petition to the Roane County Court asking for the right to "construct a grist mill in Sequacha Valley for the public utility."

In the summer of 1808 John Hankins claimed and held by right of settlement, occupancy and pre-emption 60 acres of land in Sequatchie Valley, Bledsoe County, "including the land he lives on."

In 1808 John Hankins was a lieutenant in the 31st Regiment of Bledsoe County, Tennessee State Militia. In 1811 he was Captain in the same regiment.

Smoke House
John Jackson Hankins' Home
Nine Mile Community
1815-1903

John Hankins was a land and slave holder, owning land in Sequatchie Valley on the Cumberland Mountains and Grassy Cove.

On September 30, 1813 John Hankins enlisted at Knoxville as a private in Captain William White's Company on the Mounted Volunteer Infantry from East Tennessee.

John left his wife Mary and children William B., Stephen G., Jane and Hannah, a baby, and took a horse to serve his country in the War of 1812. He was discharged December 29, 1813.

His terms of service was for two months and twelve days. His pay was $8.00 per month. His allowance was less than 26 cents a day. The allowance for the horse was 40 cents per day. His total pay including his horse was $48.69. In addition to his military service, he served as a coroner in the early days of the county.

John Hankins was drown in the Tennessee River September 26, 1826. Mary (Gallant) Hankins died at her home August 4, 1861.

At this time the Hankins family was divided. Grandsons were enlisted in both the Union and Confederate Armies.

John Hankins and Sarah (Gill) Hankins became the parents of William B. Hankins born 1790-1800. He moved to Morgan County, Illinois before 1830. In 1835 he sold his land to his brother John Hankins Jr. for $210.00. The land described as "being part drawn by said William B. Hankins in a division of his father land." William B. Hankins died April 16, 1836.

John Hankins and Mary (Gallant) Hankins became the parents of Stephen G. born October 28, 1805. He married Lucy Smith, the daughter of Thomas and Mildred Smith. In the early 1830s Stephen moved his family to Illinois but was back in Bledsoe County in 1835. In the fall of 1861, Stephen and his family moved to Warren County. Stephen died October 21, 1887. Stephen and Lucy's children were: Polly Ann, Fanny Jane, Milly Angeline, William Carroll, Susan S., John S., Thomas J., Sarah Malissa and Patrick Henry.

John S. and Thomas J. joined the Confederate Army. John S. did not return; he died in October 1861 in Hunterville, Virginia.

Jane Hankins, oldest daughter of John and Mary, was born ca.

1809, married William McDowell. They became the parents of John H., Joseph, William, James, Mary, Sarah, Hannah, Isabella, Thomas, Jesse M. and Nancy L. Jesse M. served in the Union Army.

William McDowell died 1860-1870; Jane died 1870-1880.

Hannah Hankins born April 17, 1812, the youngest daughter of John and Mary, married Thomas Swafford Jr., later known as Thomas Y. Swafford. They became the parents of: Mariah, Matilda, Mary, William, Nancy, Nasson, Samuel, Thomas, James, Martha Jane, Allen H. and Ersaline China. William, James and Samuel served in the Union Army. Thomas Y. died June 2, 1880. Hannah died January 6, 1881.

John Jackson Hankins, youngest son of John and Mary, was born June 15, 1815, after his father returned from his service in the War of 1812, he was eleven years old when his father was drown crossing the Tennessee River.

John Jackson, known as "Jack" married Sela McDowell. They became the parents of Jane C., James, Joseph, Mary, John, Nancy, Caroline and William. John Jackson married second Mary Walker, the daughter of David Walker. They became the parents of George, Steve, Samuel, David, John, Isaac E., Matthew, Martha Jane, Hannah, Elizabeth and Sallie. Joseph joined the Union Army and died in a hospital in Nashville.

John Jackson Hankins died 1903. Mary Walker Hankins died in Grand Pass, Missouri.

Richard Hankins born ca. 1775-1780 married Barbara (Camp) Cooke, May 28, 1801 in Grainger County.

Richard Hankins was in Bledsoe in 1813-1814 as he signed a petition to the Tennessee General Assembly. "That whereas the war like and gloomy attitude of the present crisis, very clearly indicates that a considerable number of the Militia of said state will inevitable be called out in defense of their country. And, inasmuch as there hath been Writs of Ejectments served on a large number of the inhabitants of the county of Bledsoe, (and it is highly probably that a considerable number more will shortly share the same fate) in consequence of their land claims - now should those suits, terminate in favor of the Plaintiffs, in the absence of the Defendants (they being in the service of their country) and their families be dispossessed, would consequently subject them to very serious inconvenience, and very probably to great injuries and hard ships. Therefore it is our earnest prair [prayer] that your honorable body would (if consistent with your policy), suspend the operation of the land law in the aforesaid state during the continuation of the present War between the United States of America, and Great Britain or so long as you, in your wisdom may deem most expedient and your humble petitioners in duty bound should ever pray."

This Petition was signed by over two hundred citizens in Bledsoe County.

Richard enlisted November 13, 1814 in Captain Miles Vernon's Company, Colonel Edwin E. Booth's Regiment East Tennessee Militia. This company was organized at Washington in Rhea County.

Richard died February 25, 1815 in service.

By the Justice of Bledsoe County Court in 1816, Barbara Hankins was given the right to administer the estate of Richard

Hankins deceased.

In 1824 Barbara sold one acre of land to Isaac Stephens for the Stony Point Methodist Church for $5.00.

In the 1830 Bledsoe Census, Barbara Hankins age is between 50 and 60, living in her household, a male (son) age 15-20 years. Richard and Barbara Hankins became the parents of Daniel, David, John, Sarah and Margaret.

Sources:

First Families of Tennessee, East Tennessee Historical Society, 2000.

Membership Roster and Soldiers The Tennessee Society of the Daughters of the American Revolution, Vol. 3, 1970-1984.

Hankins Bible Records.

Tennessee Homesteaders and Landowners, Fourth Surveyors District, by Willis Hutcherson, 1964.

Bledsoe County Census, 1830, 1840, 1850, 1860, 1870, 1880.

Brushy Cemetery - Nine Mile Community

HIXSON/HIXON

William Hixson was in the colony of New Jersey in the late 1600s listed as a land owner. Several Hixons took part in the American Revolution.

Joseph Hixson born ca. 1746, in New Jersey, was in Greene County, later Tennessee, in 1786. He married Suzannah Stringfield. Joseph died in Greene County ca. 1804. Joseph and Suzannah were the parents of nine children: Andrew, William, Timothy Stringfield, Joseph Jr., Ephraim, John, Suzannah, Benjamin and James. Four of these came to Bledsoe County: William, Timothy S., Joseph Jr. and Ephraim. Their sister Suzannah, who married William Davis, also came to Bledsoe.

The oldest son of Joseph and Suzannah, Andrew, drown in the Mississippi River on his way west; William married Ingola Hughes; Timothy Stringfield married Rebecca Hughes, sister of Ingola Hughes.

The large Hixson family was in Sequatchie Valley in early 1800. Ephraim Hixson signed the Petition in February 1809 as a citizen of Bledsoe County, "for some provisions to be made for the citizens who had settled below the Indian Boundary line before it was run and had left their improvements."

The following Hixsons were in Bledsoe in 1815 and signed the Petition to delay the land laws during the War of 1812 or the Second War with Great Britain: Ephriam Hixson Sr., John Hixson, Joseph Hixson, William Hixson and Ephriam Hixson Jr.

Ephraim Hixson was captain in the Bledsoe 31st Regiment Militia 1808. John Hixson was lieutenant in the 31st Regiment in 1811. Ephraim served as a private in Colonel Edwin Booth, Captain Miles Vernon East Tennessee Militia.

In 1830 the following Hixsons were heads of households in the county: Joseph, Ingola, David, Joseph Sr., Alexander, William, John and Ephraim. The Hixson family were large land owners in the 1830s in District IX, those being Mary, Rebecca, William Jr., Joseph Sr., William Sr., Joseph Jr. and Reuban. In 1840 the Hixsons head of households in District IX were Joseph, John, William, Mary, Joseph Jr., William Jr. and Rebecca.

In 1850 the Hixsons heads of households were William C. Hixson 22, Joseph Hixson 51, William Hixson 46, Rebecca Hixson 68, John M. Hixson 21, James Hixson 41, William Hixson 54 and Joseph 48. They all listed their occupation as farming and all born in Tennessee. Also listed was Mary Hixson age 83, born in Tennessee living in household of Jacob Skiles. Ingy Hixson age 80 born in North Carolina was living in household of Joseph Hixson age 48.

By 1860, on the eve of the Civil War, some of the descendants of the early Hixsons had moved to the new county Sequatchie, or Hamilton County, with the exception of Joseph (George) and his large family.

James, Joseph, J.M. and W.C. Hixson were listed as original stock holders in 1860 for the newly organized Sequachee College.

In 1880 a list of young gentlemen at the popular well-known school included E.M. Hixson, Samuel Hixson, their post office Fillmore in Sequatchie County. In 1881 the list included E.M.

Hixson, W.C. Hixson and Timothy Hixson their address was Stephen Chapel, Bledsoe County. M.L. Hixson was listed in 1881 on the roll of young ladies address Pitts X Roads Bledsoe.

T.J. (Thomas J.) served as Bledsoe County trustee in the late 1800s.

Sources:

A Narrative Genealogy of the Alexander Kelly Descendants and Related Families, by Erma Kelly, 1976.

Hixon - Hixson of Tennessee, by James E. Hixson.

History of Sequachee College, 1860-1881.

National Society Colonial Dames XVII Century Ancestor Roster, 1915-2005.

First Families of Tennessee, East Tennessee Historical Society, 2000.

Membership Roster and Soldiers, Tennessee Society American Revolution, Vol. I, Vol. II.

Hixson Cemetery

HOGE/HOGG/HOGUE

The Hoge name is found in the colony of New Jersey in the early 1700s. A William Hoge was in Virginia, a land owner and Juryman in the mid 1700s. He was listed as a patriot of the American Revolution. Joseph Hoge, the son of James and Elizabeth (Howe) Hoge, born September 25, 1770 in Virginia, married Barbara Brawley November 15, 1790. Barbara was born March 12, 1768.

Joseph Hoge was in Anderson County, Tennessee in 1805, on the Tax List. In 1807 Joseph signed a Petition to be presented to the Roane County Court, "To permit George Skillern to erect a grist mill in Sequacha Valley - will be of public utility."

Section 8 "First Session of the Seventh General Assemby 1807. John Tollett, Joseph Hoge and James Standefer were appointed commissioner to fix on most suitable place for holding court (in Bledsoe County) until otherwise provided by law."

Joseph Hoge in 1809 signed a petition with several other citizens of Bledsoe County asking that some provisions be made to those that "settled below the Indian Boundary Line, before it was run." That some "provision to be made to restore their property when the Indians title is extinguished."

In 1813 Joseph Hoge was listed as Lieutenant, Volunteer Company, men not subject to military duty in the Tennessee Militia, Bledsoe County. Several Hoges from Tennessee served in the War of 1812.

Joseph Hoge and Barbara (Brawley) Hoge became the parents

of: James born September 1, 1791, married Nancy Kelly September 4, 1817; John born September 10, 1793, married Mary Oats December 13, 1827; Pollie born December 26, 1795, married William Standefer May 24, 1814; Robert born March 21, 1798, married Ann Wheeler; Elizabeth born June 26, 1800, married James Gardner August 20, 1818; Sarah born December 22, 1802, married Riley Wheeler; William born May 22, 1805, married Matilda Coulter May 22, 1827; Joseph Jr. born July 3, 1807, married Nancy Wheeler; Daniel born May 30, 1810, married Rebecca Wheeler; Samuel (Lemel) born July 26, 1812.

Hoges listed in Bledsoe County in 1830 were Barbara Hoge and three of her sons, William S., James and Joseph Jr. John Hoge had moved to Marion County.

In 1840 only Joseph Hoge was in Bledsoe County and John was in Marion County. Joseph Hoge Sr. died before 1830. Barbara (Brawley) Hoge died between 1830-1840.

Joseph Hoge Jr. and Daniel, sons of Joseph Sr. and Barbara, were on the Bledsoe County Tax List 1837, 1838, 1839 in District X.

Joseph Hoge Jr. born July 3, 1807 was a farmer. He married Nancy Wheeler. They became the parents of Lafayette, Joel W., Sarah Jane, Barbary, Lemuel, Preston, Amelia, Mary, John R., Elizabeth J. and Joseph.

In 1850 Joseph Hoge Jr. lived in southern Bledsoe County. This area, the Tenth Civil District, later was attached to Hamilton County and later to Sequatchie County in 1857.

The Hoge family, like others in Sequatchie Valley was

divided by the Civil War.   Lafayette born 1830 joined the
Confederacy. Preston born ca. 1840 joined the Union Army.

Sources:

Colonial Dames XVII Century Ancestor Roster, 1915-2005.

John Hoge with History of Tennessee 1823 - 1988, by Joe F. Hoge, 1988.

Tennesseans in the War of 1812, by Sistler, 1992.

Census Records, Bledsoe County 1830, 1840, 1850, Marion County 1830, 1840.

Bledsoe County, Tennessee 1836 Tennessee Civil Districts and Tax List, by James L. Douthat, 1993.

HOODENPYLE

Phillip Gysherti Hoodenpyle, born 1756 in Amsterdam, Holland was raised and educated in Amsterdam. He was a graduate of the University. His parents were of "royal descent on the paternal side."

After the American Revolution about 1780, Phillip G. Hoodenpyle came to Philadelphia, Pennsylvania. He married in Holland and with him was his wife and young son. He had $75,000, a supply of merchandise and the Hoodenpyle Coat of Arms.

After a few years as a merchant in Philadelphia, his inheritance was almost depleted. The wife became dissatisfied and returned to Holland and divorce followed.

The next move for Phillip was to North Carolina. There he married Jane Ronceville in Buncomb County. After buying land and farming a few years, he was on the move again.

In 1813 Phillip was in Bledsoe County, when he petition the Tennessee General Assembly "to go into sheep raising on the Cumberland Plateau on 3000 acres of land," he claimed it is, "no good except for sheep raising."

By 1819 Phillip was buying land in the valley and became among the first to purchase lots in the new town of Pikeville. He served as trustee of the county in the early days.

In 1829 Phillip purchased from Charles J. Love two hundred and twenty-five acres located in lot number XIII for $550.00. The land was described as being on the northwest side of Sequatchie Creek, bordered by Cumberland Mountains.

The Bledsoe Census shows Phillip Hoodenpyle and four of his sons, James M., David, Thomas J. and Peter as heads of households in 1830. In 1840 only Peter and Jane, Phillip's widow, are living in District VI Bledsoe County. Thomas J. is living in Marion County.

Hoodenpyles on the Bledsoe County Tax List in 1836, 1837, 1838 were Peter, Phillip, Jane, Andrew and Thomas all in District VI.

In the last years of Phillip's life, he devoted his time to the study of the Bible, writing a commentary on the Bible for each of his children. Phillip G. Hoodenpyle died July 28, 1834. Jane (Ronceville) Hoodenpyle died November 3, 1845.

Phillip and Jane (Ronceville) Hoodenpyle were the parents of Peter born 1789 in North Carolina. He married Margaret (Peggy) Thomas. Peter served in the War of 1812 in Captain Charles Conway Unit in the East Tennessee Militia. Peter owned the town's blacksmith shop, located near the town's spring. After John A. Murrell was released from the State Prison he came to Pikeville. By being an excellent blacksmith, he worked at Hoodenpyle's shop. Murrell died in 1844. John Billingsley, brother-in-law of Hoodenpyle, took care of the burial of Murrell.

Peter was a farmer, merchant and surveyor, a Whig in politics. He was a builder of roads. In 1813 a petition to the General Assembly of Tennessee requested for Peter Hoodenpyle "to improve, at his own expense, a certain wagon road, which crosses the Cumberland Mountain from Bledsoe County into White, Warren and others counties along the Kioky Trace on completion of the work, he requested permission to erect a toll gate".

Peter died December 9, 1870. Margaret (Thomas) Hoodenpyle born 1794, died July 20, 1845. Both were buried in the Pikeville City Cemetery.

James M. lived in Sequatchie Valley, moved to Arkansas. Thomas J. lived in Sequatchie Valley, served in the Indian Wars of 1836-1838. David lived in Sequatchie Valley. Phillip Jr. lived in Warren County. He married Phoebe Smith, married second Hixie McGreger. Darcus married Samuel Shockly, lived in Van Buren County. Sallie lived in Arkansas, Polly lived in Arkansas. Jane, born April 21, 1812 in Raleigh, North Carolina, was married September 13, 1831 to John Billingsley. She lived in Bledsoe County and died in September 1894. She was buried in the Billingsley Family Cemetery, Smyrna.

Sources:

History of Phillip Bysberthy Hoodenpyle, by H.W. Hoodenpyle, 4100 Panadero Drive, Single Springs, California.

Bledsoe County, Tennessee, A History, by Elizabeth Robnett, 1993.

Tennesseans in the War of 1812, by Sistler, 1992.

Pikeville City Cemetery.

HOUSTON/HUSTON

The Houston name is found early in the American colonies of Pennsylvania and South Carolina. Several served in the American Revolution.

A Benjamin Houston was in Abbeville County, South Carolina in 1800.

A William Houston was in Roane County in 1805.

In 1808 Absolom Houston was a sworn chain carrier for a surveyor in Overton County.

In 1815 William Houston of Bledsoe County signed a petition to "delay the enactment of the land laws during the War of 1812."

James Houston was born February 10, 1791 in South Carolina, the son of Benjamin Houston. James Houston enlisted November 9, 1814 near Sparta in White County to serve in the War of 1812. He was a private in the Tennessee Militia. He was discharged June 10, 1815. He served 125 days at 26 cents a day, a total of $32.50. He received 40 cents a day for the use of his horse, a total of $50.00.

James married Hester Rhea who died 1825-26. James married second Delilah Bulluck, 1827-28, a Cherokee Indian born ca. 1803-04.

In 1830 William and James Houston were in Bledsoe County. In 1840 James Houston and family were living in the 2nd Civil

District of Bledsoe County. James and Delilah became the parents of Greenbury, Benjamin, Nancy, James, Martha, William, Mary E. and Delilah.

In 1850 James' occupation was a stone mason. James received a land grant in 1850 for forty acres for his military service. James Houston died June 7, 1855 and was buried in the Houston Cemetery. Delilah, James' widow, received 120 acre land grant in 1859. She was approved for a pension of $12.00 a month. Delilah died January 6, 1894.

Sources:

Bledsoe County Census 1830, 1840, 1850

Houston Family History, by Wesley S. Houston, 1985

Family information, Kyle Wear, Valley View, Ohio

Stephen Bradford Houston/Houston Genealogical Search by Robert Athol and Charleen K. Huston.

HUGHES

The large Hughes family is found in the colonies of Virginia and Maryland in the 1600s and 1700s. They were land owners, local officials and transportees.

Several served in the American Revolution. Hughes were in Tennessee in the late 1700s before Tennessee became a state in the counties of Sullivan, Greene and Washington. Several served in the War of 1812 from Tennessee.

Aaron and John Hughes were in Bledsoe County by 1815, as they signed a petition to delay the Land Laws during the War of 1812.

By 1830 the Hughes were in both Bledsoe and Marion county. The 1830 Bledsoe Census list as head of households Aaron, Ephraim, John and Hezekiah.

The 1840 census gives head of households as Margaret, Ephraim and Ann in District IX and Elizabeth Hughes in District X. This area is in southern Bledsoe.

In 1850 Hughes listed as heads of families were Benjamin, Aaron, John, Izakiah and John Jr.

Hughes on the Bledsoe County Tax List 1837, 1838, 1839 in District IX were Morgan H., Ephraim, Aaron, John, Ezekiah and Margaret. Aaron Hughes' place was the designated place of holding elections in District IX. This district included Lots Number 13 and 14.

Francis Hughes was born 1757 in Augusta County, Virginia. He was living in Burke County, North Carolina in June 1776 when he volunteered as a ranger against the Cherokee and Creek Indians. After two months he volunteered under General Rutherford and served four months fighting the Indians.

In January 1777 he was at Fort Gallagher on the Nolichucky River. In September 1780 he volunteered under Samuel Williams to march to North Carolina. Later he was at the Battle of Kings Mountain with General John Sevier. He made five tours and served a total of twenty-one months.

Francis Hughes applied for a pension on his service during the Revolution while living in Greene County in July 1833.

In November 1839 Benjamin F. Bridgeman requested that Francis Hughes' pension be transferred to Knoxville. Francis Hughes died 1841 in Bledsoe County. His pension was $51.66 annually.

Sources:

Membership Roster and Soldiers, The Tennessee Society of the Daughters of the American Revolution, Vol. II, III, IV.
National Society of the Colonial Dames XVII, Century Ancestor Roster, 1915-2005.

First Families of Tennessee, East Tennessee Historical Society, 2000.

Tennesseans in the War of 1812, by Sistler, 1992.

Bledsoe County Census, 1830, 1840, 1850.

Pension Records.

HUTCHERSON/HUTCHINSON/ HUTCHESON

The Hutcheson/Hutchinson name is found in the American colonies of New Jersey and Virginia in the 1600s. They were land owners, ministers, civil servants and transportees. In the late 1700s some were Revolutionary War patriots.

Charles Hutcheson married Sarah Estes. They were living in Amelia County, Virginia in 1743. Sarah was the daughter of Elisha Estes. Charles Hutcheson II, the son of Charles and Sarah was born in 1763 in Amelia County. Charles II married Rebekah Skillman born 1767 in Maryland, daughter of Christopher Skillman. Charles Hutcheson II was in Grainger County, Tennessee in 1797 when he purchased 100 acres of land on Hat Creek. His next move was to Sequatchie Valley.

The Hutchesons were in Bledsoe County by 1813. Charles Hutcheson, Lewis Hutcheson and William Hutcheson Jr. signed a petition for Peter Hoodenpyle "to improve at his own expense, a wagon road which crosses Cumberland Mountains from Bledsoe to Warren and White counties." Hoodenpyle had permission to erect a "toll gate".

In 1815 Charles and Thomas Hutcheson signed the petition to delay the land laws during the War between the United States and Great Britain.

The Blythe Ferry, located in Rhea County was the most important crossing of the Tennessee River between Knoxville and Ross Landing, in the early 1800s, according to the *Tennessee*

Gazetteer.

The ferry was operated from about 1809 to the removal of the Cherokee Indians, by William Blythe, a Cherokee. After 1838 the ferry was operated by the Hutcheson brothers, Alfred, William and Charles III.

After Charles, III death in 1842, his widow Sarah (Worthington) Hutcheson married Burton Holman. After Holman's death in 1863, the ferry was operated by his son Napoleon (Pole) Holman for many years.

Charles Hutcheson II died in Bledsoe County, August 1st, 1829. Rebekah died October 1848. Both were buried at Big Spring Cemetery.

John and Alfred Hutcheson were the administrators of Rebekah Hutcheson's estate in 1850.

Charles II and Rebekah (Skillman) Hutcheson became the parents of Nancy, Lewis, William, Martha, Christopher, Hezekiah, John, Mary Rebekah, Sarah, Elizabeth, Charles III and Alfred Leander.

The 1830 Bledsoe Census show Hutchesons listed as head of households as Charles III, William, Phillip, Alfred and Rebekah.

The 1840 census list Phillip and John. Rebekah was in the household of son John.

The 1850 census list John Hutcheson, Phillip S. Hutcheson and Abraham Hutcheson, a free Black.

Nancy Hutcheson, oldest child of Charles and Rebekah, born ca. 1786, married Joseph Peters. He was one of the acting commissioners for the town of Pikeville in 1816. Lewis Hutcheson born ca. 1788, married Mary Hutcheson (a cousin) in 1808 and moved to Alabama where she died in 1866. William Hutcheson, third child of Charles and Rebekah, born February 20, 1790, married Margaret (Peggy) Sigler July 20, 1809. They became the parents of Phillip Sigler, Matilda N., Charles, William Caswell, George Washington, Isaac Lafayette, Oliver Perry, Fannie F., Czarina M., and Calvin Thomas. This family lived in Rhea County. After the death of William in 1839, Margaret married Rev. Henry Gotcher. After his death, Margaret went to Texas. She died in 1880.

Martha (Patsy) Hutcheson, fourth child of Charles and Rebekah, born ca. 1792, married John Vernon, a Church of Christ preacher.

Christopher Hutcheson, fifth child of Charles and Rebekah Hutcheson, born ca. 1794, moved to Alabama.

Hezekiah Hutcheson born ca. 1797, married Priscilla Runion in 1819. He died in 1848 in Alabama.

John Hutcheson, seventh child of Charles and Rebekah, born January 20, 1800 in Grainger County, married August 25, 1825, Nancy Billingsley and lived in Bledsoe County. Nancy was born March 7, 1807, and died January 7, 1867. John died March 7, 1873. Both were buried in Billingsley Family Cemetery (Smyrna).

Mary Rebekah, eighth child of Charles and Rebekah, born November 28, 1801, married Robert Vernon Jr., May 8, 1822. Mary Rebekah died September 14, 1849 in Arkansas.

Sarah Hutcheson born July 9, 1803, became the second wife of Major James Roberson on July 12, 1828. This family lived in Bledsoe County. Sarah died August 24, 1876. She was buried in the old Roberson Cemetery. Charles Hutcheson III, born April 10, 1807 in Grainger County, married Sarah Worthington, born January 5, 1809 in Bledsoe County, the daughter of Samuel Worthington Jr. After Charles' death, Sarah married Burton Holman. Three sons of Charles III and Sarah (Worthington) Hutcheson; Alfred Leonidas, James Caswell, and William Lafayette served in the Union Army.

Elizabeth Hutcheson, youngest daughter of Charles and Rebekah, was born ca. 1808. She married William Vernon. They lived in Bledsoe County.

Alfred Leander Hutcheson, youngest child of Charles and Rebekah, born March 22, 1809, married Matilda Sigler born February 23, 1811 in Virginia. This family moved from Rhea County to Texas. Alfred Leander died January 30, 1890. Matilda died January 27, 1886. They were living in Tarrant County, Texas in 1880.

Phillip Sigler Hutcheson, oldest son of William and Margaret (Sigler) Hutcheson, born January 15, 1812, lived in Bledsoe County. He married August 28, 1832, Sarah Brown, daughter of Reuban Brown.

Phillip Sigler and Sarah were members of the Cumberland Presbyterian Church, Cedar Grove. Phillip Sigler served as Justice of the Peace for many years, some times serving as chairman, from the Fourth District in the county.

Five of his brothers and two of his sisters moved to Texas. Only William Caswell remained in Tennessee. Three sons, Frank,

James L. and Reuban Brown, of Phillip Sigler's family served in the Confederate Army. Phillip Sigler died August 31, 1890. Sarah died June 5, 1891; both were buried Hutcheson Family Cemetery.

Sources:

Here It Is Hutcheson Genealogy, by Martine Hutcheson Greenwood, Fort Worth, Texas, 1966.

Bledsoe Census, 1830, 1840, 1850.

The Tennessee Historical Quarterly, Summer 1987.

National Society Colonial Dames XVII Century, Ancester Roster, 1915-2005.

Tennesseans in the War of 1812, by Sistler, 1992.

Iron Hill Cemetery
Cold Springs area of Bledsoe County, Tennessee

JOHNSTON/JOHNSON

The name Johnson is found in the American Colonies of Virginia, Maryland, Pennsylvania, Connecticut and South Carolina in the 1600s. They were land owners, planters, transportees, proprietors, and in the military. Several served in the American Revolution.

Several Johnsons were in Tennessee before Tennessee became a state in 1796, in the counties of Greene, Knox, Hawkins and Washington.

Johnson was a common name in the War of 1812 in both officers and enlisted men that served from Tennessee.

Aquilla Johnson, born May 4, 1770 in Virginia, was in Bledsoe County in 1808 when he purchased 115 acres of land on the south east side of the river, including the improvements, "where he now lives" for $232.00.

Aquilla Johnson married Mary Ann Scarborough October 24, 1799. She was born May 15, 1780. This family of Aquilla Johnson was in Anderson County in 1803. He was listed as an esquire.

In 1813, Aquilla Johnson signed a petition to be presented to the Tennessee General Assembly for Peter Hoodenpyle "to improve at his own expense a wagon road across the Cumberland Mountains from Bledsoe County to White County."

Another early petition signed by a number of the citizens of the county was "to build a road to begin at the foot of Walden Ridge near Aquilla Johnson and cross Walden Ridge a direct line to the town of Washington in Rhea County." This is said to be the shortest route and is highly important to travel from the northeast and Kentucky.

Aquilla Johnson was an acting commissioner for the town of Pikeville in 1816. The commissioners purchased 16 acres on Sequatchie Creek in Lot Number VIII, from Charles Love of Virginia for $110.25. This was the new county seat, Pikeville. Other commissioners were Joseph Peters, Adam Sherrell and Eli Thurman.

By the Bledsoe Census of 1830, nine Johnsons were listed as heads of households. Aquilla, Right, Bright and James B. Johnson were listed on the Bledsoe County Tax list in 1837, 1838 in District V. In 1840 Aquilla Johnson was living in District V, also two of his sons, Bright and Right.

Aquilla and Mary Ann Johnson became the parents of: Kinsy born February 27, 1801, died February 28, 1801; Ruby born August 16, 1802, married Moses Lowe; Ala, born September 12, 1804, died January 20, 1805; Right, born May 8, 1806, married Frances N. Humble; Bright, born August 20, 1808, married Nancy H. Brown; Mary Ann born September 15, 1810, married John Ogle; Mark P. born September 19, 1813, married Margaret J. Porter; James Baxter born February 25, 1816, married Frances Ann Payne; Francis A. born January 20, 1818; Abigail P. born March 5, 1820, married Wiley F. Merriman; Elba H. born February 3, 1823, married Carroll L. Standifer; Rachel S. born August 6, 1825, married Thomas D. Lewis.

Mary Ann Johnson died June 13, 1846. Aquilla died February 28, 1850. They were both buried at the Old Baptist Church Cemetery. Aquilla requested that his funeral sermon be preached, "at the grave side from Psalms Fifty Chaper, fifth verse."

Sources:

Members and Patriots The Tennessee Society Daughters of the American Revolution, Vol. III, IV.

Tennesseans in the War of 1812, by Sistler.

National Society Colonial Dames XVII Century Ancestor Roster, 1915-2005.

Register of Deeds Office, Pikeville, Tennessee.

Family Bible Record of T.A. and Vesta Lewis.

KEEDY

The Keedy family was in the American Colony of Maryland in the mid 1700s in Frederick and later Washington County. This family came from Germany. The name was Gutting and was Americanized to Keedy.

The Keedys were in Tennessee in early 1800. They were in Sequatchie Valley early and settled in a cove on the eastern side of the valley that became known as Keedy's Cove. Lewis and William Keedy served as enlisted men in Captain William Christian's Company in the East Tennessee Militia during the War of 1812.

In 1830 Bledsoe Census gives Lewis Keedy as head of a household. In this household were six males and five females, with the oldest male as being between 70 and 80 years of age. David, Lewis and William Keedy were on the Tax List of the county in 1838 and 1839 in District VII. In the 1840 census Lewis Keedy was listed in District VI as head of a household, with seven males and four females, the oldest male being between 80 and 90 years of age. According to census records, Lewis, David, William and Jacob Keedy Sr. came from Maryland to Sequatchie Valley in early 1800s.

Jacob Keedy born ca. 1794 in Maryland, married [unknown] Rosecrans. Jacob died in Bledsoe County ca. 1821. Jacob's children are listed as: Mary born ca. 1814 Bledsoe County, married Newton Pike; Sara (Sally) born March 4, 1816, married Buckner Howard, died October 16, 1904; William born ca. 1821, married Nancy Powell, died before 1880 Franklin County; Jacob born March 2, 1822, married Delilah Walker, died June 15, 1888.

Jacob Keedy Jr. born March 2, 1822, the son of Jacob Sr., served as a private in Company D, the 6th Tennessee Infantry. His occupation was farming. He married Delilah Walker August 1, 1844. Delilah was born June 11, 1823. They became the parents of: Mary Ann born ca. 1846, married Gaines Hatfield; Nancy married John James; Zachariah Taylor born ca. 1859, married Mrs. Mollie Day, died May 2, 1916; Rachel Emmaline born October 12, 1850, married William Harrison Alexander July 21, 1875, died July 3, 1919 in Hamilton County; James Crispon born March 1, 1858, married Margaret Emmaline Gadd, died December 6, 1942; Tennessee Ada born ca. 1860, married Jacob Krichbaum, married second Henry Smith; Jacob Rosecrans born November 18, 1861, died Hamilton County November 11, 1927; Richard born February 7, 1864, died May 25, 1891; Delilah Virginia born ca. 1869, died 1932 Hamilton County.

Jacob died June 15, 1888. Delilah (Walker) Keedy, as a widow drew a United States Civil War pension of $8.00 a month. She died May 26, 1904.

Lewis Keedy born ca. 1790 in Maryland died after 1850 and before 1860. Lewis was a blacksmith by trade. His wife Sarah born ca. 1800 in Maryland. Also in their household was William, age 46, a blacksmith in 1850.

Sources:

History and Biographical Records of Washington County, Maryland.

Keedy Information, Carl F. Stein, Family Historian, 369 Bell St. S.E., Marietta, GA 30060.

Keedy Family of Bledsoe County, by Ralph G. Bowman, 4333 Woodlawn Pike, Knoxville, TN 37920.

Census Records of Bledsoe County, 1830, 1840, 1850.

Tennesseans in the War of 1812, by Sistler.

KELLY/KELLEY

A John Kelly was in the New World, America, in the mid 1600s. The name Kelly was in Tennessee before Tennessee became a state, in Greene County.

Several served in the American Revolution.

The Kellys were in Sequatchie Valley in the early 1800s. Several served in the War of 1812, both as officers and enlisted men from Tennessee.

Alexander Kelly Sr. born in Armagh County, Ireland, ca. 1755, came to America as a young child. During the American Revolution he lived in Virginia. He served as a captain in the Greenbriar County Militia, 1780-1781.

By the mid 1790s, Alexander was in Knox County. Alexander Kelly was a delegate to the Territorial Legislature in 1794, representing Knox County.

He was in Blount County, Tennessee in 1796 as he was a senator in the First and Second General Assemblies, 1796-1799.

He married Nancy Robinson in 1778. In the early 1800s, the Kelly family moved to Sequatchie Valley, probably after the Indian Treaty of 1805.

Alexander Kelly was listed in the 1830 Marion County census. He died between 1830 and 1840 in Sequatchie Valley, Marion County.

Children of Alexander Kelly Sr. and Nancy Robinson Kelly: John born 1779, married Nancy Mayo. He lived in Bledsoe and Marion Counties. Alexander Jr. born ca. 1781, married Sally Prigmore in 1817 in Roane County. In 1840 this family lived in Marion County. William born ca. 1887, married Ruth Prigmore, daughter of Joseph Prigmore, in Roane County. He served in the War of 1812. William lived in Marion County in 1830. Margaret born ca. 1789, married Ephraim Prigmore. This family lived in Marion County in 1840; Viny born ca. 1793, married Adam Lamb in 1815. This family lived in Bledsoe County in 1840. Annie born ca. 1795, married Richard Stone. This family lived in Marion County in 1840.

John Kelly born June 12, 1779 in Greenbriar County, Virginia was the son of Alexander Kelly Sr. He married Nancy Mayo, born 1772 in North Carolina. John was a farmer and surveyor. He served as sheriff of Bledsoe County in 1809. He was a large land owner and slave holder.

John Kelly was a Lieutenant Colonel Commander in the Tennessee Militia, 31st Bledsoe in 1815.

He was on the Bledsoe County Tax List, District VI in 1838, 1839. In the 1840 Bledsoe Census he is listed in District VI.

John Kelly was a member of the House, Tennessee General Assembly in 1817-1819, representing Bledsoe County.

John and Nancy (Mayo) Kelly became the parents of: Esther, Nancy, Alexander, Polly, Adeline, Thomas, Martha, Jane, Valentine, James, Margaret and William Jasper.

John Kelly later moved to the new county, Marion. This was

after the Indian Treaty in which the Indians gave up the southern part of Sequatchie Valley. John Kelly became a leading citizen in Marion County. He died November 26, 1845.

Sources:

Tennesseans in the War of 1812, by Sistler, 1992.

First Families of Tennessee, East Tennessee Historical Society, 2000.

National Society Colonial Dames, XVII Century Ancestor Roster, 1915-2005.

Membership Roster and Soldiers, The Tennessee Society of the Daughters of the American Revolution, 1970-1984 Vol. 3, 1985-2001 Vol. 4.

A Narrative Genealogy of the Alexander Kelly Descendants 1750-1975, by Erma Kelly, 1976.

Biographical Directory of the Tennessee General Assembly, by Robert M. McBride and Dan M. Robison, Vol. I, 1796-1861.

KERLEY/KEARLEY

The Kerley family, the mother, two sons and a daughter were in Bledsoe County by 1810. Several Kerleys from Tennessee served in the War of 1812. Kerleys were listed, both as officers and enlisted men.

The 1830 Bledsoe census list William and Daniel Kerley as heads of households. William Kerley and Jermia Kerley (Daniel's widow) were on the Bledsoe County Tax List in District III in 1838 and 1839. The 1840 Bledsoe census shows William, James and Jermia Kerley as heads of households in District III.

The William Kerley family settled on the eastern side of the Cumberland Plateau in northwest Bledsoe County in an area that became known as Kerley Hollow.

Daniel Kerley, born 1780-1790 in North Carolina, married Jermia Oxsheer, daughter of Samuel and Sarah (Wilson) Oxsheer. Jermia was born November 29, 1801. They became the parents of Elizabeth born ca. 1829, married Shamuel Selby; Samuel O. born ca. 1828, married Catherine Selby, second Rebecca (Sherrill) Kerley; James born ca. 1830; Daniel born ca. 1832, married Rebecca Sherrill, after Daniel's death, Rebecca married Samuel O., her brother-in-law; George born ca. 1834.

In November 1841, William Kerley was appointed guardian of the minor heirs of Daniel Kerley. Daniel died 1830-1838, Jermia died 1840-1850.

In 1850 George Kerley, age 16, was living with sister

Elizabeth Selby. Samuel was married and James and Daniel were living with their uncle George Oxsheer.

By 1860 this District III was added to form part of Cumberland County. The Kerleys living near the head of Sequatchie Valley in Cumberland County were Columbus, William and Samuel. Their post office was Ormes Store.

William Kerley born October 9, 1799 in Burk County, North Carolina, married Nancy Owens born ca. 1798 in Kentucky. William and Nancy became the parents of: James born ca. 1824, Daniel born ca. 1826, Parmelia born ca. 1828, Columbus born ca. 1830, Elizabeth born ca. 1832, Manery born ca. 1835, Eliza born ca. 1837, Benjamin born ca. 1840, Calvin born ca. 1843.

William Kerley in politics was a Whig, a Union man and a Republican. He joined the Stoney Point Methodist Episcopal Church, in 1824. Seven of his children became members of the Methodist Episcopal Church. William Kerley died in 1886.

James Kerley born ca. 1824, the oldest son of William, married Millie Hale. He lived in Bledsoe County, a farmer and blacksmith. James and Millie became the parents of: Permelia Ann born February 1859, married Charlie Roberts, died 1950; Nancy Sue born March 1, 1861, married Samuel J. Thurman, died December 28, 1940; William Carroll born 1863, married Elizabeth J. Thurman; Mary C. born 1865, married Jim Thurman; Elis S. born ca. 1868; Emaline born November 26, 1869, married James Wright; Daniel born March 1872, married Louise Swafford; David C.; James C. born November 20, 1878, died May 1, 1975, married Nannie Tollett; Robert Kerley born September 7, 1883, died January 28, 1967, married Ada Dunn. James Kerley died June 8, 1906. Millie (Hale)

Kerley died June 17, 1915.

Columbus Kerley, son of William, born ca. 1830, married Sarah Rector. They became the parents of: William O., James, Nancy Jane, Annie, Sarah, M.L., John, Ben, Alice and Ellen.

William O., the oldest son of Columbus and Sarah (Rector), was born December 3, 1859, was educated at Grant Memorial University in Athens, Tennessee and taught school for several years. He married Letitia Brown. He served as superintendent of schools in Cumberland County, county trustee and clerk of the county court.

Sources:

Crossville Times 2/17/1887, Calvin Kerley's death certificate.

Census Records, Cumberland County 1870.

Bledsoe County Census Records, 1830, 1840; Bledsoe County Tax List 1830s.

Compendium of Local Biography Part II, Cumberland Region of Tennessee, 1898.

Spanning the Century with the Hale Family, by Muriel Nadine (Hale) Lynch, Independence, Missouri, 1990.

****

LEE/LEA/LEIGH

The large Lee family was in the colonies of Virginia and North Carolina in the 1600s. They were land owners, colonial officials and served in the colonial military. Several served in the American Revolution.

The Lees were in Tennessee before Tennessee became a state. A large number served in the War of 1812 from Tennessee.

Burrell Lee of Dinwiddie County, Virginia was a planter and slave holder. He was born ca. 1766 in Virginia. He married Martha Jones. He made his will October 18, 1804. He requested that his estate both real and personal be equally divided between all his children. He also requested his wife's mother, Mary Jones be supported during her life time. He directed his brother, Randolph Lee, the executor of his will, to sell the land and plantation where they lived and purchase another tract, "for the benefit of his children for raising and support."

Burrell (Burl) was in the tobacco trade. He was a teamster hauling tobacco to market. He was killed by lightning sometime before June 1805.

Robert Lee born October 6, 1798 in Virginia, the son of Burrell and Martha (Jones) Lee married Elizabeth Swafford in 1818. They became the parents of: John Anderson, William E., Burrell, Aaron, Russell, Nancy, Mary, Thomas and Elizabeth. Robert married second, Elizabeth Evitt in 1834. They became the parents of James, Henry, Robert and Jake C. Robert married third Matilda Warner in 1845. They became the parents of Martha and Bluford.

Robert Lee and family moved to Bradley County after 1850. During the Civil War the family divided. Robert Lee was a strong Union man. His son, John Anderson Lee, was living in Texas at the time joined the Confederate Amry. Jake C. Lee joined the Union Army and Thomas Lee refused to fight and "hid out".

Burrell Russell Lee born October 6, 1804 in Virginia, the son of Burrell and Martha (Jones) Lee, was in Bledsoe County in 1823 when he purchased from William Hutcheson 163 acres of land in Lot Number I.

He married Louhaney Swafford, daughter of "Big" Aaron Swafford. She was born February 15, 1800 in South Carolina. Burrell Russell was on the Bledsoe Tax List in 1837, 1838, 1839. He served as Justice of Peace in Bledsoe County in the 1830s and 1840s.

Burrell Russell and Louhaney (Swafford) Lee became the parents of sixteen children: John C. born ca. 1825, married Dorthula McClellan and moved to Kentucky after 1850; Eliza born ca. 1826, married Edward Tilley, lived in Rhea County; Mary (Polly) born ca. 1827, married Thomas N. (Long Tom) Swafford (a cousin); this family moved to Texas. Thomas born ca. 1828, married Barbara McClelland; Burrell Russell Jr. born ca. 1829, married Elizabeth Nail; this family moved to Ray County, Missouri; Robert born ca. 1832, married Frances Crawley; Louisa born ca. 1833, married Joseph R. Burchfield, a Methodist minister; they moved to Kansas; William born ca. 1835, married Elizabeth (Betty) Brown; this family lived in Bledsoe County; Anderson Andrew born ca. 1837, married Louise "Lou" Branham; this family lived in Bledsoe County; Benjamin Franklin born 1838, married Mary Isbella Thurman, married second Eliza Jane Broyles. Benjamin Franklin enlisted as a private in 1865 First Lt. Andrew Payne's Company Sixth Regiment,

Tennessee Mounted Infantry. This company was organized for the "purpose of scouting the Cumberland Mountains for numerous guerilla bands that had infested the region". Martha born ca. 1841, died July 13, 1859; tradition was she was struck by lightning as she sought shelter under a tree during a rain storm. James C. born ca. 1843, died December 1855; twins, died young; twins, died young.

Louhaney (Swafford) Lee died July 6, 1863. She was buried in the Oxsheer-Lee Cemetery. Burrell Russell Lee died May 15, 1877 in Bradley County and buried there.

Martha (Jones) married second Michael Miser. Tradition was they moved west to California.

Nancy Lee born ca. 1800 in Virginia, the daughter of Burrell and Martha (Jones) Lee, married Nasson Swafford. Nasson (Nace) was born in 1802 in South Carolina. They were the parents of: Thomas Nasson (Long Tom) born in 1818, married Mary E. Lee, a cousin. This family moved to Marshall County and later to Wise County, Texas; Nathaniel C. born July 12, 1822 in Mississippi, married Seraphina J. Sloan on March 16, 1845 in Bledsoe County. She was born October 15, 1827 in Tennessee, the daughter of Thomas and Lettie (Russell) Sloan. This family moved to Marion County, later to Ray County, Missouri.

Nancy (Lee) Swafford died in Monroe County, Mississippi after 1820. By 1830 Nasson and sons had returned to Bledsoe County, and Nasson had married for the second time. Nancy (Lee) Swafford inherited two slaves from her father Burrell Lee, Rachel and Lizzie. The slaves were in the possession of Nasson Swafford at the time of his death in the early 1850s.

****

Sources:

Robert Lee of Tennessee Loyal Union Farmer, by Raymond and Melba Lee Murray, 2006.

Colonial Dames National Society XVII Century Ancester Roster, 1915-2005.

Members and Patriots The Tennessee Society Daughters of the American Revolution, Vol. III, Vol. IV.

Bledsoe County Census, 1840, 1850.

John Lee, Esquire Captain Thomas Lee, John Lee Jr. and Descendants, by Ernest L. Ross, Cleveland, TN 1978.

Bledsoe County Courthouse
Built in 1907 and burned in 1909

McDONOUGH

Andrew McDonough, born November 30, 1756 in Beaufort County, North Carolina, enlisted November 1779 to serve three months in the American Revolution. He served under Captain Matthew McCollough in Colonel John Shepard's Regiment. He enlisted again in June 1780 and served three months in Captain Edmund McKell's Company. After the American Revolution, Andrew moved to Tyrrell County and later to Raleigh. After some time in Raleigh, ca. 1809, Andrew and part of his family moved to Bledsoe County. Children of Andrew were: Elizabeth, Andrew Jr., Calvin, Mary "Polly", Henry, Ransom, James and John; Mary married Jacob Johnson and they became the parents of the future president Andrew Johnson. Sometime after 1816 Andrew married Rhoda (Sartin) Roberson, the widow of William Roberson. According to a letter written by a grandson of Rhoda, he was not too happy about "Grandma marrying that cranky old man."

The 1830 Bledsoe census gives Andrew McDonough age 70-80 and wife Rhoda Sartin Roberson McDonough age 60-70. Also, Calvin, William and Andrew McDonough Jr., as heads of households. Bledsoe Tax records list Andrew Jr., Calvin and Henry McDonough in 1837-39 in Districts VI, VII and VIII. The 1840 Bledsoe census list Andrew McDonough in District VI and Calvin in District VIII as heads of households. In 1833, Andrew applied for pension on his Revolutionary War service while living in Bledsoe County. His pension was granted, $36.36 a year.

Sometime after Rhoda Roberson McDonough's death in 1837, Andrew moved to Marion County with Andrew Jr. He died January 20, 1846 and was buried in the Roberson Cemetery in Bledsoe

County. The Bledsoe County Court Minutes Book 1841-1846 records Andrew McDonough's death and three surviving children as Elizabeth Langley, Andrew Jr., and Calvin, all residents of the state as required by the regulations of the War Department.

Andrew McDonough Jr. served in the War of 1812 as a private in Colonel Edwin Booth and Captain Miles Vernon East Tennessee Militia. Calvin McDonough served in the Cherokee War, Indian Removal in 1836.

Sources:

Pioneer Families, by John Wilson, Chattanooga Free Press, August 25, 1996.

Bledsoe County Court Clerk Book, 1841-46.

Bledsoe County Census, 1830-40.

William Roberson Cemetery

William Roberson, Andrew McDonough
Of the American Revolutionary War

James Roberson, War of 1812

Rufus Brown Roberson,
Mexican War

McDOWELL

The McDowell name is found in the American colonies in the

1700s. The McDowells were patriots of the American Revolution.

John and Isabella McDowell were living in Pennsylvania in 1790. By the mid 1790s this family were living in Stokes County, North Carolina where they had purchased land on Belew Creek. After John's death, Isabella married Grabrial Jones.

Sometime before 1820, Isabella lost her second husband Grabrial Jones. By 1820 Isabella and her children had made another move, their last to Sequatchie Valley, Bledsoe County.

In 1837 Joseph and William McDowell were on the Bledsoe Tax List in the IV District of Bledsoe County. In the 1840 Bledsoe census, Joseph McDowell was living in District III and William was living in District IV.

In 1850, Isabella was age 87 and daughter Elizabeth was 54. They were living near Joseph and William which had large families. Isabella McDowell Jones died 1850-1860, and was buried in McDowell Cemetery.

John and Isabella McDowell were the parents of: Mary born ca. 1790 in Pennsylvania, married Jesse Day; Joseph born ca. 1792 in Pennsylvania, married Nancy Close; Elizabeth born ca. 1794 in North Carolina, never married; William born ca. 1800 in North Carolina, married Jane Hankins.

Children of Isabella and Grabrial Jones: Isabella, married Anderson Clark; Martha married William N. Farmer; and William.

Joseph McDowell born ca. 1792 in Pennsylvania was the oldest son of John and Isabella McDowell. While a small child his parents moved to Stokes County, North Carolina. This county is located in the northwest part of the state on the Virginia line.

In 1816 Joseph sold land he inherited from his father. This same year he married Nancy Close, a native of the same state. Nancy was born ca. 1802. By 1820 the McDowells were in Bledsoe County.

In 1838 Joseph bought seventy-seven acres of land in Lot Number IV for $8.00 an acre. The land bordered "a wagon road, included a spring, bottom and ridge." The McDowells were Presbyterians. Joseph represented the Cedar Grove Prebysterian Church in 1848 at district meeting in Rhea County.

Joseph was appointed post master of the new rural post office, Nine Mile in 1850, two of his sons William and Kinsy, later served this office.

Joseph died in 1870-1880 and was buried near the Cedar Grove Church; Nancy died 1860-1870.

Joseph and Nancy (Close) McDowell became the parents of: Sela born ca. 1820, became the first wife of John Hankins; William J. born ca. 1825, died after 1880; Eleanor G. born ca. 1828; Thomas C. born ca. 1830, married Letitia McDaniel; Kinsey S. born ca. 1831, was a tanner by trade; Hiram born ca. 1836, married Kitturah Worthington; Joseph born ca. 1838, died 1860-1870; Lucy J. born November 29, 1939, never married, died June 19, 1913 and buried at Brushy Cemetery; Martha E. born ca. 1842; Jesse F. born ca. 1845; James A. born ca. 1848.

William McDowell was born ca. 1800 in North Carolina. In 1820 he had sold his land he inherited from his father and was living in Bledsoe County.

William married ca. 1825 a neighbor Jane Hankins, daughter of John Hankins. In 1838 William bought fifty-eight acres of land from the Glenworth Estate for $8.00 per acre. The land was described as on Cosby's Creek (later McDowell Branch) with a spring and a bottom. William, a farmer, lived the rest of his life on or near this land. William died 1870-1880, Jane died 1880-1900, buried at the McDowell Cemetery.

William and Jane (Hankins) McDowell became the parents of twelve children: John H. was born ca. 1826. He married Mary Hankins, his cousin, the daughter of Stephen Hankins. This family moved to Warren County; Joseph was born ca. 1826. Joseph left sometime before 1860 for California. Joseph left his mother, Jane, a his real and personal property in 1883, according to his will; William born ca. 1829, married Mary Smith, lived in Bledsoe County; James F. born ca. 1832; Mary born ca. 1834, never married, died 1800-1900; Sarah (Sal) born ca. 1837, never married, lived at the old home place. She died April 14, 1913; Hannah born ca. 1840, married James Worthington; Isabella (Isa) born ca. 1842, never married, lived with her sister at the old home (the home of her grandfather and mother) John and Mary Hankins. Isabella died June 6, 1915; Thomas born ca. 1844, married Martha Biddy. This family lived in Warren County; Jesse M. was born ca. 1846. At the age of 18 he volunteered October 9, 1864 at Athens, Tennessee to serve in the Union Army. His personal description was, "gray eyes, dark hair, fair complexion, five feet five inches tall." He served in Company D, 7th Regiment Mtd. Inf. He was discharged at Nashville July 1865. Jesse's occupation was farming. Jesse died 1870-1880 and was buried at McDowell Cemetery near his home; Nancy Loretta born ca. 1849, married John Worthington, brother of James Worthington. She died before 1900;

Elizabeth died young.

Sources:

Stokes County, North Carolina.

Bledsoe County Census Records.

Bledsoe County Register's Office.

McDowell Cemetery.

McDowell family information.

The McDowell Cemetery
Nine Mile Community

McREYNOLDS

The McReynolds were in the American colonies of Maryland, Virginia and Pennsylvania in the 1700s. Several took part in the American Revolution. They were soldiers or patriots from Pennsylvania, Virginia and North Carolina.

The McReynolds were in Tennessee before Tennessee became a state, 1796, in Knox, Greene and Blount counties. The McReynolds were in Sequatchie Valley in early 1800s. Joseph McReynolds and his son Samuel coming from Blount County. From the dates 1812 to 1839 the McReynolds received almost 800 acres of land in grants from the state. John McReynolds served in the War of 1812 in the East Tennessee Volunteer Mounted Infantry.

Samuel McReynolds born 1749, Cecil County, Maryland, married Sarah Margaret Woods. This family lived in Washington and Campbell Counties, Virginia before moving to Blount County and later Sequatchie Valley. The McReynolds brothers, James and Joseph, owned much real estate in Virginia.

In 1830 Bledsoe Census, Stephen and Samuel McReynolds Jr., were living in Marion County. Samuel McReynolds Sr. and Rachel McReynolds (widow of Joseph) were heads of households in Bledsoe. The Tax Records of Bledsoe show 1836, 1837, 1838, Samuel in District VII and Rachel in District VIII. The 1840 census gives the same Samuel Jr. in District VII and Rachel McReynolds in District VIII.

Samuel and Margaret (Woods) McReynolds became the parents of: John born 1778, married Jane McReynolds November 27,

1799 in Blount County, daughter of Joseph and Mary Margaret (Mitchell) McReynolds. John died September 27, 1822; Joseph born ca. 1780 Washington County, Virginia, married January 11, 1798 Rachel Rainey. Joseph was in Bledsoe County in 1807, he later moved to Marion County; Robert born ca. 1782, married Celia Snider; Sarah born ca. 1784, married David Rainey January 28, 1802 in Washington County, Virginia; James born ca. 1785 in Washington County, Virginia; Margaret born April 22, 1786 in Washington County, Virginia, married Alexander Coulter, January 1804. This family lived in Blount, Roane, Bledsoe and Marion counties, Tennessee and finally moved to Walker County, Georgia.

Samuel McReynolds Jr. born June 1797 in Washington County, Virginia, youngest son of Samuel Sr. and Sarah Margaret (Woods) McReynolds lived in Blount County before moving to Bledsoe in early 1800. He married May 10, 1821 Jane Hale born December 10, 1797, the daughter of Alexander Hale. Samuel Jr. became a leading citizen, large land owner and slave holder. He was appointed on the committee in 1835 to divide the county into Civil Districts and designate a place for holding elections.

In 1839 he reported he owned nine slaves able to work, only those able to work were taxed. In 1860, eve of the Civil War, Samuel owned 1200 acres of improved land, 1400 acres of unimproved land. His main crops were corn, wheat, oats, livestock, eight horses, fifteen mules, two oxen, twenty milk cows, 180 other cattle, 156 sheep, and 200 hogs.

Samuel and Jane (Hale) McReynolds became the parents of Margaret, Alexander H., Mary Jane, Samuel M., Sarah J., Clayborn Delaney and James W.

Margaret, the oldest daughter, born November 8, 1824, became the second wife of Judge Thomas N. Frazier on April 10, 1845.

Alexander Hale McReynolds, oldest son of Samuel Jr. and Jane, born June 20, 1826, married Emily C. Greer December 2, 1847, daughter of Weatherston S. and Mary (Kyle) Greer. Emily C. was born September 30, 1827. His father gave him a farm of 320 acres. He was educated at the Lafayette Academy in Pikeville and became a teacher in the public schools.

During the Civil War, Alexander H. and his brother Samuel M. McReynolds' store in Pikeville was burned by the Union soldiers. He later reported he lost seven slaves and a great deal of livestock and grain, and was "taken prisoner for a while." In 1874 he was serving as a trustee of People College. Alexander and Emily became the parents of Elizabeth A., Mary J., Weatherston S., John S., Gathner A. and Ida.

Samuel M. McReynolds, second son of Samuel Jr. and Jane, was born June 20, 1828. In 1850 Samuel M., age 20, was a clerk. In 1851 he formed a partnership with T.J. Wilson and started a mercantile business in Pikeville.

During the Civil War his entire stock was taken by the Union soldiers. However, by 1887 Samuel M. was again in business in partnership with W.S. Loyd. Three years later he bought out his partner and continued in business until 1892 when he sold out to G.W. Ault. He was a large land owner and a successful farmer.

Samuel M. married May 2, 1858, Elizabeth Henson who was born September 1839. They became the parents of: Charles, Joseph,

James and Hallie. Elizabeth (Henson) McReynolds died June 16, 1875. Samuel W. married May 30, 1876 Miss Kate Bell, born October 15, 1843 in Rhea County, daughter of Rev. William H. and Nancy (Rainey) Bell.

Sarah J. McReynolds, youngest daughter of Samuel and Jane (Hale) McReynolds born 1832 became the second wife of Thomas Alexander Pope.

Claiborne Delaney McReynolds was born ca. 1834. In 1850 Claiborne D. was listed as a student age 16 at the home of his parents. He later went to Texas and became a farmer and stock raiser.

James W. McReynolds born February 19, 1836, the youngest son of Samuel and Jane (Hale) McReynolds, was educated in the school at Pikeville and later attended Burritt College at Spencer. In 1861 he enlisted in Company I Eighth Tennessee Confederate Cavalry, commissioned as Captain, which was part of General Joe Wheeler's command. He took part in the Battles of Parkers Cross Roads in West Tennessee and the Battle of Chickamauga. He was held a prisoner a short time. After the war he returned to Pikeville and married Sarah Loucretia Worthington, born 1845, the daughter of James Worthington. This family moved to Texas and became the parents of one daughter, Loucretia, born October 26, 1866. Sarah Loucretia died November 3, 1866. Later James W. McReynolds, known as "Captain James" returned to Tennessee and settled in Marion County. There he became a large land owner and served on the Marion County Court. On November 26, 1872 he married Martha Graham, daughter of Pope Graham. They became the parents of Hope, Joe and Jim.

Samuel McReynolds Jr. married second Anna D. Stephens,

daughter of Isaac Stephens on August 10, 1844. Anna D. was born December 24, 1813. They became the parents of Isaac Stephens, Thomas S. and Martha. Samuel Jr. died February 13, 1865; Anna D. (Stephens) McReynolds died April 4, 1873. Both were buried on their farm north of the home.

Isaac Stephens McReynolds born September 17, 1845, attended the local schools and Burritt College. He married July 14, 1868 Adeline Davis, born September 5, 1847, the daughter of Robert R. Davis of Meigs County. Isaac became a large land owner and stock raiser. Isaac and Adeline became the parents of: Tulloss Vander (T.V.), Samuel Davis (Congressman Sam D. McReynolds), and Bertie Lew. Isaac Stephens died July 9, 1915; Adeline died March 23, 1930. Both buried in Pikeville City Cemetery.

Thomas S. McReynolds, youngest son of Samuel Jr. and Anna D. (Stephens) McReynolds, born August 22, 1849, married Jennie Davis, born November 9, 1850. She was a sister of his brother's wife. They became the parents of: Walter H., John B., Margaret "Maggie", William Isaac, and Annie H. Thomas S. McReynolds died August 21, 1922; Jennie (Davis) McReynolds died February 15, 1928. Both are buried in Pikeville City Cemetery.

Martha (Mattie) McReynolds, the only daughter of Samuel Jr. and Anna D., was born December 6, 1846, married William Rankin Pope. Martha died June 12, 1911; William died 1932.

Sources:

First Families of Tennessee, East Tennessee Historical Society, 2000.

Tennessee Land Grants, Vol. 2, Byron and Samuel Sistler, 1998.

The McReynolds A Noble Clan, by William Howard McReynolds, Mercer, Missouri, 1980.

Compendium of Local Biography, Cumberland Region of Tennessee.

Cemetery Records.

MORRIS

The Morris name is found in colonial America, in the colonies of Pennsylvania, Connecticut, Maryland, Virginia and North Carolina in the early 1700s.

Several served in the American Revolution from the states of Maryland, Virginia and North Carolina.

James Morris born ca. 1790 in Georgia, was the son of Sherod Morris born ca. 1762 in North Carolina. James married Lucy Parham September 8, 1811 in Elbert County, Georgia. Lucy was born May 5, 1791 in North Carolina. Sometime between 1812 and 1814, James and Lucy moved to Bledsoe County.

James enlisted as a private to serve in the War of 1812 at Thurman, November 13, 1814. He was discharged May 1815 at Knoxville. He served in the Captain Miles Vernon's Company, East Tennessee Militia.

Two children were born to James and Lucy. John Dixon born July 10, 1812 in Georgia, married Mary Tollett. Elizabeth born May 24, 1815 in Bledsoe County, married Simeon Selby. James died June 4, 1837.

John Dixon Morris was on the tax list in 1837, 1838, 1839 in the 3rd Civil District.

In 1840 Simeon and Elizabeth Selby were living in the 3rd Civil District as well as John Dixon and Mary. John Dixon Morris and family, and Simeon and Elizabeth Selby are listed in the 1850 census. Lucy Morris is in the household of Simeon and Elizabeth Selby.

In May 1853 Lucy Morris, widow, applied for "bounty land" on her husband's service in the War of 1812. Lucy (Parham) Morris died May 15, 1856 and was buried in the Tollett Cemetery.

Sources:

In A Pear Tree, by Margorie Parham Hailey, 1987.

Tennesseans in the War of 1812, by Byron and Samuel Sistler, 1992.

National Society Colonial Dames XVII Century Ancestor Roster, 1915-2005.

Members and Patriots.

The Tennessee Society Daughters of the American Revolution, Vol. 4, 1985-2001.

NAIL/NALE

The Nail name is found in the American colonies before the American Revolution in Pennsylvania and Virginia.

Aquilla Nail born ca. 1758 in Amherst County, Virginia, married Priscilla Gilmore born 1760. Sometime after the Revolution 1783, Aquilla Nail obtained land grants for land in Lincoln County, Georgia. Some of the Nail family was in Tennessee in the early 1800s. Several served in the War of 1812 from Tennessee, both as officers and enlisted men. The Nails were in Bledsoe County in the late 1820s. Aquilla Nail and three of his sons, John, William and Thomas came to Bledsoe County. Aquilla was in Bledsoe County in 1830, age 40-50 years.

John Nail born ca. 1784 in Georgia is listed in Bledsoe County in 1830 as head of a household. He is listed in 1840 in District V. He is also listed on the Bledsoe Tax List in District IV in the late 1830s. John and his wife, Fannie, are also in the 1850 census.

Nicholas Pope (N.P.) Nail, son of John grew up in the Sequatchie Valley, but moved to Hamilton County as a young man before the Civil War. He became well-known in the Confederate Army as one of the "Hamilton Grays". He served as second lieutenant, Company A of the 19th Tennessee Regiment. He was wounded at the Battle of Baton Rouge, Louisiana; was discharged July 4, 1863 after the Battle of Vicksburg.

William Nail, son of Aquilla Nail born ca. 1786 in Georgia, was a farmer living in northern Bledsoe County in 1850. He married Delila Hamilton. They became the parents of Abraham Hamilton,

John B., Elvira, Sophia, Benjamin A., Aquilla F., Elizabeth and James B.

William was a Methodist circuit rider serving Bledsoe County and other nearby counties. His 80 mile circuit was from his home at Tolletts Mill. It is reported he ministered to Indians, as well as whites. Family tradition has been that the Nail family intermarried with the Cherokee and Choctaw Indians.

Thomas Nail, son of Aquilla born ca. 1790 in Georgia, was in Bledsoe County in 1830 and 1840 as head of a household. He was living in 1850 in Bledsoe County. He married Mary ?. They became the parents of: Newton born ca. 1816, married Eliza Worthington, they moved to Arkansas; James R. born ca. 1818, married Carrie Elizabeth Wilson, they moved to Arkansas later to Oregan; Mary Ann born ca. 1822, married Abraham Hamilton lived in Bledsoe County; Sarah Gilmore born ca. 1824, married James D. Hamilton, moved to Dickson County; Margaret born ca. 1829; Isabella born ca. 1831, married George Sherrill lived in Bledsoe County; Elizabeth Jane born ca. 1833, married John Jackson Tollett, lived in Cumberland County; Manervy born ca. 1835, married W.W. Colling and second James Nail, a cousin.

Thomas Nail served in the War of 1812. He enlisted November 13, 1814 at Washington in Rhea County. He was listed as First Corporal, East Tennessee Militia, under Captain Miles Vernon, Colonel Edwin Booth and General Thomas Coulter. He was discharged May 13, 1815 at Knoxville. He served six months and one day, his pay $10.00 a month, total pay $60.32. He later received an eighty acre Bounty Land Warrent in Bledsoe County. Neighbors and friends signing his application to obtain this land were Moses Ormes; George H. Finley, Justice of Peace; Jesse Worthington; James

Pankey, county court clerk; Charles K. Sherrill and William Ormes.

Abraham Hamilton Nail, oldest son of William and Delila (Hamilton) Nail born December 18, 1818 in Bledsoe County. He married Matilda J. Roberson, the daughter of Isaac and Elvira Roberson. Matilda was born February 1, 1827 in Bledsoe County. In 1850 they were living in southern Bledsoe County. This family moved to Dallas County, Texas, later to the Indian Territory, Durant in the Choctaw - Chickasaw Nation. Abraham Hamilton Nail and Matilda (Roberson) Nail became the parents of eight children all born in Bledsoe County. Elvira Marilda born 1845, Isaac Roberson born 1847, Alexander Hamilton born 1850, Benjamin Nail born 1855, John Nail, William Nail, James Polk born 1864, and Aaron Lea Nail born 1867.

Abraham Hamilton Nail moved to the Indian Territory to claim his Cherokee and Choctaw Indian descent. After a few years Abraham and sons, John and Aaron, had large acreage of land 550 acres in cultivation, 1500 acres in pasturage and an extensive herd of cattle and horses. Years later, Abraham's Indian claim was disputed. He finally lost his claim and had to give up his land and property. However, this family still claimed their Indian descent. Abraham Hamilton Nail died February 6, 1907 in Indian Territory. Matilda (Roberson) Nail died February 1913, Crawford, Texas. Both were buried in Purcell, Oklahoma.

In 1856 the 1st, 2nd and 3rd Civil Districts of Bledsoe County were detached and used to form Cumberland County. John B. Nail's, son of William, residence fell in the 3rd District. He served as Cumberland County Court Clerk from 1860 to 1864.

Sources:

Tennesseans in the War of 1812, by Sistler, 1992.

Bledsoe County Census, 1830, 1840, 1850.

Nail Family, by John Wilson, News Free Press, staff writer, August 8, 1993.

Bledsoe County Tax List 1836 Tennessee Civil Districts and Tax Lists, by James L. Douthat.

Hamilton Family, by Betty McAndrews.

The Schoolfield Family Tree" and Allied Families, by Cleopatra Doss Schoolfield.

NARRAMORE

John Narramore was one of the well-known Revolutionary War Veterans to make Bledsoe County his last home. John Narramore was born January 22, 1762 in South Carolina. He first enlisted in January 1779 at age 17. His second enlistment later that same year was for his father, Edward Narramore. His third enlistment was in May 1780 after the British had taken Charleston. He rose to the rank of Lieutenant after completing almost two years of service.

John Narramore was in Jefferson County, Tennessee before Tennessee became a state. He later moved to Knox County. He was in Sequatchie Valley as early as 1807. He was a member of the first Bledsoe County Court and served as chairman. The commissioners appointed in addition to Narramore were John Tollett, Michael Rawling, John Anderson, William Roberson, James Standefer and Thomas Coulter. The commissioners were to "fix a seat of justice and lay off the town, build a courthouse, prison and stocks" for the town of Madison.

In 1809 John Narramore applied for 300 acres of land "held by the right of settlement, and occupancy in Sequatchie Valley on the east side of the creek including the place he now lives on." John Narramore Jr. was one of the sworn chain carriers in the survey.

In 1815 John was one of the signers of the petition to delay the land law during the War between Great Britain and the United States.

John Narramore married Mary Walker in July 1780. She was born in 1761. John and Mary became the parents of Sarah, Frederick,

John Jr., Martha and Nancy.

John was married the second time in 1803 to Nancy Adkins. She was born in 1775 in Virginia. They became the parents of Lucia K., Calvin W., Sophia M., Serepta, Fielding M., James, Malissa and Nelson.

John Narramore was a member of the Vale Temple Lodge in 1825. This early lodge had been organized in Pikeville in 1823.

In the early 1830s John Narramore was living on the Cumberland Plateau. In 1833 the Narramore Post Office was established with John Narramore as postmaster. However, by 1836 the name was changed to Crossville.

In 1833 John Narramore made application for pension, while living in Bledsoe County, based on his services in the War for Independence. Character witnesses were the Rev. William Nail, Scott Terry and Eli Thurman.

According to family tradition, when President Andrew Jackson, traveling from the Hermitage to Washington in the 1830s on his accustomed route of travel, would stop at the Crab Orchard Inn and inquire about the Old Revolutionary war veteran, John Narramore. They were both natives of South Carolina and had the War of Independence a common memory.

The 1840 Bledsoe census shows John Narramore living in the First Civil District of Bledsoe County. Three of John's sons, James, Fielding and Nelson, were on the tax list in the same district in the late 1830s.

In October 1850, John, age 88, and Nancy, 75, are listed in household of son James L. and family, with Fielding and his family living nearby.

John Narramore died June 11, 1851 and was buried in the Crossville City Cemetery, being the first adult to be buried there. He was the last Revolutionary War veteran living in Bledsoe County. A few weeks later Nancy died and was buried in the same cemetery.

In 1974 members of the Ford - Narramore Chapter of the Sons of the American Revolution placed a memorial marker at the grave of John Narramore in the Crossville City Cemetery. This are was in the First Civil District in Bledsoe County until 1856.

Fielding Narramore, son of John and Nancy Narramore, was born July 8, 1811 in Bledsoe County. He married Martha Taylor. She was born September 30, 1811. They became the parents of Mary, Mallissa, John, Nancy, Martha, Julia and Emily. John served in the Union Army. Fielding and Martha lived a few miles east of Crossville during the Civil War.

The Second Regiment of the Indiana Volunteer Cavalry were camped about two miles from the Narramore farm in December 1863. This regiment was on the march to Knoxville. Fielding Narramore reported on his claim to the United States Government for products taken by the soldiers, corn, hay, bacon and potatoes. His claim was for $559.00, however, he received only $250.00. His claim was witnessed by John F. Greer, neighbor; Bazel Hedgouth, son-in-law; Julia A. Hedgouth, daughter; and Martha Narramore, wife. He also reported a gun taken from him by Captain Gass's Company of the Confederate Army.

****

Sources:

First Families of Tennessee, East Tennessee Historical Society, 2000.

Member and Patriots The Tennessee Society.

Daughters of the American Revolution, Vol. 4, 1985-2001.

Tennessee Homesteaders and Landowners Fourth Surveyors District, 1808-1810.

Civil District and Tax List, Bledsoe County.

Bledsoe County Census, 1830, 1840, 1850.

NORWOOD

The Norwood name is found in the American colonies of Maryland and Virginia in the 1600s. Some received land grants. By the mid 1700s, American Revolution, the Norwoods were in North Carolina and served in the War for Independence.

By the time of the War of 1812, the Norwoods were in Tennessee, Blount County. Several served in this second war with Great Britain from Tennessee both as officers and enlisted men. John Norwood was in the service with Sam Houston. When Sam was wounded in battle, John accompanied him home to Blount County where both lived. St. Clair (S.C.) Norwood was born February 27, 1822, the son of John and Sarah (Crouch) Norwood.

The Norwoods were in Bledsoe County in 1840 in District VI. In 1841 S.C. Norwood married Catherine J. Hoodenpyle, daughter of Peter Hoodenpyle. Catherine was born October 10, 1821. In 1850 S.C. Norwood's occupation was a tailor. In 1860 he was serving as clerk of the Chancery Court in Pikeville. He was a business man and a farmer. In his many business investments, he witnessed success and failures. He became an extensive stock dealer, and a general merchant. He served as a trustee of People College, Pikeville.

He became a writer, writing on religion and the Bible. He wrote a history of the life of John A. Murrell, "the great western land pirate, after his discharge from the state prison to the date of his death at Pikeville, of his peculiar burial, the disinterring of his body and his decapitation by two medical students."

Colonel S.C. Norwood and Catherine (Hoodenpyle) Norwood

became the parents of Peter J., Sarah M., Laura, John M., Henry B., James W., and Fannie. The Norwoods lived on the farm land that Catherine inherited from Peter Hoodenpyle. Several members of this family were buried in the Pikeville City Cemetery. Sarah Norwood born 1785, died 1841; Nancy Norwood born 1805, died 1873; Sarah Norwood born 1847, died 1855; James W. Norwood born 1857, died 1883; S.C. Norwood born 1822, died 1901; and Catherine J. born 1821, died 1901.

Sources:

National Society Colonial Dames XVII Century Ancestor Roster, 1915-2005.

Memorial and Biographical Compendium of Biography, Geo. A. Ogle Co., 1898.

Census of Bledsoe County, 1840, 1850, 1860.

ORMES

Moses Ormes born ca. 1757, served in the American Revolution, died 1827 in Kentucky. He married Elizabeth Davis in Maryland.

Sometime after the American Revolution, Moses Ormes moves west, the great western movement, to Kentucky. After the War of 1812, the Ormes family from Kentucky moved south into Tennessee, Sequatchie Valley, Bledsoe County.

In the census of 1830 four heads of households were listed. Those being James, Nathan, Moses Jr., and Elly Jr. In 1832 Walter Ormes sold to Isaac Stephens a Negro boy, 18 years old for $450.00. The Ormes listed on Bledsoe County Tax List of 1837, 1838, 1839 were Elly Jr., James, John, Moses Sr., Moses Jr., Shilor and Thomas. They were in District III.

Ormes Stores post office was established in 1839 with James Ormes as postmaster. William M. Ormes also served as postmaster of this rural post office. Later the name was changed to Melvine in 1892 in memory of Melvin Ormes.

Ormes school house, the first in this area, was used as a place of learning as well as a place of worship. The building was described as being log with a stone fireplace at one end. Later a school, Hickory Grove, was in this area.

In 1840 five households of Ormes were listed. These five had a total of twenty-nine persons all listed in District III. There was Moses Jr., Elly, James, Shilor and Elizabeth, widow of Moses Sr.

The 1850 census gives William T. Ormes, age 27, born in Tennessee; James Ormes, 62, born in Maryland; William M. Ormes, 27, born in Kentucky and Elly Ormes, 64, born in Maryland.

Elly Ormes was born ca. 1786 in Maryland. In November 1814 he was in Kentucky. He volunteered at Columbia for the War of 1812 for a period of six months to serve in the state militia. He served as a private in the company commanded by Captain Robert Paxton. He was in the regiment of Colonel Parker at the Battle of New Orleans, January 8, 1815. He was honorably discharged at New Orleans/Nashville, May 1815.

By 1818 Elly was in Bledsoe County. Elly married Mary (Polly) Wilson, daughter of Greenbury Wilson, September 24, 1818 (her date), November 23, 1821 (his date). They were married by John Narramore, a Justice of the Peace. The wedding took place at Mary's mother's home. Drucilla (Selby) Parham and Rebecca (Parham) Selby attended the wedding.

Mary was born in 1796 in North Carolina, the youngest daughter of Greenbury and Temperance (Bradshaw) Wilson. Elly and Mary made their home near the Greenbury Wilson home. Elly was a farmer and slave holder. He received a 160 acre land warrent for his services in the Second War with Great Britain. He applied for this bounty land in 1855. "Uncle Elly and Aunt Polly", as they were known by many, were "unfortunately deprived of the household comfort of children." However, several orphans from family members and neighbors found a home at this Ormes home. Elly died January 29, 1875, Polly died May 1881. Both were buried in the Wilson Cemetery.

James Ormes was born ca. 1788 in the state of Maryland. In

August 1813 James was in Kentucky. He volunteered at Columbia to serve ninety days during the War of 1812. He served as a private in the company of Thomas W. Atkinson's 5th Regiment. This regiment of the 23rd Brigade was commanded by Governor Shelby. In November he was honorably discharged. He again volunteered in October 1814 for a term of six months.

James was described at this time as being a farmer, height about six feet, complexion dark, dark eyes, and dark hair. James married Catherine "Kitty" White, April 23, 1820, in the county of Franklin, Kentucky by a Baptist minister of the Gospel.

After their marriage, James and Kitty lived in Adair County for about ten years before moving to Bledsoe County. James Ormes became a leading citizen in his last home. In 1832 he purchased 100 acres of land on the east side of Sequatchie River for $1,100.00 "with good and lawful money," from Samuel and Moses Lowe. The land bordered "where John Hinch lives," also Selby land and the river. The deed was witnessed by Craven Sherrill and John Tollett. The two witnesses were early settlers and neighbors. A year later James Ormes bought sixty acres for $25.00 on the east side of Sequatchie Valley from the William Witten heirs. James was a farmer and slave owner. He served as Justice of the Peace, and revenue commissioner. He served in the Tennessee House, General Assembly 1847-1849, representing Bledsoe and Morgan counties. He was a member of the Vale Temple Lodge in Pikeville. James Ormes died at his home March 1852. After his death Kitty received a land warrent which her husband had made application prior to his death for services in the War of 1812.

William M. Ormes born 1823 in Kentucky, the son of James and Kitty (White) Ormes, married Harriet Ann Greer September 4,

1845. Harriet Ann was born in 1825 in Virginia, the daughter of Wetherston S. Greer. To this couple was born two children, Emma Elizabeth and Wetherston Shelton "Wed" Ormes.

William served as county clerk in the 1840s. After the death of William ca. 1861, Harriet Ann married James A. Vernon February 17, 1864. They became the parents of Gaither, Mary Tennessee and Edna. James A. Vernon was born April 11, 1862 and died April 7, 1891. Harriet Ann was born September 5, 1825 and died March 5, 1897. Both were buried at the Wesley Chapel Cemetery.

Sometime in the 1870s, Kitty (White) Ormes moved to Pikeville to live with her daughter-in-law Harriet (Greer) Ormes Vernon. In 1878 Kitty applied for a pension on the services of her husband, James Ormes, in the War of 1812. Living in James A. Vernon's household in 1880 was his wife Harriet Ann; their three children, Gaither, Mary and Edna; a step-son Witherson S. Ormes; a school teacher; Harriet Ann's mother Mary Greer; and Kitty Ormes, Harriet Ann's first husband's mother. Kitty (White) Ormes died August 28, 1882 and was buried in Wesley Chapel Cemetery.

William T. (Taylor) Ormes born June 3, 1822 in Tennessee married Martha Ann (Patsy) Parham October 28, 1846. She was born November 19, 1822, the daughter of Johnson and Drucilla (Selby) Parham. They became the parents of Melvin, James, Mary Tennessee, Nicholas, and Thomas Allen. Martha Ann died May 20, 1890 and William Taylor died January 20, 1900.

FIRST FAMILIES OF BLEDSOE COUNTY, TENNESSEE   147

****

Sources:

Daughters of American Revolution Magazine, p. 495, May 1995.

Bledsoe County Census, 1830, 1840, 1850.

Pension Records War of 1812, General Service Administration, Washington, D.C.

Leaves From The Family Tree, by Penelope J. Allen, 1933.

Great Grand Children at the official marking of the
grave of Johnson Parham, War of 1812.

OXSHEER/OXIER/AUXIER

The name is found in Philadelphia, Pennsylvania in the mid 1700s.

Michael Auxier, a Huguenot, born in France ca. 1685, was in the American colonies in the mid 1700s. Michael Auxier II, born ca. 1720 in France, was in Virginia in the late 1700s. He married Martha Jane Horbeck. All five of their sons, Simon, Abraham, George, Michael III and Samuel, served in the American Revolution.

Samuel Oxsheer was in Bledsoe County in 1819 when he purchased 315 acres of land from John McIven for $1,200.00. This land was in Lot No. I "where Samuel Oxsheer was living and made improvements bordering Walden Ridge and Bob Worthington."

Samuel Oxsheer was born May 18, 1777 in Russell County, Virginia. He married Sarah (Sally) Wilson, daughter of Greenbury Wilson. Sarah was born January 30, 1780 in North Carolina. Samuel and Sarah (Wilson) Oxsheer were the parents of twelve children: Mary (Polly) born December 16, 1799, married Jonathan Crawford, moved to Rusk County, Texas, died March 26, 1894; Jemina born November 29, 1801, married Daniel Kerley, died before 1850, Bledsoe County; George born January 27, 1804, married first Jane Walker, second Elizabeth Ann Kerley, moved to Texas after 1850; Elizabeth born March 8, 1806, married William G. Lewis, a Methodist minister, moved to Texas; Nancy born March 11, 1808, married William Bryant, moved to Kansas after 1850, Nancy died 1869; Sarah (Sally) born September 12, 1810, married Joseph Grimes; Samuel Jr. born December 7, 1812, never married, died before 1850, buried Oxsheer Cemetery; tradition Samuel Jr., a "cripple" and a "great singer"; William Wilson born March 29, 1815, moved to Texas 1837, died December 1905, married Martha Elizabeth Kirk; Jane T. born January 23, 1816, married Preston McClanahan; Cary (Kary) born May 21, 1820, married John Lee, moved to Rusk County, Texas; Kitturah (Kitty) Ann born May 29, 1823, married William Lee; Rebecca born February 27, 1816, married John Thurman, lived and died August 19, 1878 in Bledsoe County.

Samuel Oxsheer died 1837, Sarah (Wilson) Oxsheer died May 28, 1859.

The Oxsheer farm land in Bledsoe County was sold in 1859 by William Wilson Oxsheer of Milan County, Republic of Texas, to Peter J. Swafford, except five rods square including graves of Samuel Oxsheer and son Samuel Jr., except the spring house, except the ten acres which is fence for Sarah Oxsheer.

Places in Bledsoe County still carrying the name are Oxier Branch, tributary of the Sequatchie River and Oxier Gap and Oxier Lee Cemetery.

Sources:

The Auxier Family compiled by Dr. Dave Auxier, 1995.

The Wilson Family History by Frances Beal Hodges, Wichita Falls, Texas, 1948.

Bledsoe County Deed Records.

Bledsoe County Court Clerk Office.

PANKEY/PANETIER

The name Pankey is found in the colony of Virginia in the 1600s. Several served in the American Revolution (1775-1781).

Stephen Pankey Sr., born ca. 1743 in Virginia, married Mary Ann Smith. He was in Jefferson County, Tennessee by 1796.

The Pankeys were in Sequatchie Valley by 1807. Several Pankeys served in the War of 1812 from Tennessee.

James Smith Pankey was born ca. 1775 in Virginia. He married Mary Montgomery who was born ca. 1780. He enlisted as a private to serve in the War of 1812. His first enlistment was December 10, 1812. His second enlistment was September 24, 1813, and his third enlistment was September 20, 1814. He served under Colonel John Brown, East Tennessee Volunteer Militia.

James Smith and Mary (Montgomery) Pankey became the parents of Bird, James and Martha.

Stephen Pankey Jr., born 1778, married Elizabeth Harris in 1807 in Bledsoe County. They became the parents of Edward born 1808, William M. born 1810 and Wiley/Wyley born 1812.

Stephen enlisted January 1814 to serve in the Creek Indian War (War of 1812). He served under Captain Jesse Reamy, Colonel John Brown's Mounted Militia. Stephen was killed May 16, 1814.

James Smith Pankey and Stephen Pankey Jr. were brothers, sons of Stephen Pankey Sr. and Mary Ann Smith Pankey. Stephen

Pankey Sr. died between 1825-1830 in Marion County, Tennessee.

Bird Pankey, born July 1818 in Tennessee, married Mary Magdalene Story, daughter of Dr. Samuel and Euphanse P. (Wheeler) Story, March 20, 1845. Mary Magdalene was born August 12, 1828.

In 1840 Bird had contracts for two mail routes. The route from Pikeville to Sparta over the Cumberland Mountains and the route from Pikeville across Walden Ridge and the Tennessee River to Athens. These contracts were transferred from Alexander H. Montgomery in 1840 to Bird Pankey with "two gray horses, one bay horse and one spotted appaloosa, also included were two mail hacks and horses, the ages of the horses were young, five to ten years." Bird was a land owner and slave holder. In 1850 he was a merchant in Pikeville.

Children of Bird and Mary M. (Story) Pankey: Samuel S., born March 22, 1848, died October 5, 1887; James S. born April 14, 1850; Antoinette (Nettie) born January 1, 1853, married James Henry, she died April 8, 1882; Hugh Montgomery born March 8, 1856, died April 5, 1856. Bird Pankey died at Pikeville, February 26, 1856. Mary M. died March 3, 1904.

James S. Pankey Jr., born August 16, 1822, married Emily Story September 16, 1850, the daughter of Dr. Samuel Story and Euphanse P. (Wheeler) Story. Emily was born August 20, 1830.

James S. was a Mason, a merchant, partner with his brother Bird. He served for several years as clerk of the County Court. He served in the Mexican War. He enlisted at Memphis July 8, 1846 and was discharge at New Orleans May 31, 1847. James S. died March 29, 1860. Emily (Story) Pankey died January 23, 1870.

****

Sources:

Pankey Family Bible, 1850.

Bledsoe County, Tennesse, a History, by Elizabeth P. Robnett, 1993.

Tennesseans in the War of 1812, by Sistler, 1992.

Compendium of Local Biography, Cumberland Region of Tennessee, 1898.

John Pankey of Manakin Town, Virginia and His Descendants, by George Edward Pankey, Vol. II, 1972.

The DAR Patriot Index Centennial Edition.

First Families of Tennessee, East Tennessee Historical Society, 2000.

PARHAMS

The Parhams were in the colony of Virginia in the 1600s. By the mid 1700s Parhams were in the colony of North Carolina.

John Parham, born September 26, 1731 in Virginia, married Mary Dickerson, born ca. 1736, in Granville County, North Carolina. John became a large land owner and slave holder in Granville County. By the late 1790s John Parham's family had moved to Elbert County, Georgia. John Parham made his will in 1804 and died in 1805 in Elbert County.

John and Mary (Dickerson) Parham's children were Elizabeth, Kennon, John Jr., Isham, Nancy, Mary, Thomas, Mildred, Dickson, Frances, Hollyberry and Lucy.

Kennon Parham, oldest son of John Parham Sr., born September 7, 1762 in Granville County, married Milley Parham July 28, 1787. Kennon served in the American Revolution.

Three of John Parham Sr.'s children, John Jr. (Jack), Dickson and Lucy were in Bledsoe County by 1814. Lucy born May 10, 1791 in Granville County, married James Morris. James served in the War of 1812. Their children were John Dixson and Elizabeth.

John Parham Jr. (Jack), born ca. 1765 in North Carolina, married September 4, 1792 Mary (Molly) Shemwell, who was born ca. 1765. John and Mary became the parents of Rebecca, Johnson, Shemwell, Allen and Elva. Rebecca, born February 19, 1793, married Loyd Selby. Johnson, born September 21, 1794, married Drucilla Selby. Shemwell, born ca. 1796, married Christiana

Gibbons. Allen, born September 14, 1798, married Lucy Bunch, second Susannah Catkins, third Elizabeth Turner. Anna, born July 10, 1801, married John Hinch. Elva was born 1803, died 1847.

The Bledsoe 1830 census shows John Jr. and two sons, Allen and Johnson, as heads of households. The 1840 census only John Jr. and Johnson Parham are heads of households, both living in District III of Bledsoe County.

Johnson Parham, oldest son of John Parham Jr., was born September 21, 1794 in Granville County. He enlisted as a private September 20, 1814 at Thurman in Bledsoe County in Captain James Tunnell's Company, East Tennessee Militia to serve in the War of 1812. He served seven months and twenty days at $8.00 per month. He was discharged at Knoxville May 3, 1815. He was allowed six days travel from Knoxville to his home in northern Sequatchie Valley - 100 miles, his total pay $61.33. Johnson married Drucilla Selby April 15, 1816. Drucilla was born April 10, 1795 in Kentucky.

Children of Johnson and Drucilla: Elizabeth, married William J. Rector; John, married Elizabeth Brown; Martha Ann, married William Taylor Ormes; William, married Sarah Brown; Isaac, married Stacy Emma Taylor; James, married Martha E. Stephens; Allen, married Mary E. Jones; Mary, married William Andrew Dial. Johnson was a prosperous farmer, sending livestock to Atlanta. Johnson died May 5, 1846.

In May 1853, Drucilla age 57, a widow of Johnson Parham, filed an application for Bounty Land on the service of her husband, which she may be entitled to under the Act of September 1850. The application was witnessed by Elly Ormes and Jesse Brown.

In 1876, Drucilla filed for a pension as a widow of Johnson Parham. She gives the place of marriage as "Mrs. Wilson's place." She was married to Johnson Parham by John Narramore, a justice of the peace. Her post office was Ormes Store. She further states her husband was at the Battle of New Orleans and Seige of Mobile. Drucilla (Selby) Parham died June 7, 1884. She and Johnson were buried in the Parham Cemetery.

Shemwell Parham, born 1796, served as a Captain in the Cherokee War (Indian Removal). He enlisted at Athens in 1836 for six months in the 1st Regiment of Smith, 2nd Brigade Tennessee Mt. Inf. He was mustered out at Pikeville April 16, 1837. Shemwell married Christiana Gibbons.

Sources:

In a Pear Tree, by Marjorie Parham Hailey, 1987.

Bledsoe County Census, 1830, 1840.

Tennessee Homesteaders and Land Owners, Fourth Surveyors District, Survey Book 1808-1810, Entry Book 1814-1815, compiled by Willis Reed Hutcheson, 1964.

Military Records.

Pension Records.

*Parham Chapel
Methodist Church
built 1905-1907*

POLLARD

The name Pollard is found in the mid 1600s in the colonies of Maryland and Virginia. Several served in the American Revolution.

Chattin D. Pollard was born ca. 1763 in Culpepper County. He enlisted in the Fall of 1780 under Captain William Jenkins of Frederick County. He was stationed to guard prisoners at Winchester. He was at the surrender of Yorktown in 1781.

In 1782 he was a wagoner to convey baggage of the French Army to New York and Boston. He served seven months as a private in the service of the American colonies. He married Mary Greer, daughter of Moses and Nancy (Bailey) Greer September 16, 1790.

Several Pollards served in the War of 1812 from Tennessee.

Hansford Pollard was in Bledsoe County in 1830.

Chattin D. Pollard applied for a pension in 1833 while living in Franklin County, Virginia. In 1839 he applied for his pension to be sent to Bledsoe County, Tennessee as "most of his children lived in Bledsoe."

In the 1840 Bledsoe census Chattin and Mary Pollard lived in District II, same district as the Greers. Children of Chattin and Mary: Joseph H., Claborn, Hensord and Chattin Jr. Chattin died October 23, 1843.

Sources:

Leaves From The Family Tree, by Penelope Johnson Allen, 1933.

National Society Colonial Dames XVII Century, Ancestor Roster, 1915-2005.

Revolution War Veterans Pension Records.

The Tennessee Society Daughters of the American Revolution, Vol. 4, 1985-2001.

POPE

The name is found in the American colonies of Virginia and Maryland in the early 1700s. They were listed as planters and land owners. Several took part in the American Revolution from New York and North Carolina.

Popes were in Tennessee, Washington County, before Tennessee became a state. Several served in the War of 1812 from Tennessee. Jonathan Pope, born August 1786 in North Carolina, married Delilah Coulter, born May 1, 1786 in North Carolina. Delilah Coulter was a sister of Alexander Coulter. The Popes and Coulters were in Sequatchie Valley in the early 1800s. Jonathan became a large landowner and a successful farmer. Jonathan served in the War of 1812 as a private in Captain Jesse G. Rainey's Company, East Tennessee Mounted Gunmen of the Regiment commanded by Colonel John Brown. He enlisted January 20, 1814 at Kingston. He was discharged May 20, 1814. His time of service four months and one day $8.00 per month, total $32.25. He also was paid forty cents per day for his horse, total for the horse $48.40, total $80.65.

In the 1830 Sequatchie Valley census, Bledsoe and Marion, Jonathan Pope is listed age 40-50, Delilah age 40-50, with five males and four females, their nine chidren. The Bledsoe Tax Record of 1837-38-39 list Jonathan and Thomas Pope in District X. In 1840 census, the Popes are in District X and VII.

In 1850 Jonathan Pope was age 63, and Delilah 64. In their household were two young grandsons age 7 and 5, Leroy M. and Jonathan P. Vaught, who was born in Texas. After 1857 most of

Jonathan Pope's land was in Sequatchie County. The X Civil District was taken to help form Sequatchie County. Jonathan Pope died March 17, 1860, Delilah (Coulter) Pope died two days later March 19, 1860. Both were buried in the Pope Cemetery.

Children of Jonathan and Delilah (Coulter) Pope: Thomas Alexander born August 14, 1810, married Ala Townsend, their children were Elizabeth, Ellen, William R. and John T. Pope. Thomas Alexander married second Sarah McReynolds. They were the parents of Lilah who married December 19, 1876, Lewis Shepherd. In 1870 this family was living in District I, Sequatchie County. Minerva Pope, born 1812, oldest daughter of Jonathan and Delilah, married William Rankin. They lived in Sequatchie County District IV in 1870. William was a well-known farmer and merchant; James Jerome, second son of Jonathan and Delilah, born January 3, 1819, married Mary Murphy Worthington, daughter of Samuel Worthington Jr.; Lilah married Ben Hawkins; Polly married Dr. Charles Rains, moved to Marion County; Peggy married Dr. James Vaught; Levander, son of Jonathan and Delilah born ca. 1823, married Musedora Black. Levander became a lawyer and lived in Warren County, McMinnville. He served in the House 29th Tennessee General Assembly 1851-53, represented Warren County. Levander and Musedora became the parents of Byon Pope. Levander died 1853; Leroy, son of Jonathan and Delilah Pope went to Texas as a young man. He lived at San Antonio and served in war for Texas Independence in 1836; Mitchell Napoleon born 1828, youngest son of Jonathan and Delilah, married Hallie Acock. This family moved to Texas, later moved back east to Dade County, Georgia. In 1850 he was listed as a student in the home of his parents. He served in the Tennessee House, the 30th and 31st General Assemblies from 1853-1857, represented Bledsoe, Rhea and Hamilton counties.

Sources:

Leaves From The Family Tree, by Penelope J. Allen, 1933.

Biographical Directory of the Tennessee General Assembly, Vol. I, 1796-1861.

Sequatchie Families, by James L. Douthat.

Tennesseans in the War of 1812, by Sistler, 1992.

Military Record, National Archives, Trust Fund.

Membership Roster and Soldiers Tennessee Society of the Daughters of the American Revolution, Vols. III and IV.

Pope Cemetery

RANKIN

The name Rankin is found in the 1700s in the colony of Pennsylvania. Several served in the American Revolution, names as David, Richard, Samuel and Thomas Rankin.

Rankins were in Tennessee before Tennessee became a state, Greene County, names as David Sr., James Sr., Richard, Thomas, Thomas Jr., and William Rankin. A James Rankin was in Sequatchie Valley, Bledsoe County, in 1808. Several Rankins served in the War of 1812, serving as officers and enlisted men from Tennessee. Four Rankins, probably brothers, from Greene County, David, Samuel, William and James, found their way in Sequatchie Valley, Bledsoe and Marion counties in the 1820s.

In 1830 census David Rankin was in Marion County and Samuel was listed in Bledsoe County. The 1840 census listed David and William in Marion County and Samuel in Bledsoe County in District V.

David Rankin, born February 17, 1799 in Greene County, was in Bledsoe County in 1826 when he married Zilpah Roberson, daughter of James Roberson. Zilpah was born September 1809. This family moved to Marion County where he became a leading citizen and took a prominent part in public affairs for many years. He was a merchant and large land owner. He served in the Tennessee House, 26th and 27th General Assemblies 1845, 47, 47-49, representing Marion and Hamilton counties.

David and Zilpah became the parents of: Laura Caroline, Peter Turney, Mary Anne, James William, Margaret, Lafayette, Eliza,

David Byron, John L., and Samuel. David Rankin died September 16, 1862. Zilpah (Roberson) Rankin died October 26, 1882.

Samuel Rankin born January 8, 1801 in Greene County, married Dicey Brown, daughter of Reuban Brown and Sarah (Worthington) Brown. Dicey born May 1, 1806 was a first cousin of Zilpah Roberson, wife of David Rankin. Samuel became a well-known citizen, a large land owner, slave holder and a successful farmer. He served as a county commissioner, justice of the peace for many years. He served in the House 23rd General Assembly 1839-1841, represented Bledsoe County, he was postmaster of the short-lived Rankin Creek post office 1844-1845.

Samuel and Dicey (Brown) Rankin became the parents of: James born ca. 1825, married Elizabeth Billingsley, this family moved to Warren County; Reuban born May 30, 1826, married Theola Billingsley, lived in Bledsoe County. Reuban died February 15, 1877; William born ca. 1829; John born April 20, 1832, married Amanda Billingsley. John died February 27, 1862. Theola and Amanda were half sisters to Elizabeth Billingsley, daughters of John Billingsley; Martha E. born ca. 1833; Sarah J. born ca. 1835; Manervy M. born ca. 1837; Elizabeth born ca. 1839, married James W. Walker; Mary A. born ca. 1842; Samuel C. born ca. 1844, married Mahala Lowery; Dicy A. born ca. 1846, married Jesse F. Day; David born 1851, married Ellen Brazwell.

James and Reuban Rankin were members of the famous Confederate Company that was organized in Bledsoe County in 1861 by John M. Bridgman, Captain and James Walker, 1st Lieutenant.

Dicey (Brown) Rankin died December 16, 1875. Samuel died December 19, 1875. They were buried on the Rankin plantation, the old Rankin Cemetery.

William Rankin born July 11, 1804 in Greene County, married Eleanor Minerva Pope, daughter of Jonathan Pope. She was born September 15, 1812. William became a large land owner and slave holder. He was a prominent merchant. In 1850 he and Eleanor Minerva were living in Marion County in District II. In 1860 William's residence was District IV, Dunlap. After 1857 his home was in the new county Sequatchie. He sold forty acres of land for the town of Dunlap, the county seat and helped to lay off the town. There he built a large colonial house. He served as the first sheriff of the new county. As he was too old for service in the Civil War, "he refugeed farther south to escape the conflict". However, tradition is his home was ravaged by soldiers. He gave the land for the Rankin Cemetery. He died January 10, 1886 and was the first person buried there. Eleanor Minerva Rankin died August 30, 1897.

James Rankin born July 18, 1809 in Greene County, in 1850 James was living in Marion County. Farming was his occupation. He married Jane Alley. James and Jane (Alley) Rankin became the parents of William, John, David, Alexander, Carrie, Nannie, Mattie, Elizabeth and James.

The Nashville, Chattanooga, St. Louis Railarod (The N.C. & St.L.) was extended from Dunlap to Pikeville in 1891.

In 1900 two Rankin families lived in Pikeville. Levin A. age 50 and his wife Mary E. and sons James W. and David; James Rankin age 34 and wife Maggie and children Ray, Milton, Jennie, Virgie and Evaline.

The following Rankins were employed by the railroad in

1900; L.A. (Levin Alexander), conductor; James W., brakeman; and David, flagman. A wreck in 1902 was reported as the "worse wreck on this railroad, a total of five men lost their lives, two, Alex Rankin and George Rollins were from Pikeville." "The Pikeville train ran ahead on into the Dixie Flyer near Hooker, Georgia." The Pikeville City Cemetery list, L.A. Rankin, January 30, 1850 - June 12, 1902; George W. Rollins, October 15, 1855 - June 12, 1902.

Sources:

Tennesseans in the War of 1812, by Sistler, 1992.

Bledsoe County, Tennessee, A History, by Elizabeth Robnett, 1993.

Tennessee Records of Sequatchie County, Tennessee Tombstone Inscriptions, 1937, copied under Works Progress Administration.

First Families of Tennessee, by East Tennessee Historical Society, 2000.

Membership Roster and Soldiers The Tennessee Society of the Daughters of the American Revolution, Vol. III.

ROGERS/RODGERS

The Roger name is common in the early American colonies in the 1600s. In the New England colonies as well as the middle and southern colonies. They were land owners, ministers, physicians, planters, several served as civil servants in local governments.

Several took part in the American Revolution from North Carolina, Maryland, Virginia and Connecticut.

Members of the Roger family were in Tennessee before Tennessee became a state, in Knox, Greene, Sullivan, Jefferson and Washington counties.

James Rogers was in Roane County in 1801. Several members of the Rogers family were in Sequatchie Valley by the time Bledsoe became a county.

Elisha Rogers signed the petition for George Skillern to erect a grist mill in "Sequacha" valley in 1807. Elisha, John and Joseph Rogers were in the militia Bledsoe County 31st Regiment in 1808. They were in the same 31st Regiment in 1812.

John Rogers signed the petition in 1809 as a citizen of the county Bledsoe, asking for some provisions be made to restore property to the settlers who had settled below the Indian Boundary line "before the line was run." Joseph and Jesse Rogers signed the petition to delay the land laws during the War of 1812.

Adenston Rogers was granted 231 acres in Bledsoe on both sides of "Sequachey Creek" joining lines with Samuel Robinette and

W. Rogers and Solomon Ozburn in May 1808, "held by right of improvements and occupancy," by the state.

Joseph Rogers was granted 300 acres in May 1808 "held by right of improvement and occupancy in Sequachy Valley." John and James Skillern were sworn chain carriers.

William Rogers was granted 278 acres of land in Sequachy Valley, "claimed and held by right of improvement and occupancy on Sequachey Creek" joining lines with Adenston Rogers.

William Rogers came to Sequatchie Valley from Hawkins County in 1806. He settled near the present town of Pikeville. His neighbors were the Andersons, Standifers, Griffiths, Thurmans and Skillerns. He is given credit for building the first school house in the valley. Anderson Skillern became the first teacher. It is said he was paid and boarded by William Rogers.

William Rogers served as a chaplain in the War of 1812 under Major-General John Cocke, East Tennessee Militia.

Several Rogers served in the War of 1812 from Tennessee as officers and enlisted men. Elisha Rogers served in this war. William S. Rogers served in the Indian War, Cherokee and Seminoles 1836-1838.

By 1830 a majority of the large Rogers family was living in Marion County, which had been created out of Indian land in Sequatchie Valley in 1817. George, Anderson, Jesse, Jeremiah, James, John, Dauswell, Emanuel, William, Joseph and William Rogers Sr. were heads of households in the new county, Marion.

Only Reuban, Frederick J., John and Johnathan were heads of households in Bledsoe.

In 1840 the census shows Thomas and Jonathan Rogers living in District VI. Delila, widow of John; and Jane, widow of Frederick; and Thomas Rogers Jr. in District VIII. William S. Rogers was in District X.

William Hurd Rogers born March 22, 1813 in White County moved with his parents to Bledsoe and later to Marion County. At the age of 20, he was licensed to preach in the Methodist Episcopal Church. He married Mary Ann Douthit who was born December 19, 1820. William Hurd became one of the greatest Methodist leaders in the southeast part of the state. He was a circuit rider, a member of the American Bible Society, a writer and historian. He served as chaplain in the Mexican War, East Tennessee Regiment. He landed in Vera Cruz, Mexico January 1848. He was in Mexico to June 1848. He left a most interesting account in detail of his time in Mexico.

John Rogers born December 19, 1782 in Virginia, married Delila Jones. She was born December 26, 1786 in Lee County, Virginia. She died after 1850. John died 1833 in Bledsoe County. They became the parents of: William born ca. 1805, married Mrs. Keziah Sawyer Hixson; Frederick J. born August 1807, married Jane Pitts; Margaret Jane born February 1810, married Buckner Howard; Rebecca born October 1812, married John O. Johnson; Mary; Thomas J., married Polly Walker; Elizabeth; James M. born May 1823, married Sarah Walker (sister of Polly); John Haywood born March 1826, married Martha Maxwell Kirklin; George W. born ca. 1829, married Amanda Carnes; Daniel Jackson born September 1831, married November 4, 1852 Keziah Kirklin born September 20, 1831 (sister of Martha).

In 1850 the following Rogers were heads of households in Bledsoe County or listed elsewhere, William S. Rogers age 54, a blacksmith, born in South Carolina; George W. Rogers 21, a student in household of Buckner Howard; Jane Rogers 50, born in South Carolina, widow of Frederick J. Rogers; James M. Rogers 27, born in Tennessee; William Rogers 45, born in Virginia; William C. Rogers 20, a clerk in Stephen Hick's store; Daniel J. Rogers 18, clerk in Bird Pankey's store; Thomas 7, home of Peter Hoodenpyle; Ann Rogers 45; Thomas Rogers 28, overseer born Missouri; Abner Rogers 25, laborer born North Carolina; Delila Rogers 63, born Virginia, living in household of John O. Johnson and Jefferson Rogers 29, laborer born in Tennessee.

In 1857 the 10th Civil District of Bledsoe County was taken and added to Hamilton County and about the same time this area was added to parts of Marion County to form a new county, Sequatchie. By 1860 the following Rogers lived in the county. James Rogers 46, a blacksmith; William C. Rogers 21, clerk of the county court and James P. Rogers 31, a farmer. Also in the household of Mathew Smith were John Rogers 12, Martha 10, William 8 and James T. 7, the children of James M. Rogers.

J.P. Rogers, W.C. Rogers, William Rogers and Rogers and Hill were original stockholders of Sequachee College in 1860. Mr. George Rogers was the first president of the college. He opened the first school in the spring of 1866. During the summer on a trip to Nashville, in the interest of the school, he died suddenly from the effect of a sun-stroke.

Miss Ida Rogers, daughter of George and Amanda (Carnes) Rogers, was a teacher of music at the college in 1878 and 1879. She also served as assistant to the president. In 1879 students listed, young gentleman: William D. Rogers, W.F. Rogers, Bryon Rogers, J.A. Rogers and John A. Rogers. Young ladies enrolled were Lula, Lola and Hester A. Rogers.

Sources:

First Families of Tennessee, East Tennessee Historical Society, 2000.

National Society Colonial Dames XVII Century Ancestor Roster, 1915-2005.

Membership Roster and Soldiers The Tennessee Society of the Daughters of the American Revolution, Vol. III, IV.

Tennessee Homesteaders and Land Owners, Fourth Surveyors District 1808, 1810, 1814, 1815.

Some Descendants of John and Delilah Jones Rogers, by Ralph Bowman, Knoxville, Tennessee.

Tennesseans in the War of 1812, by Sistler, 1992.

Bledsoe Census, 1830, 1840, 1850.

Sequatchie College History, W.E. Stephens, President, 1860-1881.

William Hurd Rogers His Life & Times, by Nancy J. Wilhite, (great grand daughter), 1992.

Oak Grove Cemetery

ROBERSON/ROBERTSON

The Robersons/Robertsons were in the American colonies in the 1600s and 1700s in Virginia and New Jersey. They were landowners and ministers of the Gospel. Several served in the American Revolution. Robersons were in Tennessee, Greene County before Tennessee became a state. Several served in the War of 1812 from Tennessee.

James Roberson born 1737 in Scotland, married Mary Fuqua of Bedford County, Virginia in the mid 1750s. He served in the American Revolution, Second Virginia Regiment, commanded by Colonel Alexander Spotwood. James Roberson died before 1830 in Bledsoe County.

James and Mary (Fuqua) Roberson became the parents of Roysdon born 1757, married Mary Ann Stovall; James born ca. 1758, married Sarah Vernon; William born 1759, married Rhoda Sartain; John; Elizabeth born 1768, married Leighton Smith; and Littleberry.

William Roberson born November 7, 1759 in Bedford County, Virginia, was the son of James and Mary (Fuqua) Roberson. William served in the American Revolution from Washington County, Virginia under Colonel Isaac Shelby, in South Carolina, and was with William Campbell at the Battle of King's Mountain. He married Rhoda Sartin, who was born in 1766 in Virginia. By 1798 William Roberson was in Knox County. In 1801 William was in Anderson County and was appointed a commissioner to locate a county seat. He was on the tax list in 1805.

By 1807 William was in Sequatchie Valley and was appointed

as a county commissioner for the new county of Bledsoe. William signed the 1809 petition, "asking that some provisions be made to the citizens of Bledsoe County who settled below the Indian boundary line (before it was run) and left their improvements and property."

William and Rhoda (Sartin) Roberson became the parents of: James born 1784, married Margaret Worthington, second married Sarah Hutcheson; Jacob born 1787; Elizabeth born 1790, married Samuel Smith; John born 1792; William born ca. 1794; Jermina; Jesse; Isham; Rhoda born 1810, married William Foster; Orpha born 1812, married Hiram Coulter.

William Roberson became a large landowner. In May 1813 William was listed as an Ensign, Volunteer Company (men not subject to military duty) in the 31st Regiment of Bledsoe County Militia. William signed the Petition to delay the land laws during the War of 1812. William died January 20, 1816 in Bledsoe County, buried in Roberson Cemetery. Rhoda (Sartin) Roberson married second Andrew McDonough who was one of the early settlers in the valley. Andrew McDonough was also in the American Revolution from North Carolina. A daughter Mary (McDonough) Johnson was the mother of Andrew Johnson, who later became governor of Tennessee and president of the United States.

Rhoda (Sartin) Roberson McDonough died 1837, and Andrew McDonough died in 1846. Both were buried in the Roberson Cemetery.

James Roberson born November 11, 1784 in East Tennessee was the oldest son of William Roberson. He was in Bledsoe County in 1807, as he was the first County Register of Deeds. In 1809 he signed a petition in Bledsoe "asking for some provisions be made for those settlers who settled below the Indian Boundary line and left their improvements and property."

In 1812 James Roberson was 2nd Major in the 31st Regiment, Bledsoe County Militia. In 1815 he signed the petition to delay the land laws during the War of 1812. From this time he was known as "Major James Roberson". However, he served as a private in the War of 1812 in Captain George Wintin's Company, Colonel Edwin E. Booth's Regiment, East Tennessee Militia. He served from November 17, 1814 to May 12, 1815. His term of service was five months and twenty-six days, his pay was $8.00 per month. He was discharged at Washington, Rhea County.

James Roberson served in the Tennessee House in the 18th and 19th General Assemblies of 1829-1831, 1831-1833 represented Bledsoe and Marion counties. He was a farmer and trader. He was a large land owner and slave holder. In 1839 James paid taxes on nineteen slaves, only slaves able to work were taxed. He was the largest slave owner in the county. In the 1820s he built a large brick residence, "Belle View".

James married Margaret Worthington, daughter of Samuel and Elizabeth (Carney) Worthington in Anderson County. They became the parents of: Sarah born September 11, 1805, married Isaac Rainey, died August 11, 1881; Rhoda born January 10, 1807, married William Standifer Griffith; Elizabeth born March 27, 1808, married William Hixson; Zilpah born September 19, 1809, married David Rankin, died October 26, 1882; Samuel Worthington born December 5, 1811, married Eliza Bridgman; William Harrison born March 18, 1814, died April 26, 1836; James Monroe born March 28, 1816, married Elizabeth Kendall, died February 5, 1896; Rufus Brown born February 1, 1818, married Elizabeth Sophia Buckingham, died March

7, 1886 in Bledsoe County; Jesse Carroll born Feburary 10, 1820, married Mary Margaret Shepherd, died in Hamilton County May 31, 1891; Margaret Augusta born May 25, 1822, married Daniel F. Cocke, died November 22, 1886 in Franklin, Tennessee; John LaFayette born November 17, 1824, died April 18, 1847 in Mexico, buried in Mexico.

Margaret (Worthington) Roberson died January 8, 1827. James Roberson married second Sarah Hutcheson, daughter of Charles and Rebecca (Skillman) Hutcheson in 1828. They became the parents of: Hester Ann born October 22, 1829, married Samuel Swafford; Martha Jane born February 9, 1832, married Isaac Easterly Swafford, brother of Samuel Swafford; Eliza born September 8, 1836, married Samuel Swafford, her brother-in-law, after the death of Hester Ann; Mary Rebecca born October 12, 1839, married Joseph Haskew; Hezekiah Charles born October 12, 1841, married Ester Ann Hall. Hezekiah Charles served in the Confederate Army. He served as a private in Company I, Thirteenth Regiment, Tennessee Cavalry. He enlisted September 15, 1862 in Bledsoe County and was in the battles of Franklin and Stones River. Pete Roberson, one of the Roberson slaves, was his "body servant" and accompanied him all through the war.

James died July 31, 1852, is buried in Roberson Cemetery. Sarah (Hutcheson) Roberson died August 24, 1876, buried in the Roberson Cemetery.

In the spring of 1846 the United States Congress declared war on Mexico - The Mexican War. The cause, the disputed boundary line of Texas. William R. Caswell, a Knoxville lawyer, became the leader of the Knoxville Dragoons. This Knoxville Company led by Captain Caswell was a part of a regiment of ten cavalry units raised in June 1846 in response to the governor's call for volunteers. The dragoons were horsemen equipped to travel and fight as either cavalry or foot soldiers. The Roberson brothers of Bledsoe County, Rufus Brown and John L., were East Tennessee University alumni; they joined the Knoxville Dragoons. This march from Knoxville to Tampico, Mexico was one of the longest marches, 1,500 miles, of the conflict, five months, horses and wagons, the first stop Memphis. The most devastating enemy the Tennesseans faced was not the Mexican Army but the climate and disease.

The Knoxville Dragoons marched to Mexico June 11, 1846, Dragoons rode out of Knoxville.

June 17, Dragoons in Sequatchie Valley, Roberson brothers Rufus B. and John L. join the Dragoons. As the Dragoons crossed Tennessee they were entertained and fed.

July 14, Dragoons reached Memphis.

September, Dragoons marching from Little Rock through eastern Texas.

October, Dragoons in San Antonio, Texas, John L. Roberson who was assigned to pick up the regiment's mail, "stood for a moment in awe" at the Alamo, where Tennesseans had died ten years earlier.

November, Dragoons at Matamoros, Mexico.

January 1847, Dragoons in Victoria, Mexico.

April 16, Dragoons were attacked by Mexican guerrillas while escorting contractors wagons at a ranch near Cerro Gordo. Private

John L. Roberson was fatally wounded. "R.B. Roberson stepped firmly in his brother's place and returned fire". John L. Roberson died two days later, April 18, 1847, and was buried near the cathedral of Plan del Rio. John L. Roberson's horse was valued at $70.00 and his equipment $23.00. Rufus Brown Roberson's horse was valued at $85.00 and his equipment at $14.00, the horse broke down and sold for $10.00 in Texas. This soldier was mustered out May 31, 1847 at New Orleans, Louisiana.

From a personal account left by Private Rufus Brown Roberson:

"June 16, 1846. This morning after having stayed with my aged father and having gotten the concent of him to volunteer into the ___ service of my dear country, I according had ___ my saddle horse saddled and mounted and rode forth to meet the Knoxville Draggons which had in its ranks many that were connected to me by the nearest ties of friendship I met ___ smiles of my youthful friend."

"June 17, This morning I set out on my march attended with my fellow volunteers ___ this 1st day's march I saw nothing that was new ___ I saw many beautiful scenes. Some of the Draggons killed one or two snakes ___ when this night I lay in camp ___ with nothing by the wide ___ canoby of heaven for a cover and old mother earth _ __ not strovd with down feathers for our resting place for ones ___ Draggon ___ unable to get over the mountains our days marching __ _ but for myself I can say that I never slept sounder or ___ in my life that I remember ___ gazing upon those beautiful gems that stud the heavens ___ how romantic my entrance into camp and this company ___. After our arrival at camp Carrole on 2nd of July we pitched our encampment alone side of Capt. ___."

"After staying at camp and ____ for 25 long days our whole regiment ___ saw the sick took up the line of march on July 27 __ 46 __ and I know for the imagination mind must have been a spectacles full of exciting interest 10 companies mostly of broyant young men start out from the bosom of friends and family to an unknown ___. Our first days march of 12 miles brough us to a kind of lake to the camp, upon a spring about 1/2 mile ___ Mexico's future destine but that lies unknow there the invisible future. This morning ____ in company with a woodsmen, I started in quest of game soon after light ____ riding into lakes ____ savannas ____ cane breaks ____ I rode in camp in the evening with out any game."

"April 1847, John L. died from wounds ___ interred early in the morning of the 19th having died the evening before."

He later described in details the location of his grave and how it is marked with "rocks ___ his initials on a small cross. He was buried 30 yds from the church ___." Later he writes of his feelings and grief of his dear brother, John L.

He tells how he wanted to bring his remains back to his native land where he could be buried in his own loved valley. He had intended to use a wagon for a hearse and obtain a suitable coffin. However, the sudden manner in which they were ordered to move prevented his plans being carried out.

Sources:

Tennessee Alumnus, by Neal O'Steen, Fall of 1987.

Military Records General Services Administration National Archives & Records Service, Washington 25 D.C.

Leaves From The Family Tree, by Penelope Johnson Allen, 1935.

Members and Patriots The Tennessee Society Daughters of the American Revolution, Vol. 4, 1985-2001.

First Families of Tennessee East Tennessee Historical Society, 2000.

National Society Colonial Dames XVII Century Ancestor Roster, 1915-2005.

Rufus Brown Roberson's Personal account in possession of the *John L. Roberson Family, 1960.*

James Roberson, son of James Roberson Sr. and Mary (Fuqua) Roberson, moved from Virginia to Tennessee in the early 1800s and later to Bledsoe County. His children were: Isaac born March 10, 1804 in Kentucky, married Elvira Cole; John born January 30, 1806 in Tennessee, married Catherine Lowery; Martha born July 17, 1808; Rebecca born May 29, 1811; Andrew J. born January 7, 1814; William C. born January 1816; Carry born August 18, 1818; Ally born October 16, 1821.

Isaac and John Roberson were living in 1850 in Bledsoe County. Isaac Roberson, oldest son of James Roberson, born March 10, 1804, married Elvira Cole. She was born October 31, 1804 in North Carolina.

Isaac was in Bledsoe County census 1830 as head of a household; in the 1840 census head of household in District VIII, on the Bledsoe County Tax list 1837, 1838, 1839 in District VIII. In 1835 the Tennessee General Assembly passed an act, counties were to be divided into civil districts and a designated place for holding elections. District VII was to include Lots numbers 11 and 12. The place of voting was at Isaac Roberson's place.

Isaac served in the state senate, 26th General Assembly 1845-1847 represented Bledsoe, Marion, Meigs and Rhea counties. A look at Senator Roberson's financial report in 1846 for a term of 120 days in the state legislature, $4.00 per day, $480.00 amount of mileage to state capital 216 miles, 16 cents a mile, $34.56, total amount due $514.56.

Isaac was on the list in Captain Scott Terry's company in the Cherokee War (Indian Removal) that was mustered in May 1836 in Bledsoe County. Isaac was a Colonel in a regiment of Tennessee Militia during the Mexican War.

Isaac Roberson became a large land owner and slave holder. He served as post master for the rural post office, Roberson's Crossroads. This post office was established in 1839 and in 1882 the name changed to Sequachee College post office. Isaac also served as Justice of Peace for many years in the county.

Isaac Roberson deeded the land for Sequachee College in 1861 for $225.00. Shares in the college sold for $25.00 each. Isaac bought eleven shares. This land was located in the VIII Civil District and described as being located on the west side of Sequatchie Valley on road leading up and down the valley. He also deeded the use of a large spring northwest of the college site, known as the Cave Spring. Sequachee College was organized in 1860 with Isaac Roberson president of the original stockholders. Other Roberson stockholders were A.H. Roberson, James M. Roberson, R.B. Roberson and S.W. Roberson. In 1874 Isaac was president of the Board of Trustees. Isaac died March 25, 1883, Elvira (Cole) Roberson died July 9, 1880.

Isaac and Elvira (Cole) Roberson's children: Marilda Jr. (twin) born January 30, 1827, married Oliver Perry Schoolfield, died July 13, 1876; Matilda J. (twin) born February 1, 1827, married Abraham Hamilton Nail, died February 13, 1913; Drucilla born May 17, 1828, died young; Nancy born June 5, 1829, married Jefferson C. Walker, died June 22, 1859; Alexander Hamilton born January 30, 1831, Confederate soldier killed in service; Martha born October 7, 1832, married James L. Schoolfield; John R. born August 23, 1834, died November 27, 1908. John R. was a member of the Tulloss Rangers, this was a company of Confederate soldiers raised in Sequatchie Valley with John M. Bridgman Captain. John R. was 2nd Corporal, Adam Roberson, the son of John Roberson, was also in this Cavalry Company; James born September 4, 1836, married Penelope Pocahontas Spears, daughter of James G. Spears. James was a student of Emory and Henry College in 1861. He returned home and joined the Confederate service in Company II of the Fourth Tennessee Regiment, commanded by Colonel John T. Murray. He was captured by Federal soldiers and spent almost two years as a prisoner of war at Johnson Island. After the war he studied law, was admitted to the bar and practiced law for more than twenty years. James died August 15, 1918 in Marion County; Elvira born October 17, 1839, married John L. Stone; Polk born December 2, 1844, married Philia Ann Vaughn. She was born March 13, 1857. Polk was a student at Sequachee College in 1879-1880. His address was Sequachee College, Tennessee. Polk, a student in 1881, was also on the Board of Trustees. Philia Ann Roberson died September 10, 1899. Polk died April 28, 1904.

BELLE VIEW
Home of Major James Roberson
1784 - 1852

Shown: Samuel Hezekiah Lafayette Swafford and family

Sources:

Isaac Roberson's Bible Records.

Leaves From The Family Tree, by Penelope J. Allen, 1933.

History of Sequachee College, 1889.

Bledsoe Register of Deeds, Pikeville, Tennessee.

History of Hamilton County, Tennessee, by Zella Armstrong.

ROBINETT/ROBINETTE/ ROBNETT

The name Robnett is found in the American colony of Pennsylvania in the late 1600s. Allen Robnett was in Pennsylvania in April 1684 in the Middletown District. He held a land grant and was a proprietor.

By the late 1700s Robinetts are in Maryland and by the mid 1700s they are in Virginia. Several served in the American Revolution. After the Revolution, Robinetts are in South Carolina and Georgia, later in Tennessee.

Samuel Robinett Sr. was in Bledsoe County in 1808. In March 1808 Samuel was a sworn chain carrier for the survey of 116 acres of land on Sequachy Creek for Solomon Ozburn. He was also a sworn chain carrier for a survey of 231 acres for Adington Rogers. Rogers held the land by right of improvement and occupancy, lying in "Sequchey [sic] Valley Creek joining lines Samuel Robinett".

In May 1808 Samuel claimed by right of improvement, occupancy land lying and being in Bledsoe County in Sequachey Valley on Sequchey [sic] Creek joining lines with Stephen Kilgore, Solomon Ozburn and Adiston Rogers.

In 1813 Samuel Robinett signed a petition to the Tennessee General Assembly for Peter Hoodenpyle to improve at his own expense a certain wagon road across Cumberland Mountains to White and Warren counties and for Hoodenpyle's permission to erect a toll gate.

In 1814 Samuel Robinett a citizen of Bledsoe County was listed to serve jury duty. Samuel Robinett Sr. was a great-great grandson of Allen Robinett I of Pennsylvania. Samuel and his wife Anne Osborne, Ozburn Robinett in early 1800 were living in southwest Virginia, Scott and Lee counties, at a place called "Flag Pond". "A short time after 1805 Samuel moved his family to land on the Sequchy [sic] river in Bledsoe County, Tennessee." Sometime after 1814 and before 1820 this Robinett family was back in Scott County, Virginia at Flag Pond where they had lived before moving to Bledsoe County.

Sources:

Tennessee Homesteaders and Landowners, Fourth Surveyors District Abstracts of Survey and Entry Books, compiled by Willis Hutcheson.

RFA Newsletter and Journal, Quarterly publication of the Robinett Family Association of American, Inc., January 1994.

Bledsoe County Circuit Court Execution Book, 1810-1824.

RUTLEDGE

John Rutledge born 1738 in South Carolina, lived during the American Revolution in the Camden District. He served in the militia and furnished supplies to the American cause. He died in 1803 in South Carolina.

Rutledges were in Tennessee before 1796, in Sullivan and Hawkins counties. William Rutledge had a land grant in 1783. Several Rutledges took part in the second war with Great Britain (War of 1812) from Tennessee.

Tradition in the Rutledge family; Jackson Rutledge, son of Edward of South Carolina came to Tennessee in early 1800. Jackson's children were Emanuel, Lorenzo Dow, Lucy and Thomas.

Thomas Rutledge born in Virginia ca. 1803 was living in Bledsoe County in 1850 south of Pikeville. According to family tradition, he was the son of Jackson Rutledge born 1778 and a grandson of Edward Rutledge born 1749 who was a signer of the Declaration of Independence from South Carolina.

By the 1830s, Thomas with his family was on the move east. First settling in East Tennessee. In the 1840s Thomas moved to Arkansas. In 1850 he is back in Tennessee, Bledsoe County.

Thomas first married a Wilson. They became the parents of ten children, James, Thomas, Stephen, Joseph, Cornelius, John, Mary, Nancy Jane, Catherine and Sarah Anne. In the late 1840s Thomas first wife died and he married Jane Hall. She was born ca. 1823 in Tennessee.

In 1850, Thomas Rutledge age 47 born in Virginia and Lorenzo D. Rutledge age 36 born in Virgina were heads of households living in Bledsoe County. Thomas' occupation was a "waggon maker".

Thomas and Jane became the parents of Harriet E., Emilie P., Benjamin F., Lorenzo D., Martha, Anderson Lee, Edward, Thomas, and Wiley Blount. Tradition is they were all born in Keedy's Cove.

Lorenzo Dow Rutledge was a farmer, living south of Pikeville, his wife was Mary. They were the parents of Sarah A., George, Elizabeth, Charles M., Nancy C., Valentine and Mary W., all born in Tennessee.

Thomas Rutledge died 1870-1880 in Bledsoe County. Jane Rutledge was widow in 1880 living with three of her sons; Anderson, Edwin and Wiley B., two sons Benjamin and Lorenzo were married with families living nearby.

Benjamin Franklin Rutledge born 1852 died 1908, married Delilah Jane Bowman, second, Martha Jane ?. Benjamin Franklin and both wives were buried in the Rutledge Family Cemetery on their farm.

Edwin T. Rutledge born September 7, 1859, married Margaret Jane Smith, daughter of Isaac N. Smith. The Rutledge's and Smith's were neighbors. Margaret Jane was born November 21, 1854 and died December 29, 1895. Edwin T. died September 24, 1894. They were both buried in the Rutledge Family Cemetery.

Wiley Blount Rutledge, youngest son of Thomas and Jane born October 21, 1861, became a Baptist minister. He was the father of Wiley Rutledge, a member of the United States Supreme Court during Franklin D. Roosevelt's administration.

Stephen Wilson Rutledge, the third son of Thomas Rutledge and his first wife, was born July 7, 1833 in Tennessee. He grew up and was educated in Hawkins County. He married Mary Massey, daughter of Richard Massey, born August 4, 1835. He tells in his diary how he met Mary.

In 1850 April, a hanging was to take place in Pikeville - Hyram Godsey was to be hung for the murder of John Morris - This was to take place on the southeast side of the river, "Hangman bottom", Stephen W. Rutledge is going to the hanging - The crossing is at the north end of Pikeville - A wet spring - several people attempting to cross - Stephen's horse gets stuck in the quicksand - floundered, but pulls out of the muddy water, a young lady, Mary Massey's horse is caught in the quicksand, Mary falls backward, her head under water - her foot slipped from the stirrup - Stephen rushes from the bank to the rescue - Mary - she is unconscious - Stephen carries her to Dr. Whitesides - where she is soon revived. After the hanging, which Stephen described in details, he returned home. After much thought he sends Mary a letter. Mary's answer to Stephen's "meet me Sunday at the old church", probably Parker's meeting house and "talk the matter over."

A few months later, December 18, 1850, Stephen and Mary were married by Elder Absolom Vernon, Baptist Clergyman. This family moved to Giles County later Lawrence County. Stephen served in the Confederate Army during the Civil War from Tennessee. He was a prisoner of war for a period of time.

Sometime after the war ca. 1868, Stephen and family moved

to Texas County, Missouri. Mary (Massey) Rutledge died December 29, 1909, Texas County, Missouri. Stephen W. Rutledge died October 12, 1910, also in Texas County.

Stephen W. and Mary (Massey) Rutledge became the parents of Mary J., John B., Sarah Elizabeth, Virginia, Chelnessie Matrina, James Harve, Jerome Packard, all born in Tennessee. Flora Josephine, Thomas Thornton, Martha and May, all born in Missouri.

Sources:

Members and Patriots The Tennessee Society Daughters of the American Revolution, Vol. IV, 1985-2001.

First Families of Tennessee East Tennessee Historical Society, 2000.

Tennesseans in the War of 1812, by Sistler, 1992.

Bledsoe County U.S. Census, 1850.

East Tennessee Roots, Vol. VI, Fall 1989.

Stephen W. Rutledge, autobiography information from Emma W. Webb, 118 Lewis Road, Clemson, S.C. 29631.

Mrs. V.H. Rutledge, 946 17th Ave., Longview, Washington 98632.

SCHOOLFIELD/SCHOLEFIELD

The Schoolfield name is found in Pennsylvania and Maryland in the early 1700s. David Schoolfield born February 10, 1736 in Pennsylvania, was the son of John and Ann (Lenoir) Schoolfield. David married April 20, 1763, Rachel Greaver, daughter of Samuel Greaver. Rachel was born February 13, 1738 in Delaware.

David and Rachel lived in Pennsylvania, Delaware, Maryland and Virginia during the years 1763-1791. They became the parents of Samuel, John, Enoch, Benjamin, Sidney, Ann, Jane, Aaron and David.

Aaron Schoolfield, son of David and Rachel, was born July 29, 1775 in Maryland. He married Malinda Doyl Lawler, daughter of James Lawler, in 1803 in Campbell County, Virginia.

Aaron was in Bledsoe County as early as 1818, as he purchased two town lots, numbers six and seven, from the commissioners of Pikeville. In 1828 he was serving as a commissioner for the town with John Billingsley, James Loyd and Kinzey Smith. Aaron Schoolfield was one of the early doctors to locate in the county seat of Pikeville. He served as one of the first post masters after Pikeville became a United States post office in 1821. He was later appointed post master of East View in 1838.

Aaron and Malinda became the parents of James L., David Rittenhouse, Charles, Letitia (Lucy), Jane Elvire, Virginia Ann, Pocahontas, William Alexander and Oliver Perry.

James L. Schoolfield, oldest son of Aaron, born April 13,

1804, married Judy Rainey. They were in Bledsoe County in 1830 and 1840 census. Sometime before 1850 the family left for Texas. However, before they reached their point of destination in Texas, James L. died and was buried on the banks of the Brazos River. The family started back to Tennessee, but when they reached the Red River, they settled near Fulton, Arkansas. However, some of the members later returned to Tennessee, including Patrick Henry. Schoolfield Store Post Office was established in 1832 with James L. Schoolfield as post master.

Children of James L. and Judy (Rainey) Schoolfield: William B., Patrick Henry, Robert Emmett, David Aaron, Charles C., John P., James L. Jr., Jane Elvira, S.L., Melinda C., Samuel B., Nicholas and Hugh Malone.

William B. Schoolfield, oldest son of James L. and Judy (Rainey) Schoolfield, born April 1824 enlisted in the Confederate Army at Washington, Arkansas. His brother, Patrick Henry born 1826, enlisted in the Confederate Army at Pikeville. He married Angeline Worthington, daughter of Samuel Worthington. This family lived in Bledsoe County.

Robert Emmett Schoolfield, born 1828, married Mary Angeline Hutcheson. This family moved to Arkansas. Mary Angeline was born March 1, 1829, the daughter of Charles Hutcheson III and Sarah Worthington. Robert Emmett died 1869 and Mary Angeline died August 27, 1931.

David Rittenhouse, second son of Aaron and Malinda Schoolfield, born 1806 and died March 12, 1844, married Elvira Rice. They became the parents of: James L., married Martha Roberson; Perry A., married Mary Haskew; Lizzie, married J.E.

Wright; Mattie; Emma; Nancy; David; Curry; and twins Ida Ella and Ella Ida. This family moved to Marion County after 1840.

Virginia Ann Schoolfield, daughter of Aaron and Malinda, married Nicholas Springs, son of John Springs. Pocahontas Schoolfield, daughter of Aaron and Malinda, married James P. Springs, brother of Nicholas.

William Alexander, born August 31, 1819, married Mary S. Brown, daughter of William Lilly Brown, on April 27, 1847. William was a farmer and blacksmith. Children of William A. and Mary Brown were: Pocahontas born 1848, Robert Brown born 1849, Lucy M., Martha Virginia 1854, Edith, Henry Floyd 1858 and William A. 1862.

Oliver Perry Schoolfield, youngest son of Aaron Schoolfield, was born March 3, 1821 in Bledsoe County, married February 1, 1843, Marilda J. Roberson, daughter of Isaac Roberson. Marilda was born January 30, 1827 and died July 31, 1876. Oliver Perry served in the Confederate Army as Captain. He later moved to Mississippi.

In 1850 Malinda Schoolfield age 69, the widow of Aaron Schoolfield, was making her home in the household of her son Oliver Perry, who was living next to William. Malinda died 1863 in Bledsoe County. Aaron Schoolfield died near Bentonville, Arkansas November 8, 1843.

James L., Oliver R., and William A. Schoolfield were original stockholders for the Sequachee College in 1860. By the late 1870s several Schoolfields were listed as students as well as members of the faculty. "This was a co-educational school of strict discipline located in the 8th Civil District between Pikeville and Dunlap, where students would be removed from usual temptations that beset their college life."

Robert Brown Schoolfield, grandson of Aaron Schoolfield, served as Postmaster of Pikeville, Clerk and Master of Chancery Court, Circuit Clerk, Clerk and General Session Judge.

Sources:

The Schoolfield Family History, by Cleopatra Doss Schoolfield, 1968.

Bledsoe County Registrar Office, Pikeville, Tennessee.

Bledsoe County, Tennessee, A History, by Elizabeth Robnett, 1933.

History of Sequachee College, 1880.

Here It Is Hutcheson Genealogy, by Martrue Hutcheson Greenwood, 1966.

SELBY

The Selby family is in the American colonies of Virginia and Maryland in the 1600s. Several of the Selbys served in the American Revolution. Soon after the Revolution the Selbys began to move west to Kentucky and later to Tennessee.

William Magruder Selby born ca. 1709 in Maryland was a Revolutionary War patriot. He lived in Maryland during the war, married Martha Wilson, daughter of Major Josiah Wilson. They became the parents of William Wilson, Samuel Wilson, James Wilson, Nathan, Josiah Wilson, Lingan Wilson, Thomas, Martha, Sarah, Elizabeth and Mary. Four of William Magruder and Martha (Wilson) Selby's sons carried her maiden name, Wilson as their middle name. Four of their sons were American patriots, (signed the Oaths of Fidelity and support of Prince George County), William Wilson, James Wilson, Nathan and Josiah Wilson Selby. William Magruder Selby died in 1783.

James Wilson Selby born ca. 1747 in Maryland married Ruth Hoskisson. After her death he married Elizabeth Bennett a widow. Sometime after this marriage, James Wilson moved his family to Kentucky. Children of James and wives were: Joshua, James, Simeon, Greenbury, Rachel, Polly, Elizabeth, Druscilla, Lloyd and Sarah. Seven of these moved to Bledsoe County, Joshua, James, Simeon, Greenbury, Elizabeth, Druscilla and Lloyd.

Joshua Selby born 1780 in Maryland, later moved to Kentucky where he married Millie Ormes May 14, 1807 in Adair County. James born 1783, married Elizabeth Morris. Elizabeth born ca. 1785, married Walter Ormes. Greenbury born ca. 1787, married

Eliza Conover. Rachel born ca. 1788, married James McDaniel. Polly married Thomas Locke. Rebecca born 1795, married Johnson Parham. Lloyd born October 5, 1798, married Rebecca Parham.

By the 1830 Bledsoe census, Joshua and James Selby were living in the northern part of Bledsoe County. On the Tax List for 1837, 1838, 1839, Simeon, Greenbury, Nathaniel and Lloyd Selby were living in the III Civil District. Their voting place was Tolletts Mill and their post office was Ormes Store.

Rebecca Selby born May 10, 1795 in Kentucky married Johnson Parham "April 16, 1816/1817 at Mrs. Wilson's home," Bledsoe County. Johnson was born September 20, 1794 in North Carolina. They became the parents of Allen, Elizabeth, John, Martha (Patsy) Ann, William, Isaac, James and Mary. Johnson Parham died May 5, 1846, Druscilla died June 7, 1884. Both were buried in Parham Cemetery.

Lloyd Selby born October 5, 1798 in Kentucky, married Rebecca Parham. Rebecca was born February 19, 1793 in North Carolina. They became the parents of Simeon, Mary Ann, Catherine, Shamuel, William, Elizabeth, Joshua, Elva, Allen, and Asberry. Lloyd Selby died October 9, 1880, Rebecca Parham died March 31, 1884. Both were buried in the Parham Cemetery.

The 1850 Bledsoe census gives the following: Simeon Selby 28, a cabinet maker; Shamuel Selby 26; G.B. Selby 37; Lloyd Selby 53 born in Kentucky; Joshua Selby 70 born in Maryland; Mille (Ormes) Selby 68 born in Kentucky; and Simeon Selby 55 born in Kentucky. These families all were neighbors living in northern part of the county near the head of the Sequatchie River, the "head of the creek" in this area is the Selby Creek and the Selby Cemetery.

Sources:

Family information by Peggy Selby Calloway, 5066 Perryville Rd., Danville, KY 40422.

Bledsoe County census, 1830, 1840, 1850.

Parham Cemetery Records.

National Society Colonial Dames XVII Century Ancestor Roster, 1915-2005.

Membership Roster and Soldiers The Tennessee Society of Daughters of the American Revolution, Vol. 3, Vol. 4.

SHERRILL/SHERRELL

The name Sherrill is found in the American colonies of Pennsylvania, North Carolina and Cecil County, Maryland in the 1700s. Several served in the American Revolution.

Samuel Sherrill was born ca. 1725 probably in Maryland. By 1741 the Sherrills were in Virginia. Samuel married Mary Carmack. The Sherrills were in Tennessee before Tennessee became a state. Sometime in the early 1770s, Samuel and family moved to the Watauga settlement in Washington County, North Carolina, later Washington County, Tennessee. Samuel and four of his sons took part in the Battle of King's Mountain.

Samuel made his will in 1800 in Washington County, Tennessee. He became a large land owner and slave holder, as his will shows, he divided his slaves and land to each of his seven children. Children named in the will: Catherine born 1754, became the second wife of John Sevier; Adam born 1758 in North Carolina moved to Sequatchie Valley; George born 1759; Uriah born 1760; John born 1764; William born 1768; Mary Jane born 1769, married Little Page Sims, second Colonel Taylor. Mary (Carmack) Sherrill died November 29, 1794.

In 1806 the Sherrills were in Roane County. By 1808 the Sherrills were in Sequatchie Valley, Bledsoe County. Several served in the War of 1812 from Tennessee. Charles and Jesse Sherrill signed the petition in 1815 to delay the land laws during the War of 1812.

Adam Sherrill, oldest son of Samuel and Mary, became a large land owner and slave holder. He married Mary McCormick, married second Rebecca Kilgore, daughter of Charles Kilgore, born 1785 in Greene County. Adam was in Bledsoe County in 1808. Adam and Rebecca became the parents of Enos born ca. 1780, married May Abernathy; Charles K. born ca. 1791, married Mary Adkisson; Craven born ca. 1801, married Mary Bronson; Henry born ca. 1802. Adam was living in July 1827, when he deeded his son Craven two slaves. Adam died in 1829. Rebecca was living in 1850 age 85 in the household of her son Craven.

The 1830 Sequatchie census, Bledsoe and Marion Counties gives Jesse Sherrill in Marion and Samuel, Craven and Charles K. in Bledsoe. The Bledsoe Tax List 1837-38-39 gives Charles K., Craven, and Henry Sherrill in District III. The 1840 Bledsoe census shows the Sherrills, Charles K. and Henry are in District III. The 1850 census shows the following Sherrills were heads of families or households, Charles K. Jr., Henry, Jesse, Craven, Charles K. Sr.

Craven Sherrill born in Virginia June 9, 1801, the son of Adam and Rebecca (Kilgore) Sherrill, lived in the northern part of Sequatchie Valley, Bledsoe County. He served in the Tennessee House in the 24th, 25th and 29th General Assemblies. In 1841-45 and 1851-53 represented Bledsoe in the 24th and Bledsoe and Morgan counties in the 25th and 29th. His post office was Orme's Store.

He was serving as sheriff in Bledsoe County when the Third Civil District was put in the new county, Cumberland. He lived in the Third District. He resigned in October 1856 and became sheriff of the new county. He served from 1856 to 1862. He married Mary A. Branson. They became the parents of: Anna, married William Hinch; Rebecca, married Samuel Kerley; Adam; Thomas; Andrew; Martha, married Sam Hoge; Samuel; Nancy, married James Nail; Jesse and

Charles Kilgore. Craven died February 10, 1864 and was buried at the head of the Sequatchie Valley, Sherrill Cemetery.

Charles K. Sherrill born ca. 1791, the son of Adam and Rebecca, served in the War of 1812. He was a private in Colonel Edwin Booth, Captain Vernon, East Tennessee Militia. He enlisted November 1814 for a period of six months and was discharged in May 1815. In 1852 Charles K. applied for "Bounty" land for his service in the War of 1812. Charles married Mary Adkisson. They became the parents of: Temperance born 1815, Willia L. born 1820, Jesse born 1825, Catherine (Katie) born 1827, Casey born 1828, Nancy born 1829, Charles K. born 1830, Francis born 1833, Samuel born 1835. Mary (Adkisson) Sherrill died before 1850. Charles K. died between 1852-60.

Nancy Sherrill, daughter of Charles K. and Rebecca, born 1829, married Elijah Goar Tollett. They lived at the Tollett Mill place on the line between Bledsoe and Cumberland Counties. They became the parents of Charles K., Nancy Elizabeth, John, Sam, Frank, James Wesley, Martha A., Mary, Major Craven, Syrene, Elijah Goar Jr., William, Wilson, Mark and Mose. Nancy died 1905 and is buried in Tollett Cemetery.

Catherine (Katie) oldest daughter of Charles K. born 1827, married James E. Roberts. They lived in the area of the Tollett Mill in 1850. Sometime after 1850 they moved to Walden Ridge and lived near the Pleasant Hill Methodist Church. They became the parents of William W., Charles M., Mary, Samuel, Sarah, James E., John and Martha Jane. James E. Roberts was killed in the early 1860s on his way to enlist in the Civil War. In 1910 Catherine (Sherrill) Roberts is listed as a widow age 84, the mother of eight children, all living. She died between 1910-20.

Sources:

Biographical Directory of the Tennessee General Assembly, Vol. I, 1796-1861.

Of Such As These, by Jane Tollett, 1980.

Tennesseans in the War of 1812, by Sistler, 1992.

SKILLERN

The Skillern family was in the colony of Virginia in the 1700s. William Skillern Jr., son of William and Elizabeth Skillern, born 1739 in Virginia, married Mary Anderson in 1763. Mary was born 1747, the daughter of William and Elizabeth (Campbell) Anderson. They became the parents of William born 1764, George born 1766, Elizabeth born 1768, John born 1770, Rebecca born 1773, James born 1777, Anderson born 1780, Anna born 1783, Isaac Campbell born 1787, Margaret born 1791. William Skillern, Jr. died 1816. Mary died 1832 in Scott County, Virginia.

Several of William and Mary (Anderson) Skillern's children came to Bledsoe County. The Skillerns were in Tennessee before Tennessee became a state, in Sullivan County when they receive a land grant in 1789. The Skillerns and Anderson families were connected by marriages. Both families received large land grants. The Skillerns were in Sequatchie Valley when the area was part of Roane County.

George Skillern, the second son of William and Mary (Anderson) Skillern, born 1766 in Virginia, married Elizabeth Miller in Madison County, Kentucky in 1795. By 1807 George was in Sequatchie Valley, this area was in Roane County. George and Elizabeth (Miller) Skillern were the parents of Mary, Priscilla, Ann, Thomas M. and Alexander, all born in Kentucky.

George Skillern petitioned the Roane County Court for permission to erect a grist mill in "Sequacha" valley, "where the old Kiuka Trace, or Lower Trace, crosses the mountain from Tennessee Valley."

A second petition was also presented. The two petitions were signed by several early settlers that the grist mill would be of public use, "we therefore pray your worships to grant an order in favor of." The order was granted. The Skillern grist mill, on Skillern Branch was Bledsoe County's first industry. Some of those signing the petitions were living in the valley at the time or were planning to move to the valley in 1807 were, Springs, Rogers, Browns, Hoges, Vernons, Elijah Hicks, Robersons, Stephens, Hankins, Wilsons, Peter Looney, Raineys, Thurmans, Coulters and Fergusons.

George Skillern signed the petition in 1809 asking some provisions be made for those settlers that went "below the Indian boundary line and left improvements and property before the boundary line was run."

Anderson Skillern was Lieutenant Regiment Cavalry 8th Brigade in 1812, Bledsoe County Militia.

In 1813 James A., John, James Jr., and George Skillern signed a petition for Peter Hoodenpyle to improve at his own expense a road from Bledsoe across the Cumberland Mountains to White and Warren counties, on completion, Hoodenpyle request permission to erect a Toll Gate.

Several Skillerns served in the War of 1812 from Tennessee.

The 1830 census gives Anderson, James, John and Nancy Skillern as heads of households. Nancy is the widow of William, Jr., oldest son of William and Mary (Anderson) Skillern. The Bledsoe Tax List of 1837 gives James, John, Anderson and Nicholas in District VI and VII. The 1840 census gives James and John living in District VI. By 1850 James Skillern age 51, born in Virginia and

William age 28 born in Tennessee were listed as heads of households.

Sources:

Record of Commissions of Officers in the Tennessee Militia, 1796-1815, by Mrs. John Trotwood Moore, 1977.

Skillern Family History, by Ethelmae Eylar Carter and Darlene R. Appell, 1971.

Skillern Cemetery
Skillern Cove

SMITH, Layton/Leighton

Born ca. 1756 in Maryland, lived in Washington County, Virginia during the war years 1775-1781. In 1775 he enlisted to serve his country. His service was in southwest Virginia defending the frontier settlers against the Indians. He served approximately twenty months. After the war he moved to Greene County. He was in Knox County 1800, and in Anderson 1802. Soon after Bledsoe was created out of Roane he moved to Sequatchie Valley.

The 1830 Bledsoe Census gives Layton Smith and son Moses as heads of households. Layton was a landowner in Bledsoe County. He married Elizabeth Roberson born 1766, daughter of James and Mary (Fuqua) Roberson.

In 1833 Layton Smith filed for pension on his service during the years 1775-1779. The Pension Act was passed June 1832 by Congress. Layton gives as reference to his character and reliability John Dalton, a well-known clergyman; Eli Thurman, Sheriff, Phillip Thurman and Elisha Kirkland, a merchant in Pikeville. His pension $80.00 a year.

Children of Layton and Elizabeth (Roberson) Smith: Phoebe; William; Patsy; Moses born 1795, married Sarah; Martha born 1798; Aaron born 1801, married Mary; Elizabeth born 1803, married John Stepp. In 1840 Layton is in Marion County in household of his son Aaron. He died December 12, 1840.

Sources:
Stepps of Bledsoe County, by Mary Stepp DeVault, 1977-1980.

Declaration of Revolutionary War Service, by Layton Smith, February 1833.

Leaves From The Family Tree, by Penelope Johnson Allen, 1933-1937.

SPEAR/SPEER

The name appears in the American colonies in the late 1600s and early 1700s in Virginia, Maryland and Pennsylvania. Edward Spears, born ca. 1745, died November 4, 1791 in Ohio, married Jane Holliday, is listed as a 1st Lieutenant in the *DAR Patriot Index Centennial Edition*, Part III P. 2751. Several Spears from Tennessee served in the East Tennessee Militia during the War of 1812.

Dr. John Holliday Spears was in Bledsoe County as early as 1811. Dr. Spears was born ca. 1782 in Virginia, Buckingham County, was the son of William Spears and a grandson of Edward Spears, veteran of the American Revolution. Dr. Spears married Sarah Gallant, born ca. 1796 in South Carolina, the daughter of James Gallant I and his second wife, Sarah (McDonough) Gallant.

Dr. Spears served as an Ensign 31st Regiment Bledsoe County Militia in 1811. He served in the War of 1812, Colonel William Johnson, Captain James Tunnell East Tennessee Militia. He signed the Petition in Bledsoe County 1815 to delay the land laws during the War of 1812. The 1830 Bledsoe census list Dr. Spears as head of a household with wife, two sons, two daughters. The 1837, 1838, 1839 Bledsoe Tax List gives Dr. John H. and son James G. Spears in District VII and VIII. The Spears became large land owners and slave holders. The 1840 census shows Dr. John H. and James G. in District VII and Delila Spears in District X.

The children of Dr. John H. and Sarah (Gallant) Spears were: James Gallant, John Gallant, Mary and Anna. John H. Spears died September 16, 1860. Sarah died 1860/1870.

James Gallant Spears, oldest son of Dr. John and Sarah (Gallant) Spears was born March 29, 1816 in Bledsoe County. He became a large land owner and slave holder. He was engaged in teaching school for a number of years, probably Lafayette Academy. In 1847 he was commissioned a Colonel in the Bledsoe Militia. He began the practice of law in Pikeville in the years 1848. He was a great admirer of Andrew Johnson, he had a family connection in the McDonough family. He was a Stephen A. Douglas Democrat.

In 1850 James was married to Adelia Kindrick Brown, daughter of William Lilly Brown and was serving as Circuit Court Clerk. Adelia K. was born March 16, 1823 in Virginia. They became the parents of J. Brown, William D. and James G. Jr.

James G. Spears enlisted September 1, 1861 at Camp Dick Robinson for a period of three years to serve in the Union Army. He was promoted to Lieutenant Colonel and later to Brigadier General, February 1862 for gallantry. He took part in battles of Wild Cat Mountain and Fishing Creek, Cumberland Gap, Stone River and Chickamauga. He was 44, 5 feet 11-1/2 inches, weight 164 lbs.

James was a large land owner and slave holder, described as a "hot temper" lawyer, a hard-line Unionist and a faithful Democrat. He was a presidential elector when Stephen A. Douglas was the nominee for the Northern Democrat party in 1860. Douglas received only 38 votes in Bledsoe County in this election. Spears opposed vigorously Lincoln's Emancipation Proclamation in 1863. He had enlisted in the Union army because of the secession of the southern states, not slavery. He was the highest ranking Union officer from Bledsoe County during the Civil War. His attitude won him his arrest and court martial in early 1864. He was dismissed from the army later the same year.

Three sons of General Spears became well-known lawyers and two served in the Tennessee State Legislature. General Spears died July 22, 1869 at his summer home, Braden's Knob on the Cumberland Mountain. He was buried in the Pikeville City Cemetery.

Ashley Lawrence Spears, a half brother of the three younger sons, J. Brown, William Douglas and James G. Spears Jr., was appointed their guardian. The oldest children of James G. Spears were Ashley Lawrence, Penelope Pocahontas and Napoleon Bonaparte.

Ashley Lawrence Spears born March 28, 1842, eight miles south of Pikeville, oldest son of James Gallant Spears, attended Emory and Henry College in Virginia and Cumberland University. He became a well-known lawyer in Bledsoe and Marion counties. He enlisted in the Union Army February 25, 1862. He was with his father in the Battles of Stone River and Chickamauga. He was mustered out April 1865. He attained the rank of Colonel. He taught school a short time, and served as County Court Clerk.

He married Martha (Mattie) J. Pitts who was born May 18, 1846. He served in the Tennessee House, 36th and 37th General Assemblies 1869, 1873, represented Bledsoe, Hamilton, Rhea and Sequatchie counties.

He later moved to Marion County where he became a large land owner and a leading citizen. He was a presidential elector in 1872 for Horace Greeley, the Democrat nomiee for president. He served as president of the First National Bank of South Pittsburg.

Ashley Lawrence and Mattie J. (Pitts) Spears became the

parents of Nellie, Grace and Alvin.

Ashley Lawrence was a strong supporter of the Pryor Institute in Marion County, contributing the sum of $7,500.00 to this popular school at Jasper. Mattie J. died November 23, 1896 and was buried in the Pine Grove Cemetery. Ashley Lawrence married second December 28, 1897 Miss Willie Cummins, a well educated woman from Franklin, Tennessee.

Ashley was classed as one of the most distinguished lawyers of East Tennessee. In 1878 he was elected Attorney General of the Fourth Judicial District. In 1898 he was serving as president of the First National Bank of South Pittsburg. Ashley Lawrence died February 14, 1900 and was buried in the Pine Grove Cemetery, Marion County.

Penelope Pocahontas born ca. 1846, married James Roberson February 25, 1869. James was born September 4, 1836 the son of Isaac Roberson. They became the parents of Isaac Gallant, Alexander Lawrence, James Napoleon, Samuel Tulloss, Anna Florence, Spears, John R., Brown, and Addie Elvira. James Roberson was educated at Emory and Henry College. He served in the Confederate Army and was a prisoner of war nearly two years at Johnson's Island. After the war he studied law, was admitted to the bar and practiced law for several years in Pikeville. This family later moved to Jasper. James died August 15, 1918. Penelope Pocahontas died September 30, 1924. Both were buried at Pine Grove Cemetery.

Napoleon Bonaparte Spears, born 1849 in Bledsoe County. In 1870 he was listed as "reading law" age 21. He married Florance Mitchell. They became the parents of James P. and Douglas B. This family lived in Marion County where he practiced law. A Democrat, he served in the House 39th General Assembly 1875, 1877, represented Marion, Bledsoe, Grundy, Hamilton, Sequatchie and Van Buren counties. He later moved to Georgia and sometime later to Alabama in 1900. He died in Florida prior to 1929.

John Gallant Spears, second son of Dr. John H. Spears born ca. 1818 in Bledsoe County, married Adaline Cooper. She was born ca. 1824 in Tennessee. Sometime before 1850 John G. and Adaline moved to Alabama. However, by 1860 this family was living in Pikeville, his occupation, a farmer. Their children were John H., Delilah J., James A., Samuel, and Martha E. They were all born in Alabama. In 1879 this family was living south of Pikeville, occupation farmer and farm hand.

Mary "Polly" Spears born ca. 1820, the daughter of Dr. John and Sarah Spears, was in 1850 living with her parents and daughter, Sarah E. age one year, south of Pikeville. In 1860 Dr. Spears and family were living in Pikeville. Mary and daughter were living in the household. Sometime before 1880 Mary became the second wife of James Swafford. In 1900 Mary (Spears) Swafford was living in the household of her daughter and son-in-law, John T. Teaters.

J. Brown Spears, oldest son of James G. and Adelia Kindrick (Brown) Spears, born 1851, married Adelia Gass June 6, 1879, the daughter of Colonel W.T. Gass of Rhea County. Adelia Gass was born 1857. J. Brown served as postmaster at Pikeville and Registrar of Deeds. He lived in the Bridgman House, (Spears House) in 1909 when the courthouse burned.

The office of Registrar of Deeds was in J. Brown's home. This may have been for convenience or the office had not been moved to the new courthouse. However, this saved the deed records.

The children of J. Brown and Adelia (Gass) Spears were Pearl A., Blanche, William B., Ralph D., and Jacob A. Adelia died 1934, and J. Brown died 1948. Both were buried in the Old Spears Cemetery, Rhea County.

William Douglas Spears born December 8, 1852, the second son of James G. and Adelia Kindrick (Brown) Spears, attended Emory and Henry College in Virginia, later Cumberland University and graduated in 1873. He married Lou R. Hall November 20, 1878. She was born November 3, 1860 in Pikeville. This family moved to Marion County and later to Chattanooga. He was a well-known lawyer in Bledsoe and Marion counties and Chattanooga. Lou R. (Hall) Spears died November 23, 1922 in Jasper. William Douglas died January 10, 1929.

James Gallant Spears Jr. born 1857, youngest son of General Spears and Adaline K. (Brown) Spears, married Lula. This family moved to Grayson County, Texas. Lula E. Spears sold the old Spears residence, the "Bridgman Brick" in 1904 to S.H. Ferguson and Sam M. Pope for $1,000.00. James Gallant Jr. died in 1927 and was buried in the Old Spears Cemetery with his brother J. Brown Spears. Mrs. Adelia K. purchased the Bridgman Brick and five town lots from the Bridgman heirs for $2,250.00. The deed was recorded May 1869. It reads "to her sole and separate use free from control of James G. Spears, her husband, or from control of any other person." Sometime during Mrs. Spears' life, she had became a lady of "independence and wealth." Mrs. Adelia (Brown) Spears married second February 18, 1872 Colonel William Thomas Gass, a well-known Confederate of Rhea County.

Mrs. Adelia K. (Brown) Spears Gass made her last will June 10, 1898.

1. To William Douglas, the old parlor set, given to me by my former husband James G. Spears.

2. To J. Brown, all debts and claims I have against him, the debt of $500.00 and interest, all claims and rent, lot and residence, known as the Wed Bridgman property.

3. To Lula Spears wife of James G. Spears Jr., the Brick house and lots in Pikeville known as the Bridgman House. She is to have the same to her sole and separate use free from the debts of her husband.

4. To Florance Spears, wife of N.B. Spears, one feather bed and pillows.

5. To Jacob Gass, a step-son one gold ring and fine quilt.

6. To Penelope Pocahontas (Spears) Roberson wife of James Roberson, one toilet table and rocking chair.

7. To Ashley Lawrence, my family Bible, it being his father's Bible.

8. To my husband William Thomas Gass, all of the balance of my property and all debts he may be due me.

9. To James G. Jr. if he and his wife returned to Tennessee to live, one bed room set.

Mrs. Adelia K. died August 28, 1902 in Jasper at the home of her son William Douglas Spears. A special train was run from Jasper to Pikeville, "bearing the remains and a large number of friends and

relatives which arrived at 10:30 A.M." Her funeral was held at the
Methodist Episcopal Church South. Services were conducted by Rev.
J.L. Cash, Pikeville and Rev. J.W. Robertson of Jasper. At the
cemetery, "the casket was reopened to allow uncle Peter Spears, age
106, who had been a trusted slave to view the features of his former
mistress." She was buried in the Pikeville City Cemetery beside her
first husband General Spears.

Sources:

Quiet Places: The Burial Sites of Civil War Generals in Tennessee, by Buckner and Nathaniel C.
Hughes Jr., 1992.

Tennesseans in the War of 1812, by Sistler, 1992.

Bledsoe County Census, 1830, 1840, 1850.

Compendium of Local Biography, Part II, by Geo. A. Ogle Co., 1898.

Cemetery records.

Records of Commissions of Officers in the Tennessee Militia, 1796-1815.

Family Obituaries.

Military Records.

Bledsoe County, Tennessee, A History, by Elizabeth Robnett, 1993.

Hankin Family Bible.

John Houston Spears
Mary Caroline Ingram Spears

Grandson of Dr. John Holliday Spears

SPRINGS

Nicholas Springs was born in Virginia in ca. 1730. He served in the American Revolution as a private in Captain Matthew Smith's Company in Augusta County, Virginia. He married Margaret Cloninger, ca. 1765. She was born 1752 in Augusta County. The Springs were in Bledsoe County in the early 1800s. In 1809 Nicholas Springs was granted 100 acres of land on the south side of Sequatchie River in Bledsoe County by the state.

Nicholas and Margaret (Cloninger) Springs became the parents of: Catherine born ca. 1768, married Augustine Kaiger; Nicholas born ca. 1770, married Elizabeth Hicks; Valentine born 1779, married Sarah; John born 1781, married Nancy Moore; Mary born 1790, married Anderson Skillern; David born ca. 1792, married Rachel Rainey. Nicholas Springs died 1824 at the age of 94 in Bledsoe County. Margaret died March 21, 1848 at the age of 96. In the 1840 Bledsoe census, in the household of Valentine Springs in addition to his wife, was a female age 80-90, probably his mother Margaret Springs.

The Springs family was in Bledsoe County in early 1800s. Valentine Springs was in Bledsoe County in 1808 as he was in the regiment of the Cavalry 3rd Brigade, Bledsoe Militia. John Springs was Lieutenant 31st Regiment Bledsoe Militia, 1812. Several Springs served in the War of 1812 from Tennessee - Valentine, John, Lawrence and Nicholas Springs signed the petition in 1815 to delay a land law during the War of 1812.

The 1830 Bledsoe census gives Valentine, John and Rachel Springs as heads of households in Bledsoe County. The tax list of

1837-38-39 gives David, James, John and Valentine Springs in District VII.

In 1836 the county was divided into Civil districts. The Springs family lived in District number VII and the place of holding elections was at Valentine Springs. In the 1840 census James Pickney and Valentine Springs were heads of households in District VII. The Springs were large land owners and slave holders. By 1850 Benjamin Franklin, Nicholas A. and Valentine Springs were in the county as heads of households.

Valentine Springs, third child of Nicholas and Margaret (Cloninger) Springs, was born in 1779 in Virginia. Valentine enlisted October 1813 at Ross' Landing to serve in the War of 1812 in the Alabama area to fight the Creek Indians. His rank was a private under Captain William Christian and Colonel John Brown's Command. He was discharged January 1814. He married Sarah, born 1782 in Virginia.

In 1852 Valentine applied for bounty land, on his services in the War of 1812. His application was prepared by William Foster, Justice of the Peace of Bledsoe and also a neighbor. Valentine Springs died June 1, 1862 and was buried in the Springs Family Cemetery.

John Springs, third son of Nicholas and Margaret (Cloninger) Springs, born at Augusta County, Virginia, August 31, 1781, married Nancy Moore April 18, 1802. Nancy was born October 10, 1780. They became the parents of: Nicholas Jr. born 1809, married Virginia Schoolfield, second Pauline Sutton; James Pickney born 1812, married Pocahontas Catherine Ann Schoolfield; Mary born 1815, married John Smith; Benjamin Franklin born 1818, married Julia

Frances Hammond; Margaret born 1820, married Thomas N. Frazier; David Valentine born 1827, married Carrie Moore. John Springs died February 20, 1864. Nancy (Moore) Springs died June 16, 1844 in Benton County, Arkansas.

David Springs, youngest son of Nicholas and Margaret (Cloninger) Springs born ca. 1792, in Augusta County, Virginia, married Rachel Rainey. He died November 24, 1828 in Bledsoe County. They became the parents of Clarinda Jane Malone, Margaret Ann, Nicholas Anderson, David Henninger. After David's death, Rachel married Jacob Spurin.

Sources:

Skillern Family History and Genealogy, by Darlene R. Appell and Ethelmai Eylar Carter, 1971.

Bledsoe Census, 1830, 1840, 1850.

Tennesseans in the War of 1812, by Sistler, 1992.

General Services Administration National Archives and Records Service, Washington.

STANDEFER/STANDIFER

The name Standifer is found in the 1600s in the colony of Maryland. A John and William were listed as land owners. Several Standefers served in the American Revolution.

Luke Standefer born 1758 in Virginia served as a Lieutenant during the American Revolution.

Benjamin Standifer born May 17, 1764 in Maryland, served as a private and later a sergeant in the mounted rifleman with the North Carolina troops during the American Revolution. He entered service in 1780 to serve under Captain Douglas and Colonel Dunley in Orange County, North Carolina. He was in the Battle of Lincoln Mill. After the war, Benjamin moved to Georgia and later to Bledsoe County. He married Rachel Forest August 14, 1781 in Oglethorpe County, Georgia. He married second Nancy (Jones) Echolls December 29, 1802. They moved to Sequatchie Valley ca. 1820.

In August 1832, Benjamin applied for a pension for his service in the Revolutionary War, while living in Bledsoe County. Benjamin died May 5, 1839. Nancy (Echolls) Standifer applied for a widow's pension May 5, 1853. She died in Hamilton County February 28, 1864. Children of Benjamin Standifer are listed as Joshua, Sarah, Mildred (Milly), Leroy and Sinthia.

Several Standifers served in the War of 1812 from Tennessee as officers or enlisted men. The Standfers were in Knox County in the late 1700s and early 1800s. James and Israel Standifer were on the Tax List in 1805 in Anderson County. By 1830 census Standifers were in the Sequatchie Valley. On the Marion County list were

William H. and Jane as heads of households. In Bledsoe were Israel Jr., Benjamin, James, Shelton C., and Israel Sr. as heads of households.

On the Bledsoe County Tax List in the late 1830s (1837, 1838, 1839) in District IX were James, Jesse and William Standifer and James Standifer's heirs.

The 1840 Bledsoe census gives Shelton C. and Jesse Standifer as heads of households in District IX. Congressman James's widow Patsy, probably living in household of son Shelton C. age 50-60.

William Standifer born 1757 in Virginia married June 24, 1779 Jemima Jones. She was born 1761 in Virginia. William died June 21, 1826 and Jemima died September 28, 1838. Both died in Marion County, Tennessee. They became the parents of eleven children: Fanny born July 29, 1781, married Luke Hendrix; James Israel born September 10, 1784, married Martha (Patsy) Standifer; Luke born May 23, 1786; William C. born May 29, 1788; Mary (Polly) born May 17, 1790, married Amos Griffith August 11, 1805 in Anderson County, she died January 25, 1872; Naomi born February 10, 1794, married Israel Standifer Jr.; Skelton born August 3, 1795, married Jane Stewart; Susannah born November 6, 1799, married Henry Yarnell; Isaac born October 12, 1801, married Elizabeth Standifer, second married Dorcus Jones, died November 6, 1855 in Milam County, Texas; Samuel born August 7, 1803, died in Milam County Texas before 1843; Alfred born June 18, 1808, married Jane Yarnell, died in Milam County, Texas August 11, 1850. Jane was born December 12, 1806, died in Missouri.

James Israel Standifer, oldest son of William, born September 10, 1784 in Virginia, married Martha (Patsy) Standifer, a cousin,

February 2, 1801 in Knox County. This family moved to Sequatchie Valley in the early 1800s with a brother-in-law Amos Griffith and wife Mary (Polly) (Standifer) Griffith. They were the first to settle in this area while part of Roane County.

In 1807 Bledsoe was officially declared a county by the General Assembly. James was appointed one of the first county commissioners. In 1809, as a citizen of the county, James signed the petition "to provide some provisions for the citizens who had settled below the Indian boundary line and left their improvements."

James Standifer with Joseph Hoge and John Tollett were appointed to "fix the most suitable place for holding court until otherwise provided by law," for Bledsoe County.

In 1811 James Standifer and John Tollett were appointed to select a place for the county seat. In 1812 James Standifer was Captain in Volunteer Rifle Company 31st Regiment State Militia, Bledsoe County. He enlisted September 30, 1813 to serve in the War of 1812. He went from private to captain in November by order of General Cocke. He served three months and was paid $93.32 for his service as a private and captain and the use and risk of his horse. He was discharged at Washington, Rhea County, December 30, 1813. He reenlisted January 20, 1814 and was promoted to Lieutenant Colonel, serving under Colonel John Brown in the East Tennessee Volunteer Mounted Gunman.

James Standifer was a large land owner and slave holder. He served in the Tennessee Senate from 1815 to 1823, represented Bledsoe, Anderson, Rhea and Roane counties, and later other counties added to his district were Marion, Morgan, Hamilton and McMinn. He was elected to the 18th congress of the United States in 1823-

1825 and later to the 21st congress and four succeeding congresses serving from March 1829 to his death 1837. Congressman Standefer died Sunday morning August 20, 1837 at Kingston on his way to Washington. He had stopped at the residence of a good friend Colonel Joseph Byrd. The Masonic Lodge in Kingston took charge and buried the congressman in the Baptist Cemetery in Kingston. When the news of Congressman Standifer's death reached Washington, the Senate and House both passed resolutions unanimously to go into mourning for thirty days by wearing crape on the left arm.

James Standifer served in the local government, Bledsoe County, the state government Tennessee Senate; and the national government Congress. He was congressman while a Tennessean (Andrew Jackson) was in the White House. He was elected five times and served with other well known Tennesseans as John Bell, David Crockett, Cave Johnson, Andrew Johnson, James K. Polk, Sam Houston, Felix Grundy and Hugh Lawson White.

James Standifer was a farmer. In a letter August 1834 to James K. Polk from his home at Mt. Airy, he discussed the good condition of his crops before informing his friend on politial news. He was a military man, considered a typical and loyal Jacksonian Democrat.

Two issues led to Standifer's split with Jackson and the Democrat Party and his joining the rival Whig Party, the removal of the Cherokee Indians. At first Standifer stood with Jackson on almost all the great questions of the day. Congressman Standifer's 4th congressional district bordered the Cherokee nation, and he took understandable interest in Indian affairs. The presidential candidacy of Hugh Lawson White was another issue. Standifer opposed

Jackson's vice-president and "hand picked" successor, Martin Van Buren from New York.

James Standifer and Hugh Lawson White were long time friends and political allies. In fact, their families were friends. James White and William Standifer served together in the Militia and the War of 1812 from Tennessee.

True, Captain or Lieutenant Colonel, James Standefer was the chief instigator of the Presidential campaign of Hugh Lawson White in 1836. How great was Congressman Standifer's vote-getting strength in his home county?

In the 1832 election for president, Andrew Jackson, a Democrat, carried the county, 176 votes to Henry Clay a Whig, four votes. In 1836 election, Hugh Lawson White a Whig 223 votes, to Martin Van Buren the Democrat, 15 votes. The Whig candidate for President carried the votes in the county for the next four presidential elections.

James and Martha (Patsy) (Standifer) Standifer became the parents of six children. William I. Standifer born 1801 was about five years of age when his parents came to Sequatchie Valley. He received a good education having graduated from Blount College, Knoxville. He became a lawyer and moved from Bledsoe to Marion County and in 1837 moved to Hamilton County. He organized a company for service in the Cherokee War (Indian removal) of 1836. He knew the Indians needed protection, not the Tennesseans. He served as Brigadier General and stoutly resisted the Removal Treaty. He served in the Tennessee House, the 23rd and 24th General Assembly 1839-1834. He represented Hamilton and Marion counties. He served as Clerk and Master of the Chancery Court in Hamilton

County. He served as Captain in Company G, 2nd Tennessee Infantry in the Mexican War. He was mustered in service June 18, 1846. His unit landed at Vera Cruz and moved toward Mexico City and fought in the Battle of Mountain Pass, Cerro Gondo. He was mustered out at New Orleans May 25, 1847. Probably the most famous act in his military career was his part in the capture of James Andrew of Andrew's Raiders. The stealing of the locomotive "The General" on April 12, 1862, during the Civil War. One of the best collection of Cherokee Indian artifacts was collected by William Standifer from William Island, Tennessee River, Hamilton County and presented to the State of Tennessee.

Luke, the second son of James and Martha (Patsy) born November 3, 1810, was educated at West Point. After leaving there he and his father became interested in government lands in the delta and had business interest in Vicksburg and New Orleans. He was employed by Texas, Louisiana and Arkansas under the government to locate the lines between these three territories. Soon after the completion of this work he disappeared. It was thought by the family that he was killed by the Indians.

Jesse H. was born September 3, 1812, died 1865 in Missouri. Skelton Carroll was born April 12, 1815, married Nancy King, born ca. 1817 in Kentucky. Skelton Carroll was a soldier in the Mexican War. He lived in Bledsoe County and died August 8, 1904. James Madison was born October 6, 1817, married Katherine Melvine Boyd. She was born 1818 and died 1860 in Bledsoe County. Eliza Ann was born August 31, 1820. Martha (Patsy) Standefer died June 15, 1848.

Sources:

Membership Roster and Soldiers The Tennessee Society of the Daughters of American Revolution, Vol. 3, 1970-1984.

National Society Colonial Dames XVII Century Ancestor Roster, 1915-2005.

Tennesseans in the War of 1812, by Sistler.

Biographical Directory of the Tennessee General Assembly, Vol I, 1796-1861.

Compendium of Biography Cumberland Region of Tennessee, 1898.

The Tennessee Historical Quarterly, by Steven D. Byas, Summer 1991.

Revolutionary Pension Records of Benjamin Standifer.

Standefer (Standifer) 300 Years in American, by Harry Standefer, 3821 Chamoune, San Diego, California.

James Standifer Military Record, National Archives and Record Service, Washington D.C.

Family History, by Maxine Botelho, 114 Addax, San Antonio, Texas 78213.

Last Will and Testament of William Standifer, Registered, Marion County, Tennessee, October 23, 1828.

Standefer Family History and Genealogy, by Jim C. Standifer, 1812 Greenwell Drive, Knoxville, Tennessee 37939, 1998.

Collier Cemetery

STORY

Samuel L. Story born 1806 in Kentucky was in Bledsoe County in the early 1830s. He is listed in the 1830 Bledsoe census in the Pikeville area.

He was an early doctor in Pikeville, a large land owner and slave holder. He served as postmaster of Pikeville, a Trustee for Lafayette Academy and Circuit Court Clerk.

In August 1830 he purchaed from James A. Whitesides the "western half of Lot number 28 (facing the public square) for $25.00," where he built the first hotel in the valley, the Sequatchie Hotel. This hotel was very similar to Bridgman house on the eastern half of Lot 28.

In 1835 Samuel L. Story, Samuel McReynolds, and Isaac Stephens were appointed by the Tennessee General Assembly, "to divide the county in ten civil districts and designate a suitable place (near the center of each) for holding elections." This was for the purpose of electing two justice of peace and one constable for each district.

Samuel L. Story was on the Bledsoe County Tax List in 1837, 1838, 1839, in District VI. In the 1840 census, Euphemia P. Story and her four daughters were living in District VI, Pikeville.

Dr. Samuel L. Story married Euphemia P. Wheeler. They became the parents of: Mary Magdalen born August 15, 1828, married Bird Pankey March 20, 1845, Mary died March 3, 1904; Emily born August 20, 1830, married James S. Pankey September 16,

1850, Emily died January 23, 1870; Lavina born ca. 1835; Matilda born December 25, 1838, died October 2, 1911.

Dr. Story's death was reported in the *Republican Banner*, a Nashville newspaper. He died at the age of 33 on September 27, 1839.

James A. Tulloss was appointed guardian of Mary, Emily, Lavina and Matilda Story, infant children of Samuel Story.

Alexander H. Montgomery and Euphemia P. Story were administrators of Dr. Story's estate. Alexander H. Montgomery died before 1846. In April 1847, Bird Pankey was appointed to replace Alexander H. Montgomery. Euphemia P. (Wheeler) Story died November 1, 1845.

During the 1860s Mary M. Pankey and Emily Pankey, daughters of the late Dr. Story and both young widows, operated the Sequatchie (Story) Hotel. During the Civil War the hotel was taken over by the Union soldiers and much of the furnishing destroyed. Sometime later the family moved to their farm north of Pikeville.

Sources:

Bledsoe County census, 1830, 1840, 1850.

Registrar of Deed Office, Pikeville, Tennessee.

Bledsoe County, Tennessee, A History, by Elizabeth Robnett, 1993.

Compendium of Local Biography Cumberland Region of Tennessee, 1898.

The Pankey Family Bible, 1850.

STEPHENS/STEVENS

The name Stephens is found in the American colonies in the 1600s in Virginia, Maryland and North Carolina. They were land owners and civil servants. Several served in the American Revolution.

The Stephens were in Tennessee before Tennessee became a state in the counties of Greene, Washington and Sevier.

Isaac Stephens born February 26, 1782 in Montgomery County, was the son of Soloman and Milly (Britt) Stephens. Soloman served in the Virginia Militia, was wounded and died 1785.

Isaac Stephens married Anna Davis January 13, 1803 in Virginia. In 1805 Isaac Stephens was on the Tax List in Anderson County. By 1808 Isaac Stephens was in Bledsoe County.

In May 1803 Isaac Stephens claimed 214 acres of land by "right of improvement and occupancy lying in Sequatchie Valley on Sequachey Creek." He was Captain of Light Infantry Company 31st Regiment County Militia in July 1808. Isaac Stephens became an active and leading citizen of the county. A large land owner and slave holder. He served as a member of Bledsoe County Court for several years between 1818 and early 1820s, county commissioner, justice of peace. In February 1809 Isaac Stephens signed the petition asking for some provisions be made to those settlers who went below the Indian Boundary line before it was run and left their improvements and property. In 1815 Isaac Stephens signed the petition to delay the land laws until after the War of 1812. Several served in the War of 1812 from Tennessee both as officers and enlisted men.

The first person to represent Sequatchie Valley, Bledsoe County, that was a county resident, in the Tennessee General Assembly, was Isaac Stephens. He served in the House in the 10th 1813-1815, representing Bledsoe; in the 11th 1815-1817 representing Bledsoe, and in the 15th 1823-1825 representing Bledsoe and Marion Counties.

In 1836 Isaac Stephens was one of the three men in Bledsoe County that was appointed "to divide the county into Civil Districts, for the purpose of electing two Justice of Peace and a Constable in each district, and to designate a suitable place near the center of the district for holding elections."

This act was passed by the Tennessee General Assembly in December 1835. The county was divided into ten districts by Stephens, Samuel McReynolds and Samuel L. Story. The placed named for holding elections were: First District, John Stewart; Second District, Pleasant Gipson; Third District, Tolletts Mill; Fourth District, Thomas Swafford; Fifth District, Jonathan Dentons; Sixth District, Pikeville; Seventh District, Valentine Springs; Eight District, Isaac Roberson; Ninth District, Aaron Hughes; Tenth District, William Jewells.

Isaac Stephens died January 8, 1862 and was buried on his farm, the Stephens Cemetery. Isaac and Anna (Davis) Stephens became the parents of: Elizabeth born August 9, 1804, married Wesley Tollett October 12, 1823. Elizabeth and Wesley moved to Texas.
Wesley was slain by the Indians in 1836. She married Joel Wafer in 1838; William born January 1, 1807, married Martha E. Lewis

February 16, 1832, who was from Marion County. This family remained in Bledsoe County; Mark born December 8, 1808, married Elizabeth Charlotte Greer December 2, 1847. This family remained in Bledsoe County; James born August 1, 1810, married Isabella Hood Beaty June 28, 1831. She was born 1809 in Knox County. This family moved to Texas; Anna D. born December 24, 1813, married Samuel McReynolds October 8, 1844. Anna D. was Samuel's second wife. This family remained in the county; Hester Ann born March 18, 1816, married William Rainey Thurman January 5, 1837. This family remained in the valley; Sarah born March 18, 1818 married Ike Broyles. This family moved to White County.

Sources:

Biographical Directory Tennessee General Assembly, Vol. I, 1796-1861.

Tennessee Homesteaders and Landowners, Fourth Surveyors District, by Willis Hutcherson, 1964.

Record of Commissions of Officers, in the Tennessee Militia, 1796-1815.

Steph   ar y History, by Carolyn Stephen Beyer.

The last home of Hester Ann (Stephens) Thurman
1816-1871
Melvine Community

SWAFFORD/SWOFFORD/ SWAFFER

The Swaffords were in the colony of Pennsylvania in the 1600s. In the 1790 census Swaffords are in Delaware County, Pennsylvania, Greenville and Lauren counties, South Carolina.

In the 1800 census, John, Jacob, James, Aaron and Abraham are in Greenville County, Thomas and Moses are in Lauren County and James in the Pendleton District of South Carolina.

Sometime after 1800 the Swaffords of Greenville County, South Carolina began to move west. Eight Swafford brothers with Biblical names Jacob, Abraham, Aaron, Thomas, William, Isaac, Paul and John began their move.

By 1813 Swaffords were in Sequatchie Valley, Bledsoe County. Of the eight, four Jacob, Abraham, Aaron and Thomas settled in Bledsoe County. After the close of the War of 1812, with the Indians defeated, four new states, Alabama, Mississippi, Indiana and Illnois were admitted to the union. Also new counties in southeast Tennessee, McMinn, Marion, Bradley, Monroe and Hamilton were created.

By 1816 the Swaffords were on the move again. This large clan with their slaves moved to Monroe County, Mississippi. However, after several members of this family died in this Mississippi climate, the Swaffords returned to the valley in the early 1820s where they had first settled.

Jacob Swafford born ca. 1762 in South Carolina, married

Sarah Larkin born in 1772 in Virginia. In 1810 Jacob was in Wayne County, Kentucky. In 1814 he was in Tennessee. In the 1820 census Jacob and family were in Monroe County, Mississippi. By 1830 Jacob is in Bledsoe County.

Children of Jacob and Sarah Larkin: Alexander was born 1791 in South Carolina. He served as a private in the War of 1812. He enlisted November 13, 1814 in Captain Miles Vernon's Company of the East Tennessee Militia. He moved to Overton County after 1840.

Larkin Swafford was born ca. 1794 in South Carolina. He served as a private in the War of 1812. He enlisted in Matthew Cowan's Company, Third Regiment Tennessee Militia, November 18, 1814. He moved to Monroe County, Indiana after the war.

Peter J. Swafford born February 28, 1805 in South Carolina, married Rebecca Igou, born in 1807 in Kentucky. Peter J. became a large land owner in Bledsoe County. Peter J. and Rebecca Igou's children were Evander, John P. (Jack), Elizabeth Caroline, and Narcissa Emmaline. Rebecca died in 1872.

Peter J. married second, Tennessee Annie Torbett. They became the parents of Mary Jane, Charles Ross, James Barnett, Hulon, Hattie and Peter J. Jr.

Charles Swafford born ca. 1807 in South Carolina moved from Bledsoe County to Bradley County after 1850.

Richard Swafford born 1808 in South Carolina, married Malinda C. Swafford, daughter of Thomas Swafford. Malinda was born February 16, 1815 in Bledsoe County. Richard served as a private in Captain Shemwill Parham's Company during the Indian removal. He entered service July 1836 to serve six months. He was discharged at Pikeville January 1837. In 1852 Richard applied for Bounty Land for his service, while living in McMinn County. Richard died April 10, 1886. Malinda died May 16, 1888.

Jackson Swafford born 1812 in Tennessee moved to Overton County after 1850; Alfred Annison Swafford born 1814 in Tennessee moved to McMinn County before 1850; Thomas Swafford born 1816 in Tennessee moved to McMinn County after 1840; Jefferson Swafford born 1820 in Mississippi lived and died in Bledsoe County.

Abraham Swafford born October 10, 1772 in South Carolina, married Jane Howard, daughter of Peter Howard. In 1810 Abraham was in Wayne County, Kentucky. He was in Bledsoe County in 1813 when he enlisted October 13, 1813 at Madison (county seat of Bledsoe). He enlisted as a private in Colonel John Brown, East Tennessee Militia. He served to January 3, 1814. He signed the petition to delay the land laws 1815.

Children of Abraham and Jane (Howard) Swafford: Moses born ca. 1780 in South Carolina, married Sarah Swafford, a cousin, October 3, 1804 in South Carolina. Sarah was born in 1784. Moses enlisted September 13, 1814, a private in Captain James Tunnell's Company, East Tennessee Militia. He died in service November 24, 1814 at Fort Clayborn, Alabama. Sarah Swafford filed for pension in 1853 while living in Marion County.

William Swafford born ca. 1792 in South Carolina; Carolina Swafford born ca. 1794 in South Carolina; Julia Swafford born ca. 1796 in South Carolina, married James Glass moved to McMinn County before 1850. Ezekiel Swafford, born ca. 1798 in South Carolina, married Susan Underwood, moved to McMinn County after

1840.

Howard Swafford born ca. 1800 in South Carolina, married Nancy Narramore April 8, 1823 in Rhea County. Nancy was born September 30, 1795 in Tennessee. Howard and Nancy's children were: Andrew J., Major P., John M. (Beatty John), Martha Manery, Nancy J., George, Howard Jr., and Eliza A. Nancy died May 6, 1850. Howard married second Elizabeth Kelch, born 1822 in Tennessee. Their children were Patrick, Samuel F., Reuban B. and William. Howard and Elizabeth moved to Indiana after 1870.

Portman (one arm Port), youngest child of Abraham, born February 5, 1816 in Tennessee married Drucilla Keltner in 1837. She was born June 18, 1816 in Tennessee. They moved to McMinn County before 1850. Portman married second Arta M. Avens. He married third Adline Nichols. Portman died August 9, 1911.

Abraham and Jane died before 1850 and were buried at Swafford Chapel Cemetery.

By 1830 there were twelve Swafford heads of households in Bledsoe County, Jacob, Alexander, Nasson, Ezekiel, Charles, James, Elizabeth, Larkin, John, Thomas, Alfred and Salley.

In 1840 in Bledsoe County Civil Districts III, IV and V, this is northern Sequatchie Valley, there were twenty-seven Swaffords heads of households, Moses, John, James, Orrison, Thomas, William, James, Peter, Thomas Sr., John, Howard, Ezekiel, Alexander, Thomas Jr., Abraham, Portman, Alfred, Nasson, Charles, John, Peter J., Jacob, Aaron, John, John Jr., Elizabeth and Aaron N.

Aaron (Big Aaron) Swafford born ca. 1780 in South Carolina,

married Elizabeth Howard, daughter of Peter Howard and Sarah Portman. Aaron was in Bledsoe County in 1815. He signed the petition to delay the land laws during the War of 1812.

Children of Aaron and Elizabeth: Louhaney born February 15, 1800 in South Carolina, married Burrell Russell Lee; James (Stingy Jim) born 1806 in South Carolina, married Elizabeth Hall; Elizabeth born September 19, 1807 in South Carolina, married Robert Lee; Peter W. born 1808 in South Carolina moved to Bradley County after 1850; Aaron W. born 1812 in Tennessee, married second Elizabeth Shirley. Aaron moved to Ray County, Missouri; Thomas Swafford born 1813 in Tennessee, married Millie Hall born 1813 in Tennessee. They moved to Bradley County before 1850; Sarah born 1814 in Tennessee married Landon J. Sherley; John Calvin born ca. 1818 in Tennessee, married Mary Ellen Sherley. John Calvin moved to Miller County, Missouri after 1850. Aaron Swafford died 1824 in Bledsoe County. Elizabeth died before 1860 in Bledsoe County.

Thomas Swafford born March 10, 1783 in Greenville County, South Carolina, married Matilda Howard, daughter of Peter Howard of Greenville County. Matilda was born ca. 1785 in South Carolina.

Thomas was in Bledsoe County in 1815 as he was listed for jury duty. Sometime after 1815, Thomas and family moved to the Mississippi Territory. Matilda died before 1820 and the family returned to Bledsoe County. Thomas after returning to the valley began to buy land and slaves. By the 1850s Thomas was a large land owner and slave holder. Thomas and Matilda Howard became the parents of ten children.

Alfred Allen Swafford, oldest son of Thomas and Matilda Howard, born June 3, 1801 in South Carolina, married China

Segraves born July 7, 1801 in North Carolina. Alfred Allen and China became the parents of: Thomas A. born 1829, married Sarah Dorsey, daughter of Jeremiah Dorsey. This family moved to Lee County, Mississipii after 1860; Kizziah Swafford born 1829, married Evander "Van" M. Swafford, a cousin; Nancy Swafford born 1830, married Henry Close; Luray "Lou" Swafford born 1832, married Mr. Guinn, married second Samuel P. Worthington, her brother-in-law; Jane Swafford born 1834, married Hugh C. Roberts; Ollie (Olly) Swafford born 1836, married Mr. Conger; Elizabeth Ann (Betty) Swafford born 1837, married William K. Day, this family lived in Rhea County; China Swafford born 1838, married Mr. Braswell; Alfred K., A.K. Swafford born October 25, 1840, married Terasda Isabel Worthington, he served in the Confederate Army during the Civil War; Martha B. Swafford born October 7, 1843, married Samuel P. Worthington; John L. Swafford born February 1, 1846, married Evaline J. Billingsley, daughter of John Billingsley and Jane Hoodenpyle, John L. served in the Confederate Army during the Civil War; Eliza Roberson Swafford born June 15, 1848, married Lafayette "Fate" Gault/Gott; Alfred Allen Swafford married second Martha Jane Cooley who was born 1841 in Tennessee, they became the parents of Mary Tennessee Swafford born 1873, she married J.M. Brown and lived in Meigs County.

China Segraves Swafford died during the Civil War. Alfred Allen died November 11, 1880.

Nasson Swafford born ca. 1802 in South Carolina married Nancy Lee. Nasson and Nancy were in Mississippi in 1820, Monroe County. They were the parents of Thomas Nasson and Nathaniel C. Sometime after 1820, Nancy died in Mississippi. By 1830 Nasson had returned to Bledsoe County. Thomas Nasson married Mary Lee, a cousin, this family moved to Marshall County and later Texas.

Nathaniel C. married Seraphina J. Sloan, daughter of Thomas Sloan. This family moved to Ray County, Missouri.

Nasson Swafford married second Eliza A. Lucker, born in 1814 in South Carolina. They became the parents of Marshall, Sarah Carolina, Emaline, Eliza J., Louise, Alfred L. and John Rufus. Nasson died 1852 in Bledsoe County.

Nancy Swafford born ca. 1804 in South Carolina, the oldest daughter of Thomas and Matilda Howard, died in 1819 in Bledsoe County. Nancy was the first person to be buried in the Swafford Chapel Cemetery.

James Swafford, third son of Thomas and Matilda Howard, born 1805 in South Carolina, married Nancy Teeters. Nancy was born in 1810 in Virginia. James and Nancy lived in Bledsoe County. They were the parents of: Kizziah born 1834, married Squire Boom Freily; Sarah Jane born in 1835, married James Calvin Shirley; Thomas born 1837; Aaron born 1840; John born 1841, married Manerva J. Curtis, a cousin. John served in the Union Army during the Civil War. Samuel born 1844, married Kizziah Curtis, a cousin. Samuel served in the Confederate Army and later in the Union Army. James born ca. 1849, moved west after 1860; Minerva Jane born 1851, married Thomas C. Morgan August 17, 1867 in Rhea County; Mary Elizabeth born 1853, married Isaac Newton Shirley; James Swafford married second Mary (Polly) Spears.

Thomas Swafford Jr. (Thomas the younger), Thomas Y. fourth son of Thomas Sr. was born June 10, 1806 in South Carolina. He married Hannah Hankins, daughter of John Hankins and Mary Gallant. Hannah was born April 27, 1812 in Bledsoe County. Thomas Y. and Hannah became the parents of Mariah, Matilda,

Mary, William F., Nancy, Nasson, Samuel, Martha Jane, James, Thomas, Alfred Howard and China Ersaline.

John T. Swafford born February 9, 1809, married Elizabeth Segraves September 27, 1832. Elizabeth was born May 20, 1814 in North Carolina. This family moved to Hamilton County before 1850. Later they moved to Illinois. John T. and Elizabeth became the parents of James Ross, Thomas Carroll, John W., Elizabeth J., Alford M., Rebecca Ann, Joel Segraves, Rufus, Teresa and William R.

William Swafford born June 24, 1811 in Tennessee, married Eliza Jane Henson born September 7, 1820 in Tennessee. In 1850 they were living in Hamilton County. In 1860 they are in Bledsoe County. William and Eliza Jane became the parents of Elizabeth, William Byrd, Christianna, Matilda, Thomas, Nancy and Eliza Emmaline.

Aaron Swafford, the youngest son of Thomas and Matilda Howard, born 1813 in Tennessee, married Mariah Mills born in 1822 in North Carolina. Aaron and Mariah became the parents of James A., Nancy, Emma, Adaline, Isaac, Alfred, Rufus, Thomas L., John Calhoun and Perdette.

Malinda C., a twin, born February 16, 1815 in Tennessee, married Richard Swafford, a cousin, son of Jacob Swafford.

Lucinda, twin of Malinda, born February 16, 1815, married Hezekiah (KY) Curtis. He was born 1812 in Tennessee. They became the parents of: Manerva J. born March 29, 1845, married John Swafford, a cousin; Kizziah born 1846, married Samuel Swafford, a cousin; John born 1848 lived and died in Bledsoe County; Evander born ca. 1850, married Minerva Karnes, married second Matilda Mercer.

Fannie moved to Texas; Hezekiah Jr. married Miss Massey.

In 1853 Thomas Swafford deeded land for a church. The deed recorded, "I Thomas Swafford, for the love and affection that I have for the Methodist Church, I do bequeath and give to Samuel Swafford, Isaac E. Swafford and John Hale, as trustees and their successors in office a certain tract or parcel of land suppose to contain 3 acres for the use of Methodist Episcopal Church, on which there is a meeting house built, known by the name of Swafford Meeting House and Graveyard, bounded by Jonathan Clark line and Sequatchie Creek June 16, 1853."

Thomas Swafford Sr. married second Elizabeth Nichols born September 26, 1788 in North Carolina. Thomas Swafford Sr. and Elizabeth (Nichols) Swafford became the parents of: Samuel Swafford, a twin, born November 17, 1823, married Hester Ann Roberson born October 22, 1829, daughter of James Roberson and Sarah (Hutcheson) Roberson. Samuel married second Eliza Roberson, a sister of Hester Ann; Sarah Jane Swafford, a twin, born November 19, 1823 (two days after Samuel), married Jesse C. Brown, son of Reuban Brown; Isaac Easterly Swafford born February 6, 1827, married Martha Jane Roberson, born February 8, 1832, a sister to Hester Ann and Eliza; Frances Swafford born 1829, married Albert Loyd, married second Colonel William Stone. This family moved to Cedartown, Georgia.

Thomas Swafford made his will February 5, 1850. He died November 2, 1856. Elizabeth died January 14, 1879. They were buried in the Swafford Chapel Cemetery.

Sources:

Swafford, Swafford Families of America, by Ray C. Swafford, 1st Edition 1975.

Swaffords of Sequatchie Valley, by Ray C. Swafford, 2nd Edition 1978.

Census of Bledsoe County, 1830, 1840.

Swafford Chapel Cemetery

TERRY

The name Terry is found in the American colonies in the late 1600s and 1700s. Several served in the American Revolution from Virginia and North Carolina.

The Terrys were in Tennessee, Knox and Hawkins counties, before or by 1796. Samuel Terry was in Sequatchie Valley, Bledsoe County in 1808. Several Terrys served in the War of 1812 from Tennessee.

Samuel Terry born ca. 1780 served for several years as deputy clerk in the office of Register of Deeds under James Roberson, first registrar in 1808. He signed the petition in 1809 that would provide some provision for the citizens of the county who settled below the Indian Boundary line and "had left their improvements;" signed the petition for building a road (turnpike) from Aquilla Johnson's to Washington in Rhea County. He served as post master for the post office in Pikeville. Samuel Terry died before 1830. Sarah Terry born 1787 in Virginia, died 1850-1860.

Scott Terry born ca. 1803 in Tennessee was the son of Samuel and Sarah Terry. In Bledsoe County he became a very active and prominent citizen, a large land owner and a slave holder. He served as clerk of the Chancery Court and clerk of the County Court. He served as captain of a company mustered in the county for the Cherokee War, 1836 (Indian Removal).

In 1837-39 he served in the State House, General Assembly, represented Bledsoe County; in the Senate 23rd General Assembly represented Bledsoe, Hamilton, Rhea and Marion counties. He later served as State Superintendent of public instruction. He was member of first Lodge Vale Temple, organized in Pikeville in 1823.

Scott Terry was on the Bledsoe County Tax List 1837, 1838, 1839 in District VI. The 1840 census list Scott Terry in District VI.

In the spring of 1834, Gerold Troost, Tennessee state geologist was exploring Sequatchie Valley for coal and iron deposits. He was a guest at the Story Hotel when he met Scott Terry. With Scott Terry "Mr. Beatty and Mr. Stephens" guided the state geologist to a place "called the gulf; a large basin more than 100 feet deep in the Cumberland Plateau."

This was the first time the state became aware of the "jewel of the Cumberland Plateau."

During the period 1830-1840, Scott Terry built the beautiful two story house in Pikeville. This house was later sold to Judge Thomas N. Frazier.

During the Civil War, Scott Terry suffered heavy financially in slaves and fine blooded horses. John Terry, a slave of Scott Terry, was one of the "color servant" that went to war with the Tulloss Rangers. Many years later John drew a Confederate pension for this service. Scott Terry died 1870-1880.

Sources:

Bledsoe County census, 1830, 1840, 1850, 1860, 1870.

Bledsoe County, Tennessee, A History, by Elizabeth Robnett, 1993.

Tennesseans in the War of 1812, by Sistler, 1992.

Bledsoe County Registrar of Deeds office.

Biographical Directory of the Tennessee General Assembly, Vol. I, 1796-1861.

Home built by Scott Terry in the 1830s

*Later became the home of Judge Thomas N. Frazier
and Robert B. Schoolfield*

THURMAN/THURMOND

Thurmans were in Virginia in the 1600s. By the 1700s Thurmans were in North Carolina and later in South Carolina. Several served in the American Revolution. Several served in the War of 1812 from Tennessee.

Charles Thurman was born February 6, 1760 in Buckingham County, Virginia. He entered service of the United States, the Virginia Militia, under Captain Thomas Redd. He first was stationed at the Albermarle Barracks guarding prisoners. Charles a private, was a great "marcher". "He marched from Buckingham County to Petersburg; from Petersburg to Hillsboro, North Carolina; from Hillsboro to Salisburg, South Carolina; marched back from Salisburg and fell in behind General Morgan who had prisoners taken at Kings Mountains; marched to Dan River; stationed between Morgan and Cornwallis, who was on opposite side of Dan River; marched after Cornwallis to Hillsboro and the Battle of Guilford Courthouse, and to the seige of Yorktown."

Private Thurman was at the surrender of Yorktown. He saw Cornwallis deliver his sword to the American officer October 19, 1781. After the surrender at Yorktown, he marched to Winchester under Captain Cunningham. He was discharged November 7, 1781. He served a total of one year and nine months.

Charles Thurman married Barbara Picknell July 29, 1790 in Lee County, Virginia. Barbara was born ca. 1765.

After the war, Charles moved from Buckingham County to Washington County in southwest Virginia. He was living in

Washington County in 1810 near the Kings Salt works. Sometime after 1814, Charles Thurman's family was in Tennessee, Bledsoe County. With Charles and Barbara and their children, was Nathaniel Evitt, step-father of Charles.

On August 15, 1832, while living in Bledsoe County, at the age of 72, Charles Thurman filed for a pension for his services during the Revolution. He gave as references, William Brown, deputy sheriff; Joseph McDowell and William Hall, Justices of Peace; and his step-father Nathaniel Evitt. Charles Thurman was placed on the pension roll May 29, 1833, his annual allowance was $70.00. He died December 16, 1848, Barbara died December 14, 1849. Barbara did not draw a widow's pension. Both are said to be buried at Lone Cedar Cemetery, near their home.

The 1830 Bledsoe census gives John and William Thurman as heads of households. The Bledsoe Tax list 1837, 1838 and 1839 in District III and IV are Charles Sr. and William, Henry and Charles Jr. The 1840 Bledsoe census gives Charles, John, William, Henry, Fredrick, and Charles Jr. living in District III and IV.

Charles Thurman and his sons, Fredrick, Henry, John and William, received from the state over 1,000 acres of land between 1832 and 1849. In 1850 Fredrick, John, William and Margaret lived on Walden Ridge in Eastern Bledsoe County.

Charles and Barbara (Picknell) Thurman became the parents of nine children: Mary Ann born ca. 1791 in Virginia, died before 1855; Thomas born ca. 1794 in Virginia, died before 1855; William born 1797 in Virginia, married Margaret, died 1860-1870, Margaret was born 1802 in Tennessee, she died 1860-1870.

William and Margaret's children were: Rebecca, Evander, Mary, Charles, William Jr., Henry, Susan and John.

John born August 6, 1800 in Virginia, married Chleoa (Clary) Rector born ca. 1799 in Virginia. John was killed by "bushwackers" during Civil War 1864 in Bledsoe County. Chleoa died 1871 in Texas.

John and Chleoa (Rector) Thurman's children were Rebecca Jane, Nancy, Eliza, John, Owen, Nail, Mary, Jesse T., Elizabeth, Phoebe and Martin.

Fredrick, Fred, born 1804 in Virginia, married Jane Carnahan born ca. 1804 in South Carolina. Fredrick died 1870-1880. They became the parents of James, Jane, John, Mary, Charles and Tabitha.

Elizabeth born ca. 1806 in Virginia, married Alexander H. Carnahan, son of William Carnahan, a brother of Jane who married Elizabeth's brother Fredrick. Elizabeth and Alexander became the parents of Alexander Jr., Sarah Elizabeth, Charles, Nancy Jane, Mary (Polly), Margaret (Peggy), Ruth and John.

Henry born 1808 in Virginia, married Matilda. She was born ca. 1811 in Tennessee. They became the parents of Minerva, Eliza A., Samuel A., John W., William H., Margaret E., Marlin M., Benjamin F. and Elizabeth C. This family moved from Bledsoe to Rhea County between 1840-1850.

Charles Jr., born ca. 1812 in Virginia, was listed on the Bledsoe Tax List in the late 1830s and the 1840 census in District IV.

Margaret born 1814 in Virginia, never married, living alone

in 1850. In 1860 she was listed in the household of William Thurman Jr., her nephew.

By 1870 the only son of the Revolutionary war soldier living on Walden Ridge was Fredrick and his wife living in District X.

Sources:

Charles Thurman's pension application.

Bledsoe County Census, 1830, 1840, 1850.

Family Information.

Descendants of William Carnahan, by Barry W. Carnahan, B.V. Carnahan, Mt. Juliet, Tennessee.

Phillip Thurman, one of the six sons of Benjamin Thurman, was born November 15, 1757 in North Carolina. He enlisted for service in the Revolutionary War in 1775 and "fought with troops from the Cheraw District, South Carolina. In 1780 he enlisted and was at the siege of Augusta. After being discharged in the fall of 1781, he returned to the Cheraw District and re-enlisted and served until he was discharged November 15, 1782."

Phillip Thurman married Kesiah Sawyer, July 7, 1783, in Anson County, North Carolina. Kesiah was born in 1765.

Sometime after 1800 the Thurman family moved to Smith County, Tennessee (formed in 1799), and later to Anderson County (formed in 1801). By 1806 the Thurmans were in Sequatchie Valley.

Phillip Thurman built a two-story log house in a little frontier village that had grown up on the west side of the Sequatchie River on a high plateau, near a large spring. As the seat of Justice for the new county, Bledsoe, Madison, was located some fifteen or more miles south near the Indian Boundary line, court was often held in Thurman's log house.

Johnson Parham enlisted in September 1814 for service in the War of 1812 for a period of six months. He gave his place of enlistment as Thurman's in Bledsoe County.

Children of Phillip Thurman and Kesiah Thurman were: Eli, oldest son, born April 22, 1784 in South Carolina, married Sarah Rainey, daughter of William Rainey. They became the parents of William Rainey, Nancy, James A., Asahel Rawlings, Elizabeth T. and Stephen Decatur. Eli became a large land owner, an influential citizen of the county, serving as sheriff, a commissioner for the town of Pikeville in 1816. He was one of the early purchasers of the new county seat (Pikeville) Lot Number 12 and half of Lot Number 13.

In 1808 Eli was Captain of the 31st Regiment of the Bledsoe Militia. He signed the Petition of Delay the Land Laws during the War of 1812. He signed the Petition in 1809 asking for some provisions be made for those citizens who settled below the Indian Boundary line and left their improvements. Eli died March 10, 1842 in Bledsoe County and Sarah died June 1859.

James, born 1786 in South Carolina, married Mrs. Elizabeth (McNair) Anderson in 1816. He died in 1818. Easter (a twin) born June 25, 1788 in South Carolina, married in 1810 Asahel Rawlings. She died August 17, 1816. Sarah born March 24, 1790 in South Carolina, married Elisha Rogers in 1809, Sarah died April 8, 1862. Mary born March 17, 1792 in South Carolina, married George Sawyer in 1809. Mary died May 30, 1849. Ephraim born January 16, 1797 in South Carolina, married Rosannah Rogers, a sister to Elisha Rogers in 1817. They moved to Walker County, Georgia. Stephen born ca. 1799 in South Carolina, married Betty Rogers. This family moved to Hamilton County. Elijah (a twin) born February 27, 1805 in Anderson County, married Minerva Rice. He moved to Hamilton County before 1836. Susannah (a twin) born February 27, 1805 in Anderson County, married Rev. John Bradfield. She died January 5, 1887 in Arkansas. John born in Bledsoe County in 1808, married Letty Lamb, daughter of Alexander Lamb. In 1849 this family joined a wagon train to travel overland to "promise land" California. Enroute Lettie died.

Phillip Thurman applied for pension in 1832 for his services in the Revolution. The Rev. John Dalton, James Standifer, John Bridgman a merchant, Elisha Kirklen and James A. Whitesides certify to Phillip's high character. His annual pension was listed as $78.31. Phillip died September 2, 1840, Kesiah died in 1845.

Sources:

Leaves From The Family Tree, by Penelope J. Allen.

Chattanooga Sunday Times, magazine section, August 16, 1936.

Membership Roster and Soldiers, Tennessee Society of Daughters of the American Revolution, Vol. III.

Pension Records, Revolutionary War, Washington, D.C.

Thurman Genealogy, Joe Cole, P.O. Box 190, Mineral Springs, North Carolina 28108.

TOLLETT

John Tollett born ca. 1757 in Augusta County, Virginia was the son of Mark Tollett who lost his life during the French and Indian War. John Tollett was a soldier in the war for American Independence. He was listed in Captain Patton's Company in March 1781.

John Tollett became a land owner early in his life. By 1782 John owned land in Montgomery County. He married ca. 1784, Margaret Brown, daughter of Abraham Brown, born 1762 in Augusta County, Virginia.

The John Tollett family was in Elbert County, Georgia in 1786. There he purchased 600 acres of land. While there John helped to organize a Methodist Church and was listed as a trustee in 1788. However, by 1790 John was selling his land. The Tollett family moved back to Montgomery County. By 1793 this family moved to southwest Virginia, Tazewell County.

Sometime in the early 1800s John Tollett began his move southwest to the new state of Tennessee. By 1805 John Tollett and family were in northern Sequatchie Valley which was in Roane County at that time. John Tollett had some experience in local government in Virginia. He was appointed one of the first Bledsoe County Commissioners in 1807. In 1811 he was appointed on the committee to select a suitable place for the new county seat.

In each new county John Tollett purchased land and became active in establishing a church. The Tollett family while in Bledsoe County between 1809 and 1826, received land grants from the state which totaled more than 1,700 acres.

In early 1800 near the head of the Sequatchie Valley "a small group of early settlers met in the home of John Tollett with the Rev. James Axley." William Witten and John Tollett were neighbors in Tazewell County, Virginia. The Wittens were staunch Methodists, had established the Methodist religion in Virginia. Again they are neighbors in Sequatchie Valley. "The need for religion had emerged on the frontier." The Tolletts and Wittens "laid the foundation of Methodism in that area." Out of this came the Stony Point Camp Grounds and Stony Point South Methodist Church and the North Methodist Church.

After the War of 1812, the Tolletts were moving again, this time across the Mississippi. In March 1819 John Tollett and Margaret, their sons Elijah, Westly, David, and Henry, Margaret's brother, Cornelius Brown and his family, the Tollett and Brown slaves, a total of twenty-six, left Knoxville. They traveled by boat on the Tennessee, Ohio, Mississippi and Red Rivers to the Arkansas Territory. After a trip of 100 days, they reached their destination in July. They settled in Hempstead County, where John became a Methodist Episcopal minister.

John Tollett Sr. died October 24, 1824 in Miller County, Arkansas. Sometime after John's death and before the Texas Revolution in 1836, Margaret (Brown) Tollett and sons Westly and Elijah moved to Texas. Margaret died sometime after May 1844 in Texas.

John and Margaret (Brown) Tollett became the parents of seven children:

Mark born 1786 in Elbert County, Georgia was the oldest son. At an early age the family moved to Tazewell County, Virginia. At the age of seventeen he was listed in the county militia. Mark married Elizabeth Witten, born 1791, the daughter of William and Letitia (Laird) Witten in 1806 in Roane County. Mark was in Bledsoe County in 1808 as a sworn chain carrier. Mark signed the petition to delay the land laws during the War of 1812. Mark also was a surveyor in the Fourth District of East Tennessee. Mark and Elizabeth (Witten) Tollett's children were Elijah W., Nancy and Elizabeth. Mark and Elizabeth were divorced in 1816. Mark married second Cynthia R. Hooper born 1801. They moved to Marion County as they were listed in the 1830 census, as his son Elijah W. was also listed as head of a household.

Mark and Cynthia (Hooper) Tollett became the parents of Daniel T., Ennis, John, Margaret, Sarah and Wesley. While in Marion County Mark received two land grants from the state; in 1826 for 140 acres and another for 150 acres. Sometime after 1830, Mark was making his last move. This time to Arkansas. He died in the Arkansas Territory in 1834. After Mark's death, Cynthia (Hooper) Tollett married the Rev. Samuel Ellis Pearce. This family was in Sevier County, Arkansas in 1850.

David was born 1788 in Elbert County, Georgia. He moved with his family to Montgomery County, Virginia, later to Tazewell County and to Tennessee, Roane County. In March 1808 David was a sworn chain carrier in Bledsoe County. In 1815 he signed the petition in Bledsoe County to delay the land laws during the War of 1812. He was a surveyor in the Fourth District of East Tennessee. David married Rebecca Parks, born 1792. They became the parents of John, Henry, Cornelius Brown, Anna, Margaret, Rebecca Parks, and William H. Rebecca (Parks) Tollett died 1826. David married

Julia Brown born 1805, his first cousin.

David and Julia became the parents of John, James Roland, Ellen Jane, Elijah, Mary, Eliza Johnson, Daniel Witten, Mayberry, Sarah P., Augustus Brown, and Agnes Rowland. David, with his family, moved to Arkansas where he became a large land owner. David died in 1852 near the town of Tollett, Arkansas. Julia died in 1855.

Margaret Tollett, born 1789 in Elbert County, Georgia, moved with her family to Virginia, Tazewell County. Later Margaret moved again with her family to Tennessee. By 1805 the Tolletts were in Roane County, in the northern Sequatchie Valley. In 1817 Margaret married William B. Wilson, born 1782, the son of Greenbury Wilson. The Tolletts and Wilsons were neighbors. Later this family moved to Morgan County, Alabama. About 1835 the Wilsons moved to Texas. The children of William and Margaret were all born in Alabama, except the youngest, who was born in Mississippi on their move to Texas. Their children were Temperance, Samuel, Clara, Margaret, Greenbury, John, Thomas Benton and Nancy. William B. Wilson died 1846 in Milan County, Texas.

John Tollett Jr., born October 2, 1790 in Montgomery County, Virginia was in Tennessee, Roane County in early 1800. In 1808 he married Nancy Wilson, born 1786 in North Carolina, daughter of Greenbury Wilson. John signed the petition of 1815 to delay the land laws during the War of 1812.

John Tollett, Jr. became a large land owner, merchant and operated a mill on the Sequatchie River. His place was designated as a voting place in the Third Civil District of Bledsoe County in 1836. This place Tollett Mill and store was an early land mark during the

1800s. A post office was later established. John Jr. was the only son of John Sr. to remain in Bledsoe County. Nancy (Wilson) Tollett died October 29, 1842. John Tollett Jr. was killed and robbed at his home during the Civil War, May 1, 1863. He and Nancy were both buried in the Tollett Cemetery.

John and Nancy (Wilson) Tollett's children: Carrie born 1810, married Robert Frazier; Henry B. born 1812, married Jane McGregor; Greenbury Wilson born 1814; Margaret born 1816, married Josiah Patton; Mary (Polly) born 1818, married John D. Morris; John Jackson born 1820, married Harriet Byrd, second Elizabeth Nail, died 1862; Elizabeth born 1823, married Clayborne Devenport, died 1903; Wesley born 1824; William S. born 1824, died 1860; Elijah G. born 1827, married Nancy Sherrill, died 1905; Nancy Ann born 1829, married John E. Young, died 1875; Sarah Letitia born 1833, married Thomas Ford, married second Charles Sherrill.

Henry was born in Tazewell County, Virginia in 1793. He was a young boy when his parents moved to Tennessee. This family lived in Roane County, the part that was in Sequatchie Valley. He was a surveyor for the Fourth District, East Tennessee. While living in Bledsoe County during the War of 1812 he served as a private in Captain Miles Vernon East Tennessee Militia. He was also listed in 1815 as a Captain in the 31st Regiment Bledsoe Militia.

Henry moved with his parents to the Arkansas Territory in 1819. Henry married Elizabeth Brown, born 1795, his first cousin. They became the parents of William Jefferson, Roland Carol, Lucinda Catherine, Margaret Jane, Ferdinand Galatin, Edward Franklin, and Harriet Louise. Henry died in 1871 in Washington County, Arkansas. Elizabeth (Brown) Tollett died in 1885.

Wesley/Westly born 1797 in Tazewell County, Virginia, moved with his parents John and Margaret (Brown) Tollett to Tennessee. In the early 1800s Wesley was living in northern Sequatchie Valley, Bledsoe County. Wesley married Elizabeth Stephens in Bledsoe County in 1823. He had moved to Arkansas with his family in 1819, but returned to marry Isaac and Anna (Davis) Stephens' daughter. Elizabeth was born 1804 in Montgomery County, Virginia. The Tolletts and Stephens had been neighbors in Montgomery County and again in Bledsoe County. Wesley and Elizabeth moved west, first to Arkansas and later sometime before 1836 to Texas.

Wesley saw service in the Texan Revolution under the service of General Sam Houston. He was a member of the Texas Rangers. For his service in the fight for Texas Independence, Wesley received a large acreage of land. Wesley and Elizabeth became the parents of Anna S., Margaret, Lucinda, Letitia, Sarah, Elizabeth and Hester Ann. In July 1838 Wesley was killed by Indians in the Red River County. Elizabeth, the widow of Wesley, married second Joel Wafer. The Wafer children were Mabry W., Sicily and Thomas Ed. Elizabeth (Stephens) Tollett Wafer died in 1862 in Wood County, Texas.

Elijah was born 1808 in Bledsoe County, the only child of John and Margaret Brown to be born in Tennessee. Elijah moved with his parents to the Arkansas Territory in 1819. Elijah settled near Ozark, Arkansas and married Jane Lynch in 1836. They became the parents of John born 1838. Elijah married second Rebecca Lynch, a sister of Jane. They became the parents of Margaret born 1844. Elijah married his third wife Mary Autry. They became the parents of America, Mary, Mordecai and Calvin B. From about 1839 to his death in 1853, Elijah lived and owned land in Sevier County, Arkansas. Mary (Autry) Tollett married second James W. Falkner.

John Tollet Sr. died October 26, 1824 in Miller County, Arkansas. Margaret (Brown) Tollett died in Texas in 1844.

Sources:

Tollett Cemetery.

Texas Trails of Our Tollett Family, by Mary Louise Donnely, 1994.

Bledsoe County United States Census, 1830, 1840, 1850.

Marion County United States Census, 1830.

Tennessee Land Grants Vol. II, Barbara, Byron and Samuel Sistler, 1998.

Tennesseans in the War of 1812, Sistler, 1993.

Manuscript of William M. Dickey, by Great Grandson of Thomas Witten, 1880.

Tennessee Homesteaders and Landowners, Fourth Surveyors District, by Willis Hutcherson, 1964.

Tollett Cemetery

TULLOS/TULLOSS

The Tullos/Tulloss name is found in the colonies of Virginia and North Carolina in the early 1700s.

James A. Tulloss was born in Virginia April 26, 1809, the son of Joshua and Ursula (Allen) Tulloss. Both parents were born in Virginia. He came to Bledsoe in the late 1820s. By 1837 he was on the tax list in District VI. He married Martha A. Loyd in 1845. She was born May 24, 1824 and died January 9, 1849.

James A. became a leading citizen in the county. He was a large land owner, slave holder, merchant and live stock dealer. He served as a trustee of the Methodist Church, member of the St. Elmo Lodge, County Court Clerk, and Postmaster. James A. was a Democrat and voted for Martin Van Buren in 1836.

John M. Bridgman organized a company of Confederate soldiers at Pikeville May 1861. "This Cavalry company became known as the Tulloss Rangers, as a compliment to James A. Tulloss for his 'liberal aid in money and other respects.' This company was 'handsomely uniformed' at the expense of some fifteen hundred dollars. The company went to war in southern style as they had seven colored servants, one being John Terry, a slave of Scott Terry."

Tradition was, Tulloss left his plantation in the care of an overseer and "went south". December 1863, after the victory at Chattanooga, as one soldier wrote, "our work was lighter our thoughts turned to pleasure and a party was given December 14th by some of our officers at Squire Tullos' house. A call was made on some lady in the neighborhood, no letter of introduction being necessary, and the invitation given was always accepted. The soldier always offered a horse to ride, as the lady's horse had generally been stolen, the music was furnished by two colored men, who accompanied by violin with singing. About 11:00 o'clock came supper, ham, chicken, wild turkey, venison, and pure coffee - then on again with dance, toward daylight - the party brok up - the girls were taken to their homes and we went to camp."

James A. was known as a "rich merchant". He lived about two miles north of Pikeville in a large two story colonial home that he had built for his wife.

In 1880 he was age 70 and listed as a retired merchant living in the boarding house of Mrs. Mary Panter.

James A. Tulloss died in Rhea County July 27, 1900 and was buried in an unmarked grave beside his wife in the Pikeville City Cemetery.

Sources:

Leaves From The Family Tree, by The Rev. Silas E. Lucas, Jr., 1982.

Bledsoe County, Tennessee, A History, by Elizabeth Parham Robnett, 1993.

History of Tennessee, Illustrated, East Tennessee Edition, The Goodspeed Publishing Company, 1887.

WALKER

The name Walker is found in the American colonies in the 1600s, as land owners and public officials in Virginia, Delaware and North Carolina. Several served in the American Revolution.

Walkers were in Tennessee before Tennessee became a state in Knox, Jefferson and Greene counties. Several served in the War of 1812 from Tennessee.

George Walker born November 20, 1745 in Fanquier County, Virginia, married Eleanor Hicks in 1767 in Rowan County, North Carolina. She was born June 1, 1752. George enlisted in the North Carolina Militia in Burk County, Salisbury District in 1767. He was in the Battle of Ramsour's Mill. He served as Lieutenant and was later promoted to Captain in July 1779. He served under Colonel Joseph McDowell. Captain Walker was discharged February 16, 1782.

By late 1700s, the Walker Family was in Knox County, Tennessee. This family was in Bledsoe County in 1807. In 1832 George Walker applied for pension while living in Bledsoe County for his services during the Revolution. He reported he fought against the "Indians and Tories."

James Standifer, Congressman, James A. Whitesides, lawyer and John Bridgman, merchant certify to Captain Walker's high character. His annual allowance was $230.00. William his youngest son, was appointed administrator of his estate.

The 1830 Bledsoe census gives George Walker and Eleanor

ages 80 to 90, also son Ephraim is listed. The 1840 census lists William, Ephraim and Jesse as heads of households living in District VIII.

George and Eleanor (Hicks) Walker became the parents of ten children: Dicey born July 21, 1768, married Rezin Howard, they lived and died in Bledsoe County; Jesse born December 28, 1770. He was serving as Justice of Peace in Bledsoe County in 1832; Ephraim born January 15, 1774, married Mary Beauchamp, this family later moved to Mississippi; Elizabeth born June 18, 1776, married William Reed. They lived in North Carolina; Bathsheba born April 13, 1779, married James Hope, this family lived in Knox County; Buckner born Janury 21, 1782, married Peggy McCain, they lived in Roane County; Sarah born January 18, 1784, married William Matlock Jr., this family moved to Monroe County, Indiana; Charlotte born March 16, 1786, married Benjamin Cherry. She died in Franklin County ca. 1840; George Jr. born November 16, 1789, died before 1833; William born November 16, 1791, married Rachel Edens January 20, 1814. Rachel was born January 28, 1798 in South Carolina.

William served in the War of 1812. He was a private in Captain Steward Company, Colonel William Johnson's 3rd Regiment East Tennessee. He enlisted September 20, 1814 and was discharged May 3, 1815. William Walker died June 26, 1868. Rachel died May 2, 1864, both were buried in the Walker-Howard Cemetery.

William and Rachel became the parents of: James born December 18, 1814, married Mary Rebecca Billingsley; Jeremiah born February 21, 1816, married Sarah A. McKinney. He served in Captain Scott Terry Company in the Cherokee War 1836; Polly born March 26, 1819, married Thomas J. Rogers; Eleanor born July 29, 1821, married Nicholas Owens; Delilah born June 11, 1823, married

Jacob Keedy; Sarah born March 22, 1825, married James M. Rogers, married second Doc. Smith; Jefferson born August 27, 1827, married Martha E. Lasater, married second Jane Laster; Nancy born July 18, 1829, married Crispen E. Shelton; William J. born January 22, 1832. William died October 18, 1863, Rutherford County; Matilda Jane born June 1834, married William McKinney Hixson.

Sources:

First Families of Tennessee, East Tennessee Historical Society, 2005.

National Society Colonial Dames XVII Century Ancestor Roster, 1915-2005.

Membership Roster and Soldiers The Tennessee Society of the Daughters of the American Revolution, Vol. III, Vol. IV.

Some Descendants of Captain George Walker 1745-1833, by G. Ralph Bowman, 1978.

Soldiers of the War of 1812 Buried in Tennessee, by Mary H. McCown, Inez E. Burns.

Walker-Howard Cemetery

WHITESIDE

Jonathan Whiteside born April 3, 1776 in Burke County, North Carolina, married July 19, 1796 Thankful Anderson in Madison County, Kentucky. Thankful, the daughter of James Anderson, was born February 7, 1775 in Virginia. By 1813 the Whiteside family was in Tennessee, Overton County. By the 1820s the Whiteside family is in Bledsoe County, Pikeville. Several Whitesides served in the War of 1812 from Tennessee.

Jonathan Whiteside was chairman of the Bledsoe County Court in the late 1840s. The Whitesides were living in the "new incorporated" town of Pikeville in 1830. Jonathan and sons, James A. and William B., were on the Bledsoe County Tax List in the late 1830s, District VI. The 1840 Bledsoe Census gives the Whitesides in District VI.

Jonathan and Thankful (Anderson) Whiteside became the parents of: Lydia born August 5, 1797, died 1815; Elizabeth born September 5, 1799, married Dr. Robert Cox, she died in 1834 in Sparta, White County; Robert Henry born October 31, 1801 (a twin) married Letha Hanna. He moved to Missouri after 1840; Sally Hall born October 31, 1801 (a twin) married Vincent B. Tate, married second Jalez G. Mitchell, lived in White County.

James Anderson Whiteside, second son of Jonathan and Thankful (Anderson) Whiteside was born September 1, 1803 in Pulaski County, Kentucky. He married February 5, 1829, Mary Jane Massengale of Grainger County. She was born May 17, 1812 and died April 12, 1843 in Knox County. They became the parents of John, Penelope, Anderson, Foster and Thankful A. James A. married second Harriet L. Straw, February 1, 1844 in Chattanooga. Harriet was born May 5, 1824. They became the parents of James L., Florence, Helen, Ann Newell, Vernon, Hugh, William M., Charles and Glenn.

While living in Bledsoe County, Pikeville, James A. Whiteside became a well-known lawyer. He was admitted to the bar in 1826. He became a large land owner, a business man, a politician and a state law maker.

He purchased Lot Number 38 in the town of Pikeville in 1829 from the town commissioners John Bridgman, Elisha Kirkland, Kingsley Smith and Aaron Schoolfield. On this lot he built a brick house. The house was described as "an elegant two story brick of southern colonial style of architecture with a center hall and sunburst windows on the front door." The bricks were molded by hand by slaves. It is tradition that the house was used as a hospital by the Union soldiers during their stay in Pikeville, while other homes of Confederate families were used for entertainment by the soliders. He also purchased lot numbers 49 and 50. These lots were used as his stables. He owned lots number 17 and 18 where his cotton gin was located.

James A. Whiteside served in the House in the 21st General Assembly 1835-1837, representing Bledsoe County. He served in Senate 22nd General Assembly 1837-1839, representing Bledsoe, Hamilton, Marion and Rhea counties. He later served again in the House 26th and 27th General Assembly, representing Hamilton County, 1845-1849. In 1836 James A. Whiteside was a presidential elector on the ticket of Hugh Lawson White, Whig candidate for president.

Seeing the potentials of Ross Landing in Hamilton County he sold his property in Bledsoe County and moved to Hamilton County in ca. 1838. Again, as in Bledsoe County he became a leading citizen and business man in Hamilton County. He died November 12, 1861.

William Bolen, third son of Jonathan and Thankful Whiteside, born October 22, 1806, married Nancy Thurman, daughter of Eli Thurman, married second Narcissa F. (Massengale) Bridgman, a sister to his brother James's wife. William Bolen became a well-known doctor in Bledsoe and Hamilton counties. Anderson D. born June 16, 1808 died 1857, Jacob Sandusky born November 22, 1811 died in infancy, Jacob Sandusky II born September 6, 1813 died in infancy. Almire Tennessee Whiteside, the youngest child of Jonathan and Thankful Anderson Whiteside was born April 9, 1816. She married Samuel Billingsley of Bledsoe County. They became the parents of Anderson and Martha Billingsley, married second Wiley Merriman, they became the parents of Jonathan, Harriet, Kitty and Lydia Merriman.

In 1848 Jonathan and Thankful (Anderson) Whiteside moved to Hamilton County. Jonathan died October 1860 and Thankful died 1859.

Sources:

Leaves From The Family Tree, by Penelope Johnson Allen, 1933.

A History of Bledsoe County, Tennessee, by Elizabeth P. Robnett, 1807-1957.

Biographical Directory of the Tennessee General Assembly, Vol. I, 1796-1861.

Bledsoe County, Tennessee, A History, by Elizabeth P. Robnett, 1993.

Register of Deed Office, Pikeville, Tennessee.

WILSON/WILLSON

The name Wilson/Willson is found in the New England colonies in the 1600s and also in the Middle and Southern colonies.

The Wilsons were land owners, some were "original land" owners, millers, civil servants, some served in the military and some came as "transportees".

Several served in the American Revolution. Several served in the War of 1812 from Tennessee.

Greenbury/Greenberry Wilson, a land owner, was living in Burk County, North Carolina in 1778. That same year he was a juror in the same county. Greenbury born 1750-55, was the son of William Wilson of Baltimore County, Maryland, who made his will in 1785.

Greenbury lived in North Carolina during the Revolutionary War. He rendered patriotic service to the colonies. He was paid vouchers for supplies in June 1783, August 1783 and September 1783, by the Board of Auditors Morgan District, North Carolina.

Greenbury was listed in the First United States Census 1790. He was in Burk County, Morgan District, North Carolina. The census shows one male over 16, one male under 16, four females and three slaves.

Greenbury married Temperance Bradshaw sometime before 1780. Temperance was born 1750-55, the daughter of Charles Bradshaw.

Greenbury was still in North Carolina in December 1796. The well-known traveler, Richard G. Waterhouse recorded in his diary, "left Morganton to accompany Tillman Walton twelve miles up Catawba to his plantation, crossed Silver Creek and Catawba River; thence to Greenberry Wilson, with whom we dined."

By 1800 Greenbury and family were in Tennessee. In 1805 Greenbury and son William were on the Tax List of Roane County. As early as 1807, Greenbury was living at the head of Sequatchie Valley in Bledsoe County.

In 1810 Greenbury made his will. He named his sons as "William, Green Jr., and Charles; his wife Tempy, and daughters Sally, Betsy, Nancy, Kary, and Polly." His estate "land on both sides of Sequacha Creek, mill shole, horses, cattle, hogs, sheep, Negro slaves." William was the administrator of his father's estate. Andrew and Samuel Lowe, neighbors, were witnesses.

By September 1812 Greenbury was dead. He was buried on a hill, Wilson Cemetery, overlooking his home on Wilson Branch. Temperance died after 1830 and before 1840.

Greenbury and Temperance (Bradshaw) Wilson became the parents of Sarah (Sally) born January 30, 1780 in North Carolina, married Samuel Oxsheer/Oxier; William B. born 1782 in North Carolina, married Margaret Tollett; Nancy born May 12, 1786 in North Carolina, married John Tollett; Betsy born ca. 1788 in North Carolina, died before 1830; (names in her father's will of 1810); Greenbury Jr. born 1790 in North Carolina, married Mary Bradshaw; Carrie (Kary) born February 20, 1794 in North Carolina, married Jesse Brown; Mary (Polly) born July 3, 1796 in North Carolina, married Elly Ormes Jr.

Greenbury Wilson Jr. married Mary Bradshaw March 9, 1820, of Adair County, Kentucky. He enlisted at Ross Landing as a private, September 1814 to serve in the East Tennessee Militia during the War of 1812. His Captain was James Tunnell. He was discharged at Knoxville May 1815. He served seven months and fifteen days. He was allowed six days travel time. A private pay wa $8.00 per month. He was living in Morgan County, Alabama in 1850 when he applied for Bounty land "for which he was entitled for his military service." He died after 1850.

Charles B. (Big B.) born 1800 in Tennessee, married second Louvassie McKenney. He lived and died at the last home place of Greenbury Wilson, that he inherited at the head of Sequatchie Valley on Wilson Branch in 1851. Louvassie died before 1850. Both are buried in the Wilson Cemetery.

His children by the first marriage were Elizabeth, married James R. Nail; William and Greenbury III, all moved west to California and Oregon.

The second family of Charles B. were: Charles B. Jr. (Bub), married first Nancy Swafford, second Ellen Robinson; Martha married Sam Sherrill; Margaret married John H. Sherrill; James Crockett (changed name to Matt Brown); Tempie married Matt Patton; Mattie married Tom Smallwood.

William B. Wilson born December 20, 1782 in North Carolina married Margaret Tollett, daughter of John and Margaret (Brown) Tollett. Margaret was born November 30, 1793 in Virginia.

William B. signed a petition to the Roane County Court in 1807 "to allow the erection of a grist mill in Sequatchie Valley."

William B. was in Bledsoe County in 1812 where he became the administrator of his father's estate. Sometime after Alabama became a state, he moved his family to Morgan County. After living in Alabama a few years this family moved to Texas. William B. died April 6, 1846 in Milam County. Margaret died February 14, 1873 in the same county.

William B. and Margaret (Tollett) Wilson became the parents of William, Goodhue, Temperance, Margaret, Greenbury, Cary, John T., Thomas and Nancy Wilson.

The following is an interesting "bear story" that has been told in the Wilson family for well over 150 years.

Greenbury Jr. referred to by his father as "Green" went for a short hunt one afternoon. The time was probably in the spring of the year and the family out of meat. He was probably just looking for a "mess of squirrel". This is also the time of year when bears come out of hibernation. The Wilson boy climbed the steep side of the ridge, just east of the Wilson home located on Wilson Branch. With him was his dog. The slope got steeper and steeper. Suddenly he came face to face with a bear. His only thought was to aim and shoot. After firing the gun he knew he hit the bear, but down, down the steep slope the bear rolled.

The bear was wounded and a wounded bear is a mad bear. The bear grabbed the boy by the leg causing the boy to drop his gun. Being in this terrible condition, the boy was able to grab hold of a sapling. On this steep slope, the boy was holding onto the sapling, the bear was holding onto the boy's leg. The boy's only hope was his dog. The dog grabbed the bear by the leg. There on this steep slope, the boy holding to the sapling, the bear biting on the boy's leg, the dog biting the bear's leg, finally with loud calls to the dog, the dog bit harder on the bear's leg. Finally the bear let go of the boy's leg and turned on the dog. Then the Wilson boy was able to let go of the sapling and recovered his gun. This time he was able to shoot and kill the bear. The happy ending was that Green recovered from his near fatal accident in this frontier environment.

Sources:

Greenbury Wilson's Will.

Cemetery Records.

Military Records.

Census Records, Bledsoe County.

First Families of Old Buncombe County.

Land Entries of Burk County, NC.

Burk County, North Carolina Land Records, Vol. II, 1779-1790.

Wilson Family, by Frances Beal Hodges, Wichita Falls, Texas, 1948.

Greenbury Wilson Home Place

Bledsoe Co., TN

WORTHINGTON

The name Worthington is found in the American colonies of Maryland and Conecticut in the late 1600s. Samuel Worthington Sr. was living in Virginia during the American Revolution and furnished beef to feed the American soldiers.

The Worthingtons were in Tennessee before Tennessee became a state, Hawkins County 1791. James, Samuel and Thomas were on the Anderson County Tax List in 1805. Samuel Worthington Sr. while living in Knox County had a license to carry on trade and commerce with the Cherokee Indians for six months, a special order by the President of the United States, 1797.

Several Worthingtons served in the War of 1812 from Tennessee. James Worthington a private in Captain James Standefer's East Tennessee Volunteer Militia died December 3, 1813. Others in Captain Standifer's company were Jesse and Robert Worthington. Samuel Worthington Jr. and brothers-in-law, Reuban Brown and James Roberson were in Bledsoe County in early 1800.

Samuel Jr. signed a petition for Peter Hoodenpyle to improve a certain wagon road across the Cumberland Mountains from Bledsoe into White and Warren counties. "On completion Hoodenpyle had permission to erect a toll gate."

The 1830 Bledsoe census list the following Worthington heads of households, John, William, Thomas and Robert. The Bledsoe Tax List gives Jesse, Samuel, James, Robert and William in Districts III, IV, V, 1838-1839. In the 1840 census Robert, Jesse, Samuel and William were in District III and IV.

Samuel Worthington Sr. born 1746 in Maryland married Elizabeth Carney 1774 in Botetourt County, Virginia. They became the parents of: Thomas born May 8, 1775, married Catherine Kuykendall, died Bledsoe County; Samuel born April 1, 1776, married Mary Murphy ca. 1802, Mary was born June 22, 1784 in Tennessee; James born July 11, 1779, married Lettice Tunnell, died December 3, 1813, Ft. Strother, Alabama; Elizabeth born October 1, 1781, married William Tunnell; Nancy Ann born June 10, 1784, married John Tunnell, died June 21, 1821 in Anderson County; Sarah born June 10, 1784, a twin of Nancy Ann, married Reuban Brown, Sarah (Sallie) died December 16, 1873, Bledsoe County; Margaret born October 26, 1786, married James Roberson, Margaret (Peggy) died January 8, 1827 Bledsoe County; William born March 1, 1789, died May 2, 1830 in Anderson County; Robert Gaston born March 17, 1791, married Frances Jacks, second married Sarah Moyers; Jesse born April 1794, married Nancy Galbraith, died May 3, 1879 Anderson County; Joseph born January 22, 1796, married Susan England, Joseph died September 10, 1840 in Anderson County.

Five of Samuel and Elizabeth Worthington's children, Thomas, Samuel Jr., Sarah, Margaret and Robert Gaston, found their way into Sequatchie Valley in early 1800s. Samuel Worthington Sr. died January 21, 1821 and Elizabeth (Carney) Worthington died October 10, 1830, both died in Anderson County.

The well-known Tunnell family and the Worthington family lived in the same area of Anderson County. Three children of Samuel Worthington Sr. married into the William and Mary (Maysey) Tunnell's family.

Samuel Worthington Jr., second son of Samuel Sr. born 1776, married Mary Murphy. They became the parents of: Rachel born ca.

1803, married Jacob Sigler, second Nemiah H. Evitt, died before 1840, family moved to Texas; William born 1804-05, married 1828 Margaret Brown (first cousin), William, known as Big Spring Bill, lived near the "Big Spring", married second Mariah Hutcheson, William died November 1896, buried at Big Spring Cemetery; Elizabeth born February 7, 1807, married William Worthington (first cousin) December 21, 1828, Elizabeth died September 3, 1891; Sarah born January 5, 1809 married 1830, Charles Hutcheson, married second Berton Holman, Sarah died September 26, 1895, Spring Town, Texas; Robert, born December 12, 1810 married Mary Jane Porter, married second Carolyn. Robert died September 5, 1873 in Bledsoe County, buried Worthington Cemetery; Kiturah (Kitty) born March 19, 1813, married John Rowan, married second Isaac Bird Henson, Kiturah died August 2, 1856, buried in Henson Cemetery; Deliah born ca. 1815, married Martin A. Smith, who served as sheriff in Bledsoe County in the late 1850s. This family moved to Texas after 1870; James (Jim) born November 29, 1816, married Minervia Brown, a first cousin, James died August 21, 1893, buried Worthington Cemetery; Mary Murphy born November 15, 1820, married James Jerome Pope, who was born January 3, 1819. Mary died June 22, 1876 and James J. died April 9, 1880. They were both buried in Pope Cemetery, Mt. Airy; Lodemia born ca. 1823, married James R. Brown, married second George W. Jones, this family moved to Laverge, Tennessee; Angeline B. born April 4, 1825, married Patrick L. Schoolfield, died October 26, 1889, buried Worthington Cemetery; Robert Gaston born March 17, 1791, married Frances Jacks, born April 13, 1791 in North Carolina, married second Sarah Moyers. Robert G. was a Baptist preacher called "Iron Jacket" or "Old Buddy".

An early school was located at his place, the Methodist held their camp meetings at the same place near the spring.

Robert G. and Frances became the parents of: Jesse born ca. 1817, married Temperance Brown born March 27, 1819, daughter of Jesse and Carrie (Wilson) Brown. Jesse served in the Cherokee Indian War 1836-1837. He made application for a bounty land warrnt in 1850. Jesse was in Captain Shamell Parham's Company 1st Regiment 2nd Brigade, Tennessee Infantry. Jesse, a private, enlisted for six months at Pikeville, was discharged January 8, 1837. Temperance died April 25, 1864, buried in the Hamilton Cemetery. Jesse and their children later moved west. Sarah born ca. 1820, married Greene J. Holden; Isabella born ca. 1825, married Samuel Gott, who died before 1850, Isabella and son, Richard, moved west; Elizabeth born ca. 1827; Margaret born December 5, 1833, married John Hamilton Sr. born May 6, 1820. Margaret died October 25, 1893 and John died June 2, 1904; both are buried in the Hamilton Cemetery. Robert G. Worthington died April 10, 1873, Frances died October 5, 1869, both were buried on their farm, later called the Hamilton Cemetery.

Sources:

Members and Patriots The Tennessee Society Daughters of the American Revolution, Vol. 4, 1985-2001.

Tennesseans in the War of 1812, by Sistler, 1992.

National Society Colonial Dames XVII Century Ancestor Roster, 1915-2005.

Family Information, by Kirby W. Gilbert, 9413 Dolton Way, Highland Ranch, Colorado 80126.

Cemetery records, Jesse Brown Bible.

Worthington Cemetery

Bledsoe's First Black Families
African Americans

Bledsoe County in 1810 (1st census), had a population of 3,259, including white, free colored and slaves, of the total 209 were slaves or free Blacks.

In 1820 the population was 4,005 with 389 slaves or free Blacks. By 1830, the population was 4,648, with 483 slaves or free Blacks. In 1840 the total population was 5,676 with 666 slaves, free Blacks and Mulattoes. In 1850 the population was 5,959 with 923 slaves or free Blacks. In 1860 the population had dropped to 4,459 with 816 persons of color. Areas had been taken Districts I, III, III and District X, to form parts of Cumberland and Sequatchie counties.

After the Civil War by 1870 Bledsoe again was divided into ten civil districts. The total population was 4,870 with 659 being classed as colored.

District I Rainey, southwest Bledsoe County.

Henry McReynolds was the head of the sole Black family.

District II Wards - Cumberland Plateau - no Black family.

District III Tollett's Mill.

Head of the Black families were R. Stephens, P. Hench, W. Tollett, R. Hinch, H. Stephens, J. Tellis, B. Stephens, D. Thurman, H. Worthington, Charlotte Crock, Green Swafford, Harriet Lee, Harry Swafford and Henry Swafford.

District IV Worthington.

The head of the Black families were H. Holman, W. Worthington, E. Hutcheson, G. Swafford, T. Worthington, B. Guess, L. Smith, S. Worthington, G. Clark, L. Swafford, E. Swafford, Gilbert Clark, A. Swafford and R. Hutcheson.

District V Cold Spring.

The head of the families were Jessie Thompson, Madison Swafford, H. Loyd, J. Billingsley, Alford Rankin, Henderson Billingsley, N. Billingsley, Charles Pankey, M.M. Billingsley, G.W. Worthington, Jack Tulloss, Sam Gadenhise, Walker Rankin, Turner Brown, Chana Brown, Agna Brown, Henry Rankin and Martin Billingsley.

District VI including the town of Pikeville.

The following were heads of households, D. Bridgman, James Springs, Ned Bridgman, Malala Berch, W. Bridgman, J. McReynolds, Stephens Tulloss, Peter Spears, Hose Bennet, Cam Springs, Thom McReynolds, Clark W. Elder, A. Bridgman, Robert Daniels, Bird Stephens, Henry Tulloss, James Swafford, Anthony Bridgman, Calvin Pankey, Ann Vernon, Jackson Brown, Jessee Skillern and M. Bridgman.

District VII Bells.

Thomas Springs, Scoot Springs, Anders McReynolds, Preston Parker, Samuel Cherman, John White, Jerry Foster, Edward Springs, Leander Foster, Lucinda Springs, Alfred McReynolds, John Bridgman, A. McReynolds, D. McReynolds, Ben McReynolds, Luke Foster, Henry McReynolds, Stephens Fraisure, Ben Schoolfield, John A. Pope and

E. Bridgman were listed as heads of households.

District VIII Nail Roberson Cross Roads.

W.C. Roberson, W.F. Roberson, John Roberson, Patrick Springs, John Schoolfield, H. Merriman, John Goen, Henry Bates, Adley Bolen and Malinda Bolen.

District IX Hughes.

Heads of Black families were Rubin Hixon, M. Roberson, George Phelps, Leander Phelps, Jane Roberson, George Hughs, Han Rankin, M. Roberson and Peter McReynolds.

District X Burditts - Walden Ridge.

No Black family. Several single, male and females old or young Blacks were listed in white families at this time as servants or laborers.

NOTE: Names were copies and spelled as in the 1870 census.

Sources:

1870 Bledsoe County U.S. Census.

Resources of Tennessee, by J.B. Killebrew, published by Bureau of Agriculture, Nashville, TN 1874.

Did You Know?

Tennessee was admitted to the union as the 16th state June 1, 1796

Signed by George Washington, 1st President of the United States

Bledsoe County was created November 30, 1807 by the General
Assembly of Tennessee

signed by John Sevier, 1st Governor of Tennessee

Little Known Facts About Bledsoe County

Bledsoe County was created from Roane 1807. Roane was created from Knox 1801. Knox was created from Greene and Hawkins in 1792. Hawkins was created from Sullivan in 1786. Greene was created from Washington in 1783. Washington was created by the state of North Carolina and named for General Washington in 1777.

Peter Looney was the first sheriff of Bledsoe County 1808, he also had the job of collector of taxes.

James Roberson was the first Register of Deeds 1808. John Narramore was the first chairman of the Bledsoe County Court, other members were John Anderson, John Tollett, Michael Rawlings, William Roberson, James Standifer and Thomas Coulter.

The first census of 1810 gives the population of the county as 3,259.

The first commissioners for the town of Pikeville 1816, Adam Sherrill, Aquilla Johnson, Joseph Peters and Eli Thurman.

Bledsoe County first official records were headed, Sequatchie 1808-1812, Madison 1812-1815, Pikeville 1816. Land was being sold and deeds recorded 1808 before a county seat was designated.

Pikeville was the first United States post office in the county

1824-1825.

General Nathan Bedford Forrest's camp, while in Pikeville, was located on the hill, southwest corner of Grove and Cleveland Avenue. This was north of Judge Thomas N. Frazier's home.

Across Cleveland Avenue (Old Spencer Road), on northwest corner of Grove and Cleveland was the well-known Lafayette Academy.

The following applied and received pensions while living in Bledsoe on their service in the American Revolution.

Brannon, Thomas

Brown, Stephen

Crawford, John

Curtis, John

Dalton, John

Davis, Andrew

Ford, John

Hale, John

Hughes, Francis

Malaby, John

McDonough, Andrew

Narramore, John

Pollard, Chattin

Rains, John

Reed, Lovett

Smith, Laton

Standifer, Benjamin

Sutherland, Daniel

Thomas, John

Thurman, Charles

Thurman, Phillip

Walker, George

The following veterans of the American Revolution were early settlers of Bledsoe County. They did not draw pensions for reason: moved elsewhere or deceased before the pension bill was passed.

Billingsley, Samuel

Clark, Thomas

Kelley, Alexander

Kerklin, George

Roberson, James

Roberson, William

Sherrill, Adam

Thompson, Bernard

Tollett, John

Wilson, Greenbury

The following filed for Revolutionary War pensions while living in Bledsoe County, but their application were rejected for various reasons.

Daffron, John

Dever, Joshua

Pruett, Micajah

Simpson, James

-A-

ABERNATHY
MAY, 195
ABLE
MARGARET ADALINE, 17
ACOCK
HALLIE, 159
ACUFF
ALMIRE CAROLINE, 2
ANDREW, 1
ANGELINE, 2
ANGELINE M., 2
ANN, 2
ANNA, 2, 4, 70, 74
BARTON, 2
BUSTER W., 1
CLAUDE HARDING, 4
DARIUS M., 2, 3
DAVID, 2
ELEANOR, 1, 3
J. FRED, 4
JAMES, 1(2), 2(3),
3, 48, 74
JAMES H., 2(2), 3, 4
JAMES H. (JIM), 3
JAMES J., 3
JASPER S., 2
JASPER SYLVESTER, 3
JOHN, 1(3), 2
JOHN D., 2
JOHN H., 1(2), 2(3),
3(2), 27
JOHN J. SPENCER, 4
JOHN SPENCER, 4
JONATHAN, 1(2), 3
JOSEPH, 2
JOSEPH R., 2, 3
MARTHA, 2
MARY, 2, 3
MARY B., 48
MARY E., 2(2)
MARY T., 4
MATILDA EMILY, 2
MATILDA EMILY
(BILLINGSLEY), 3
MICHAEL, 1
MOSE SCOTT, 4
NANCY, 1
NANCY (BILLINGSLEY),
74
NANCY (HUTCHESON),
1, 2
NANCY ANN MATILDA, 2

NICHOLAS, 1(3), 27
REBECCA, 1(2)
ROBERT, 1, 2
ROBERT BATES, 4
ROBERT D., 2, 3
SAMUEL JACKSON, 2, 3
SARAH, 1
SARAH (HENDERSON),
2, 3
SARAH (SALLIE
HENDERSON), 3
SARAH (SALLIE), 4
SERENA J., 1
SIDNEY, 4
TIMOTHY, 1
WILLIAM, 1(2), 2(3),
3(2)
WILLIAM B., 4
WILLIAM J., 2
WILLIAM L., 2
WILLIAM, JR., 2
ADKINS
NANCY, 138
ADKISSON
MARY, 195, 196
AGEE
MARGARET, 78
ALEXANDER
WILLIAM HARRISON,
109
ALLEN
MISS, 10
ALLEY
JANE, 163
ALLISON
ROBERT, 5
THOMAS, 5
ANDERSON
AUDLEY, 9
AUDLEY M., 8
BETSY, 9
ELIZABETH, 9
ELIZABETH
(CAMPBELL), 198
ELIZABETH (McNAIR),
9, 10, 243
ELIZABETH ANN, 10
ISAAC, 42
JAMES, 257
JAMES MADISON, 10
JANE, 8, 11
JOHN, 8, 9(3), 10,
51, 137, 274
JOHN, JR., 8(2),
9(2)

JOHN, SR., 8(2), 10,
11
JOSIAH McNAIR, 10
JOSIAH S., 8
LOUISE, 8
LOUISE MAXWELL, 9
MARTHA, 8
MARY, 8, 10, 198
REBECCA, 10, 11
REBECCA (MAXWELL), 8
REBECCA (SKILLERN),
8(2)
THANKFUL, 257
VIRGINIA, 8
WILLIAM, 8(5), 198
ANDREW
JAMES, 219
ANNIS
ALFRED H., 14
CHARLES, 13
DANIEL C., 13
DEWEY, 14
ELIZABETH, 13
ETHEL, 14
FANNIE E., 13
GEORGE, 13
HENRY, 13
JOHN, 13, 14(2)
JOHN R., 13(2),
14(2)
LAURA, 14
LAURA (WHITE), 14
MARTHA, 13, 14
MARTHA (LOVE), 13
ROBERT, 13(2)
ROBERT R., 13, 14
SAM, 13
VIDA, 14
WILLIAM F., 13
ASHBY
F., 3
ATKINSON
THOMAS W., 145
AULT
ALBION, 16
ANN, 15
CATHERINE, 15
CHARITY, 15
CHARLES W., 16
CHARLES WESLEY,
16(4)
CLINTON, 17
CONRAD, 15(3),
16(5), 17
DOCTOR, 18

EMMA, 17
ETHEL, 17
EVE, 15
FREDRICK, 15
G.W., 128
GEORGE, 15, 16
GEORGE W., 16
GEORGE WASHINGTON, 16(3), 17
GERTRUDE, 16
HENRY, 16
ICIE DELLE, 17
IDA LATITIA, 17
JACOB, 15, 16
JAMES FRANKLIN, 17(2)
JOHN, 15
LEAH (SMITH), 16
LEAH SMITH, 16
LOLA, 17
LORINDA JANE, 17
MARGARET A., 17
MARGARET ANN, 16, 17(2)
MARY, 15
MARY EMMA, 17
MARY J., 16
MICHAEL, 15(5)
MICHAEL, SR., 15
NELLIE, 15
OLINDA, 16
OTTO, 17
PERRY W., 17
RUTH (HOWARD), 17(2)
SAM WESLEY, 17
SUANNA ADALINE, 17
SUSANNA, 16
SUSANNA (NEWMAN), 16(2), 17
THOMAS, 16, 17
VERSAILLES, 17
VESTA, 16
VESTA A. (DARWIN), 17
WILEY ALLISON, 17(2)
WILEY NEWMAN, 16, 17(4)
WILLIAM HENRY, 17(3), 18
WILLIAM L., 16
AUTRY
MARY, 250
AUXIER
ABRAHAM, 148
GEORGE, 148

MICHAEL, 148
MICHAEL, II, 148
MICHAEL, III, 148
SAMUEL, 148
SIMON, 148
AVENS
ARTA M., 229
AXLEY
JAMES, 246

-B-

BAILEY
NANCY, 72
BALLARD
GEORGE WASHINGTON, 53
JOSEPH, 53(2)
NANCY, 53(2)
SAMUEL, 53(2)
WILLIAM, 53(2)
BATES
HENRY, 272
WILLIAM, 67
BEATTY
MR., 237
BEATY
EDWARD, 19
HUGH, 19(3), 20
ISABELLA, 19, 20
ISABELLA HOOD, 20, 225
J.M., 20
JANE, 19, 20
JOHN M., 19
JOHN M./J.M., 20
MARGARET, 19, 20(2)
NANCY, 19, 20
BEAUCHAMP
MARY, 255
BELL
JOHN, 217
KATE, 129
NANCY (RAINEY), 129
WILLIAM H., 129
BENNET
HOSE, 271
BENNETT
ELIZABETH, 191
BIDDY
MARTHA, 124
BILLINGSLEY
AMANDA, 23, 26, 162
ANDERSON, 259
ANDREW BLACKWOOD, 25

CROCIA, 59
ELIJAH, 23
ELIZABETH, 27, 43, 162
ELIZABETH E., 25
EVALINE J., 231
EVALISTA JANE, 26
FRANCIS, 23
HENDERSON, 271
HIXIE O., 26
J., 271
JAMES, 23
JANE, 26
JANE (HOODENPYLE), 26
JEPHTHA, 23
JOHN, 23(2), 24(2), 25(3), 26(2), 60, 94, 95, 162, 187, 231
JOHN CALVIN, 25
JOHN DAVIS, 25
JOHN M., 27
JONATHAN, 27(2)
JOSEPH B., 27
LEANDER TRAVIS, 26
LEANDER TRAVIS (LEE), 26
LEE, 26
LENA, 60
M.M., 271
MAHALA, 25
MARTHA, 259
MARTHA (BLACKWOOD), 25
MARTHA JANE, 25
MARTIN, 271
MARY, 23, 25, 27, 47
MARY REBECCA, 255
MARY THEOLA, 26
MATILDA, 2, 27
MATILDA EMILY, 2
N., 271
NANCY, 2, 23, 25, 27, 102
NANCY (MULKEY), 27
PHILLIP MARSHALL, 26
REBECCA, 27
SALLIE, 27
SAMUEL, 23(4), 24, 25(2), 26, 27, 43, 259, 276
SAMUEL, JR., 24, 27
SAMUEL, SR., 26
SARAH, 23

THOMAS, 249
FOREST
  RACHEL, 214
FORREST
  NATHAN B., 68
  NATHAN BEDFORD, 275
FOSTER
  JAMES, 42
  JERRY, 271
  LEANDER, 271
  LUKE, 271
  ORPHA, 73
  WILLIAM, 171, 212
FRAILEY
  MAMIE, 2
FRAISURE
  STEPHENS, 271
FRAZIER
  ABNER, 66(3), 67
  ABNER, JR., 67
  BARBARA, 66
  BERIAH, 66, 67
  JAMES B., 67, 68
  JULIAN, 66
  LOUISE, 59
  MARGARET, 67
  MARY (EDMONSON), 66, 67
  MARY ELLEN, 67
  MINERVA T., 16
  REBECCA, 66(2), 67(2)
  REBECCA (JULIAN), 66
  ROBERT, 249
  SAMUEL, 66(5), 67
  SAMUEL J., 67
  SARAH J.M., 67
  THOMAS, 66
  THOMAS N., 46, 67(2), 128, 213, 237, 238, 275
  THOMAS NEAL, 66, 67(3), 68
  TOM, 67
FREILY
  SQUIRE BOOM, 232
FUQUA
  MARY, 170

-G-

GADD
  MARGARET EMMALINE, 109
GADENHISE

SAM, 271
GALBRAITH
  NANCY, 266
GALLANT
  JAMES, I, 81, 202
  MARY, 232
  MARY (POLLY), 81
  SARAH, 202
  SARAH (McDONOUGH), 202
GARDNER
  JAMES, 91
GARRISON
  JACOB, 56
GARVIN
  JAMES A., 45
GASS
  ADELIA, 206(2)
  ADELIA K., 208
  ADELIA K. (BROWN) SPEARS, 207
  JACOB, 208
  W.T., 206
  WILLIAM T., 42
  WILLIAM THOMAS, 207, 208
GAULT/GOTT
  LAFAYETTE "FATE", 231
GENTRY
  ALLEN, 70(4)
  AMY LOU, 70
  ANNA J., 71
  CAL, 2
  CORA, 71
  ELIZA E., 70
  FLORA, 71
  FRANCIS MORGAN, 70(2)
  HUGH, 71
  JAMES K., 70(2), 71
  JAMES K. POLK, 70
  JAMES K. POLK (J.P. OR POLK), 71
  JAMES POLK, 71
  JOHN, 70
  JOHN A., 70
  JOSHUA, 70
  JOSHUA C., 70
  JOSIE, 71
  LEROY (LEE), 71
  LEROY (LEE)/R.L., 71
  LIZZIE, 71
  MARY, 71
  MARY (DWIGGINS), 71

MARY E., 2, 3
SARAH, 70
SARAH E., 70
THOMAS H., 70
ZELZY, 70
GIBBONS
  CHRISTIANA, 154, 155
GILL
  SARAH, 81
GILMORE
  PRISCILLA, 133
GIPSON
  PLEASANT, 224
GLASS
  JAMES, 228
GODSEY
  HYRAM, 185
GOEN
  JOHN, 272
GOTCHER
  HENRY, 102
GOTT
  RICHARD, 268
  SAMUEL, 268
GRAFTON
  CHARLOTTE, 42
GRAHAM
  MARTHA, 129
  POPE, 129
GREAVER
  RACHEL, 187
  SAMUEL, 187
GREELEY
  HORACE, 204
GREER
  ALEXANDER CAMPBELL, 74, 75
  ANNA, 74, 75, 76(2)
  ANNA (ACUFF), 74, 75(2)
  BETSY, 72
  ELIZABETH CHARLOTTE, 73, 225
  EMILY C., 128
  EMILY CALLOWAY, 73
  HARRIET ANN, 73, 145, 146
  HENRY CLAY, 60, 73(2)
  HORTENSE (RANDALS), 73
  ISAAC S., 60
  ISAIAH, 2
  ISIAH, 74(3), 75(4), 76(2)

ISIAH STEPHENS, 74
JAMES, 72
JAMES L., 74(2)
JOHN, 72
JOHN BARTOW, 74, 75
JOHN F., 72(2), 139
JOHN W., 60
JONAH CLARK, 74, 76
KITTY, 72
LAURA, 60
LAURILLA, 74
LAURILLA (LAURA), 76
LOUISE EVALINE, 74,
  75
MARY, 72, 146, 156
MARY (FINCH/FITCH),
  72
MARY (KYLE), 73(2),
  128
MARY ANN, 74(2), 75
MATILDA, 74
MOLLIE, 72
MOSES, 72, 73, 156
MOSES, JR., 72(2)
MOSES, SR., 72(3)
NANCY, 72(2), 74
NANCY (BAILEY), 156
NANCY MATILDA, 75
NELLIE, 72
SALLY, 72
SARAH MARGARET, 74,
  75
SHADRACK, 72
SUSANNAH (WOODS), 72
THOMAS, 73
THOMAS BAILEY, 72
WALTER, 72
WALTER ACQUILLA, 72
WEATHERSTON S., 72,
  73(2), 128
WEATHERSTON S., JR.,
  73
WEATHERSTON SHELTON,
  SR.(W.S.), 72
WETHERSTON S., 146
WILLIAM, 72(4)
WILLIAM CARNES, 74,
  75
WILLIAM HENRY, 73
GRIFFITH
AMOS, 215, 216
JAMES, 25
MARY, 23, 26
MARY (POLLY)
  (STANDIFER), 216

WILLIAM STANDIFER,
  172
GRIMES
JOSEPH, 148
GRIMSLEY
ELIZABETH, 2
GRUNDY
FELIX, 217
GUESS
B., 271
GUINN
MR., 231

-H-

HALE
ALEXANDER, 127
ANDREW JACKSON, 78
AQUILLA, 78
ARRANZENA, 78
ELIJAH, 78
ELIZABETH, 78
HEZEKIAH, 78
ISHAM, 78
JANE, 127
JOHN, 77(2), 78(3),
  234, 276
JOHN N., 78
JOHN T., 78(2)
JOHN T., JR., 78
KING, 78
MARTHA, 78
MARTHA JANE, 78
MARY ANN, 78(2)
MICHAEL, 78
MILLIE, 114
SARAH, 78
SUZANNAH, 78
T.F. (FRANK), 80
THOMAS, 78(2)
THOMAS HALE, 78
WILLIAM, 78
HALL
BENJAMIN, 59
ELIZABETH, 230
ESTER ANN, 173
JANE, 183
JESSE, 26
LOU R., 207
MARY ANN, 59(2), 78
MILLIE, 230
WILLIAM, 240
HAMILTON
ABRAHAM, 79(2), 134
ABRAHAM, JR., 80

BENJAMIN, 34, 79(4),
  80(2)
DELILA, 79, 133
DELILAH, 79
GEORGE, 79
HARVEY, 79
ISAAC, 80
JACOB, 80
JAMES, 80
JAMES D., 134
JOHN, 79(2), 80, 268
JOHN, SR., 268
MARGARET, 268
MARTHA J., 80
MARY, 79, 80(2)
MARY A., 80
NANCY E., 80
RACHEL, 79, 80
SARAH, 80
SARAH E., 80
WILLIAM, 79
WILLIAM E., 80
HAMMOND
JULIA FRANCES, 213
HANKINS
ABSOLEM, 81
BARBARA, 85, 86(2)
CAROLINE, 84
DANIEL, 86
DAVID, 84, 86
ELIZABETH, 84
FANNY JANE, 83
GEORGE, 84
HANNAH, 82, 84(2),
  232
ISAAC E., 84
JAMES, 84
JANE, 82, 83, 122,
  124
JANE (SHARP), 81
JANE C., 84
JOHN, 81(6), 82(2),
  83(4), 84(4), 86,
  123, 124(2), 232
JOHN JACKSON, 82,
  84(2)
JOHN JACKSON (JACK),
  84
JOHN S., 83(2)
JOHN, JR., 83
JOSEPH, 84(2)
LUCY, 83
MARGARET, 86
MARTHA JANE, 84
MARY, 82, 83, 84(3),

-J-

JACKS
  FRANCES, 266, 267
JACKSON
  ANDREW, 9, 138, XI
JAMES
  JOHN, 109
JENKINS
  WILLIAM, 156
JEWELLS
  WILLIAM, 224
JOHNSON
  ABIGAIL P., 106
  ALA, 106
  ANDREW, 69, 120,
    171, 217
  ANN (ANGELINE), 2
  AQUILLA, 105(4),
    106(6), 236, 274,
    XXI
  BRIGHT, 106(3)
  CAVE, 217
  ELBA, 11
  ELBA H., 106
  ERASMUS (RAS), 2
  FRANCIS A., 106
  JACOB, 120
  JAMES B., 106
  JAMES BAXTER, 106
  JOE, 60
  JOHN O., 167, 168
  KINSY, 106
  L.C., 60
  LOUISE, 50
  MARK P., 106
  MARY (McDONOUGH),
    171
  MARY ANN, 106(3)
  MISSOURI, 56
  RACHEL S., 106
  RIGHT, 106(3)
  RUBY, 106
  WILLIAM, 9, 202, 255
JONES
  DELILA, 167
  DORCUS, 215
  GABRIEL, 59
  GEORGE W., 267
  GRABRIAL, 122(3)
  ISABELLA, 122(2)
  ISABELLA McDOWELL,
    59, 122
  JEMIMA, 215
  MARTHA, 116, 118,

122
  MARTHA ANN, 59
  MARY, 116
  WILLIAM, 122
JULIAN
  REBECCA, 66

-K-

KAIGER
  AUGUSTINE, 211
KARNES
  MINERVA, 233
KEEDY
  DAVID, 108(2)
  DELILAH (WALKER),
    109
  DELILAH VIRGINIA,
    109
  JACOB, 108(2), 109,
    256
  JACOB ROSECRANS, 109
  JACOB, JR., 109
  JACOB, SR., 108, 109
  JAMES CRISPON, 109
  LEWIS, 108(5), 109
  MARY, 108
  MARY ANN, 109
  NANCY, 109
  RACHEL EMMALINE, 109
  RICHARD, 109
  SARA (SALLY), 108
  SARAH, 109
  TENNESSEE ADA, 109
  WILLIAM, 108(4), 109
  ZACHARIAH TAYLOR,
    109
KELCH
  ELIZABETH, 229
KELLEY
  ALEXANDER, 276
KELLY
  ADELINE, 111
  ALEXANDER, 110(2),
    111
  ALEXANDER, JR., 111
  ALEXANDER, SR., 110,
    111(2)
  ANNIE, 111
  ESTHER, 111
  JAMES, 111
  JANE, 111
  JOHN, 110, 111(6),
    112
  MARGARET, 111(2)

MARTHA, 111
  NANCY, 91, 111
  NANCY (MAYO), 111
  NANCY ROBINSON, 111
  POLLY, 111
  THOMAS, 111
  VALENTINE, 111
  VINY, 111
  WILLIAM, 111
  WILLIAM JASPER, 111
KELTNER
  DRUCILLA, 229
KENDALL
  ELIZABETH, 172
KERKLIN
  GEORGE, 276
KERLEY
  ALICE, 115
  ANNIE, 115
  BEN, 115
  BENJAMIN, 114
  CALVIN, 114
  COLUMBUS, 114(2),
    115(2)
  DANIEL, 113(4),
    114(3), 148
  DAVID C., 114
  ELIS S., 114
  ELIZA, 114
  ELIZABETH, 113, 114
  ELIZABETH ANN, 148
  ELLEN, 115
  EMALINE, 114
  GEORGE, 113(2)
  JAMES, 113(2),
    114(5), 115
  JAMES C., 114
  JERMIA, 113(3)
  JOHN, 115
  M.L., 115
  MANERY, 114
  MARY C., 114
  MILLIE, 114
  MILLIE (HALE), 114
  NANCY, 114
  NANCY JANE, 115
  NANCY SUE, 114
  PARMELIA, 114
  PERMELIA ANN, 114
  REBECCA, 113
  REBECCA (SHERRILL),
    113
  ROBERT, 114
  SAMUEL, 114(2), 195
  SAMUEL O., 113(2)

SARAH, 115
SARAH (RECTOR), 115
WILLIAM, 113(5),
  114(6), 115
WILLIAM CARROLL, 114
WILLIAM O., 115(2)
KILGORE
  CHARLES, 195
  REBECCA, 195
  STEPHEN, 181
KING
  NANCY, 219
  SARAH (FINE), 70
KIRBY
  MR., XIII
KIRK
  MARTHA ELIZABETH,
    149
KIRKLAND
  ALLEN, 9
  ELISHA, 201, 258
  LOUISE (ANDERSON),
    10
KIRKLEN
  ELISHA, 77, 244
KIRKLIN
  KEZIAH, 167
  MARTHA MAXWELL, 167
KRICHBAUM
  JACOB, 109
KUYKENDALL
  CATHERINE, 266
KYLE
  MARY, 72

-L-

LAMB
  ADAM, 30, 111
  ALEXANDER, 244
  HUGH, 10
  JANE, 10
  LETTY, 244
  NANCY, 10
LANGLEY
  ELIZABETH, 121
LARKIN
  SARAH, 227(2)
LASATER
  MARTHA E., 256
LASTER
  JANE, 256
LAWLER
  JAMES, 187
  MALINDA DOYL, 187

LAY
  LUKE, 78
  RICHARD, 78
LEE
  AARON, 116
  ANDERSON ANDREW, 117
  BENJAMIN FRANKLIN,
    117
  BLUFORD, 116
  BURREL (BURL), 116
  BURRELL, 116(3),
    117, 118(2)
  BURRELL RUSSELL,
    117(2), 118, 230
  BURRELL RUSSELL,
    JR., 117
  ELIZA, 117
  ELIZABETH, 116
  HARRIET, 270
  HENRY, 116
  JAKE C., 116, 117
  JAMES, 116
  JAMES C., 118
  JOHN, 149
  JOHN ANDERSON, 116,
    117
  JOHN C., 117
  LOUHANEY (SWAFFORD),
    117, 118
  LOUISA, 117
  MARTHA, 116, 118
  MARTHA (JONES), 116,
    117, 118
  MARY, 116, 231
  MARY (POLLY), 117
  MARY E., 118
  NANCY, 116, 118, 231
  RANDOLPH, 116
  ROBERT, 116(2),
    117(3), 230
  RUSSELL, 116
  THOMAS, 116, 117(2)
  WILLIAM, 117, 149
  WILLIAM E., 116
LEIGH
  ANNA, 1
LEWIS
  MARTHA E., 224
  THOMAS D., 106
  WILLIAM G., 148
LOCKE
  FRANCIS, 23
  THOMAS, 192
LOONEY
  PETER, 199, 274

LOVE
  CHARLES, 106, VII,
    XXI
  CHARLES J., 93
  MARTHA, 13
LOWDEN
  NANCY, 64
  WILLIAM, 64, 65
LOWE
  ANDREW, 261
  MOSES, 106, 145
  SAMUEL, 145, 261
  SARAH ANN, 78
LOWERY
  CATHERINE, 177
  MAHALA, 162
  ROBERT, 27
LOYD
  ALBERT, 10, 234
  BENJAMIN, 54
  ELIZABETH, 10
  ELIZABETH (McNAIR),
    8
  ELIZABETH ANDERSON
    THURMAN, 8
  ELIZABETH/BETSY, 10
  H., 271
  JAMES, 10(3), 187
  JANE, 10
  MARGARET, 10
  MARTHA, 10
  MARTHA A., 252
  R.P., 11
  ROLAND, 10
  ROLAND PETERSON, 10
  W.S., 128
LUCKER
  ELIZA A., 232
LUTTRELL
  PURLYMLY, 10
LYNCH
  JANE, 250
  REBECCA, 250

-M-

McCAIN
  PEGGY, 255
McCALL
  NANCY, 19
McCLANAHAN
  MARTHA, 149
McCLELLAN
  DORTHULA, 117
  JOHN, X

McCLELLAND
  BARBARA, 117
McCLELLEN
  JOHN, VII
McCLUNG
  CHARLES, VII, X
McCOLLOUGH
  MATTHEW, 120
McCORMICK
  MARY, 194
McDANIEL
  JAMES, 192
  LETITIA, 123
McDONALD
  ROWLAND F., 42
McDONOUGH
  ANDREW, 120(4),
    121(2), 171(3),
    276
  ANDREW, JR., 120(4),
    121(2)
  CALVIN, 120(4),
    121(2)
  ELIZABETH, 120
  HENRY, 120(2)
  JAMES, 120
  JOHN, 120
  MARY, 120
  MARY "POLLY", 120
  RANSOM, 120
  RHODA (SARTIN)
    ROBERSON, 171
  RHODA ROBERSON, 120
  RHODA SARTIN
    ROBERSON, 120
  WILLIAM, 120
McDOWELL
  ELEANOR G., 123
  ELIZABETH, 122(2),
    125
  HANNAH, 84, 124
  HIRAM, 123
  ISABELLA, 84, 122(3)
  ISABELLA (ISA), 124
  JAMES, 84
  JAMES A., 123
  JAMES F., 124
  JANE, 124
  JANE (HANKINS), 124
  JESSE F., 123
  JESSE M., 84, 124
  JOHN, 122(3)
  JOHN H., 84, 124
  JOSEPH, 84, 122(5),
    123(3), 124, 240,

254
KINSEY S., 123
KINSY, 123
LUCY J., 123
MARTHA E., 123
MARY, 84, 122, 124
NANCY, 123
NANCY (CLOSE), 123
NANCY L., 84
NANCY LORETTA, 124
SARAH, 84
SARAH (SAL), 124
SELA, 84, 123
THOMAS, 84, 124
THOMAS C., 123
WILLIAM, 84(3),
  122(4), 123(2),
  124(3)
WILLIAM J., 123
McGREGER
  HIXIE, 95
McGREGOR
  JANE, 249
McIVEN
  JOHN, 148
McKELL
  EDMUND, 120
McKENNEY
  LOUVASSIE, 262
McKINNEY
  JOHN, 48
  SARAH A., 255
McMINN
  JOSEPH, XIV
McNAIR
  ELIZABETH, 9
  JAMES, 9
McREYNOLDS
  A., 271
  ADELINE, 130(2)
  ALEXANDER, 128
  ALEXANDER H., 73,
    127, 128
  ALEXANDER HALE, 128
  ALFRED, 271
  ANDERS, 271
  ANNA D., 130
  ANNA D. (STEPHENS),
    130(2)
  ANNIE H., 130
  BEN, 271
  BERTIE LEW, 130
  CHARLES, 128
  CLAIBORNE D., 129
  CLAIBORNE DELANEY,

129
CLAYBORN DELANEY,
  127
D., 271
ELIZABETH (HENSON),
  129
ELIZABETH A., 128
EMILY, 128
GATHNER A., 128
HALLIE, 129
HENRY, 270, 271
HOPE, 129
IDA, 128
ISAAC, 130
ISAAC STEPHENS,
  130(3)
J., 271
JAMES, 126, 127, 129
JAMES W., 127,
  129(2)
JANE, 126, 128(2)
JANE (HALE), 127,
  129(2)
JENNIE (DAVIS), 130
JIM, 129
JOE, 129
JOHN, 126(2), 127
JOHN B., 130
JOHN S., 128
JOSEPH, 126(2),
  127(2), 128
LOUCRETIA, 129
MARGARET, 51,
  127(2), 128
MARGARET (MAGGIE),
  130
MARGARET (WOODS),
  126
MARGARET M., 67
MARTHA, 130
MARTHA (MATTIE), 130
MARY J., 128
MARY JANE, 127
MARY MARGARET
  (MITCHELL), 127
PETER, 272
RACHEL, 126(2)
ROBERT, 127
SAM D., 130
SAMUEL, 51, 67,
  126(3), 127,
  129(2), 221, 224,
  225
SAMUEL DAVIS, 130
SAMUEL M., 127,

****

SLOAN
  LETTIE (RUSSELL),
    118
  SERAPHINA J., 118,
    232
  THOMAS, 118, 232
SMALLWOOD
  TOM, 262
SMITH
  AARON, 201
  DOC., 256
  ELIZABETH, 201
  ELIZABETH
    (ROBERSON), 201
  HENRY, 109
  ISAAC N., 184
  JAMES, 59
  JERUSHA, 78
  JOHN, 212
  KINGSLEY, 258
  KINZEY, 187
  L., 271
  LATON, 276
  LAYTON, 201(3)
  LAYTON/LEIGHTON, 201
  LEAH, 16
  LEIGHTON, 170
  LUCY, 83
  MARGARET JANE, 184
  MARTHA, 201
  MARTIN A., 267
  MARY, 124, 201
  MARY ANN, 150
  MARY M., 26
  MATHEW, 168
  MATTHEW, 211
  MILDRED, 83
  MOSES, 201(2)
  PATSY, 201
  PHOEBE, 95, 201
  SAMUEL, 171
  SARAH, 201
  SUSAN P., 78
  THOMAS, 83
  WILLIAM, 201
SNIDER
  CELIA, 127
SPEARS
  ADALINE, 206
  ADALINE K. (BROWN),
    207
  ADELIA (BROWN), 207
  ADELIA (GASS), 207
  ADELIA K., 203
  ADELIA KINDRICK

  (BROWN), 206, 207
  ALVIN, 205
  ANNA, 202
  ASHLEY LAWRENCE,
    204(4), 205(2),
    208
  BLANCHE, 207
  DELILA, 202
  DELILAH J., 206
  DOUGLAS B., 205
  EDWARD, 202(2)
  FLORANCE, 208
  GENERAL, 207, 209
  GRACE, 205
  J. BROWN, 203, 204,
    206, 207(2), 208
  JACOB A., 207
  JAMES, 203
  JAMES A., 206
  JAMES G., 42, 179,
    202(2), 203, 204,
    206, 207(2), 208
  JAMES G., JR., 203,
    204, 208(2)
  JAMES GALLANT, 202,
    203, 204
  JAMES GALLANT, JR.,
    207
  JAMES P., 205
  JOHN, 203, 206
  JOHN G., 206
  JOHN GALLANT, 202,
    206
  JOHN H., 202(4),
    206(2)
  JOHN HOLLIDAY, 202,
    210
  JOHN HOUSTON, 210
  LOU R. (HALL), 207
  LULA, 207, 208
  LULA E., 207
  MARTHA E., 206
  MARY, 202
  MARY "POLLY", 206
  MARY (POLLY), 232
  MARY CAROLINE
    INGRAM, 210
  MATTIE J., 205
  MATTIE J. (PITTS),
    204
  N.B., 208
  NAPOLEON BONAPARTE,
    204, 205
  NELLIE, 205
  PEARL A., 207

  PENELOPE POCAHONTAS,
    179, 204, 205
  PETER, 209, 271
  RALPH D., 207
  SAMUEL, 206
  SARAH, 202, 206
  SARAH (GALLANT),
    202, 203
  SARAH E., 206
  WILLIAM, 202
  WILLIAM B., 207
  WILLIAM D., 203
  WILLIAM DOUGLAS,
    204, 207, 208(2)
SPOTWOOD
  ALEXANDER, 170
SPRINGS
  BENJAMIN FRANKLIN,
    212(2)
  CAM, 271
  CATHERINE, 211
  CLARINDA JANE
    MALONE, 213
  DAVID, 211, 212, 213
  DAVID HENNINGER, 213
  DAVID VALENTINE, 213
  EDWARD, 271
  JAMES, 212, 271
  JAMES P., 189
  JAMES PICKNEY,
    212(2)
  JOHN, 67, 189,
    211(4), 212(2),
    213
  LAWRENCE, 211
  LUCINDA, 271
  MARGARET, 211(2),
    213
  MARGARET
    (CLONINGER), 211,
    212(2), 213
  MARGARET A., 67
  MARGARET ANN, 213
  MARY, 211, 212
  NANCY (MOORE), 213
  NICHOLAS, 189,
    211(5), 212(2),
    213
  NICHOLAS A., 212
  NICHOLAS ANDERSON,
    213
  NICHOLAS, JR., 212
  PATRICK, 272
  RACHEL, 211
  SARAH, 211, 212

CHINA SEGRAVES, 231
CHRISTIANNA, 233
E., 271
ELIZA A., 229
ELIZA EMMALINE, 233
ELIZA J., 232
ELIZA JANE, 233
ELIZA ROBERSON, 231
ELIZABETH, 116,
  229(3), 230(3),
  233(2), 234
ELIZABETH (NICHOLS),
  234
ELIZABETH ANN
  (BETTY), 231
ELIZABETH CAROLINE,
  227
ELIZABETH J., 233
EMALINE, 232
EMMA, 233
ERSALINE CHINA, 84
EVANDER, 227
EVANDER "VAN" M.,
  231
EZEKIEL, 228, 229(2)
FANNIE, 234
FRANCES, 10, 234
G., 271
GEORGE, 229
GREEN, 270
HANNAH, 84, 232
HARRY, 270
HATTIE, 227
HENRY, 270
HEZEKIAH, JR., 234
HOWARD, 229(4)
HOWARD, JR., 229
HUGH B., 21
HULON, 227
ISAAC, 226, 233
ISAAC E., 234
ISAAC EASTERLY, 39,
  173, 234
JACKSON, 228
JACOB, 226(4), 227,
  229(2), 233
JAMES, 84(2), 206,
  226(2), 229(3),
  232(4), 233, 271
JAMES (STINGY JIM),
  230
JAMES A., 233
JAMES BARNETT, 227
JAMES ROSS, 233
JANE, 229, 231

JANE (HOWARD), 228
JEFFERSON, 228
JESSE, 21
JOEL SEGRAVES, 233
JOHN, 20(3), 21,
  226(2), 229(5),
  232, 233
JOHN CALHOUN, 233
JOHN CALVIN, 230
JOHN EDWARD, 21(2)
JOHN L., 26, 231
JOHN M. (BEATTY
  JOHN), 229
JOHN P. (JACK), 227
JOHN RUFUS, 232
JOHN T., 233(2)
JOHN W., 233
JOHN, JR., 229
JULIA, 228
KIZZIAH, 231, 232
L., 271
LARKIN, 48, 227, 229
LOUHANEY, 117, 230
LOUISE, 114, 232
LUCINDA, 233
LURAY "LOU", 231
MADISON, 271
MAJOR P., 229
MALINDA, 228
MALINDA C., 227, 233
MARGARET, 20, 21
MARIAH, 84, 232, 233
MARSHALL, 232
MARTHA B., 231
MARTHA JANE, 21(2),
  84, 233
MARTHA MANERY, 229
MARY, 84, 233
MARY (SPEARS), 206
MARY ELIZABETH, 232
MARY JANE, 227
MARY TENNESSEE, 231
MATILDA, 78, 84,
  230(2), 232, 233
MATTIE, 21
MINERVA, 39
MINERVA JANE, 232
MOSES, 226, 228, 229
NANCY, 84, 229,
  231(2), 232(2),
  233(3), 262
NANCY (LEE), 118(2)
NANCY J., 229
NARCISSA EMMALINE,
  227

NASSON, 84, 118(3),
  229(2), 231(2),
  232, 233
NASSON (NACE), 118
NATHANIEL C., 118,
  231, 232
OLLIE (OLLY), 231
ORRISON, 229
PATRICK, 229
PAUL, 226
PERDETTE, 233
PETER, 229
PETER J., 149,
  227(2), 229
PETER J., JR., 227
PETER W., 230
PORTMAN, 229
PORTMAN (ONE ARM
  PORT), 229
REBECCA, 227
REBECCA ANN, 233
REUBAN B., 229
RICHARD, 227, 228,
  233
RUFUS, 233(2)
SALLEY, 229
SAMUEL, 84(2),
  173(3), 232,
  233(2), 234(2)
SAMUEL F., 229
SAMUEL HEZEKIAH
  LAFAYETTE, 180
SARAH, 228(2), 230
SARAH CAROLINA, 232
SARAH JANE, 39, 232,
  234
TERESA, 233
THOMAS, 84, 224,
  226(3), 227, 228,
  229(2), 230(4),
  232(3), 233(3),
  234(3)
THOMAS A., 231
THOMAS CARROLL, 233
THOMAS L., 233
THOMAS N. (LONG
  TOM), 117
THOMAS NASSON,
  231(2)
THOMAS NASSON (LONG
  TOM), 118
THOMAS Y., 84(2),
  232(2)
THOMAS, JR., 84,
  229, 232

FIRST FAMILIES OF BLEDSOE COUNTY, TENNESSEE   301

****

www.ingramcontent.com/pod-product-compliance
Lightning Source LLC
Chambersburg PA
CBHW081428270326
41932CB00019B/3127